HERACLES AND OTHER PLAYS

EURIPIDES was born in Attica (the country whose main city was Athens) about 485 BCE. By the time of his death in 406 BCE he had written at least eighty plays, which were performed at the Great Dionysia, the Athenians' major drama festival. Seventeen of these survive complete. The universality of the conflicts he explores, and the startling realism of his characterization, ensure that he has also been by far the most often adapted, staged, and filmed of the ancient dramatists from the Renaissance to the present day. The first three plays in this volume are typical of Euripides: filled with violence or its threat, and with controversial psychological insights into friendship and enmity, hope and despair, duty and betrayal. The fourth, *Cyclops*, is our only surviving example of a genuine satyr play, with all the crude and slapstick humour that characterized the genre. There is death in *Alcestis*, which explores the marital relationship of Alcestis and Admetus with pathos and grim humour, but whose status as tragedy is subverted by a happy ending. The blood-soaked *Heracles* portrays deep emotional pain and undeserved suffering; its demand for a more humanistic ethics in the face of divine indifference and callousness makes it one of Euripides' more popular and profound plays. *Children of Heracles* is a rich and complex work, famous for its dialogues and monologues, in which the effects of war on refugees and the consequences of sheltering them are movingly explored. In *Cyclops* Euripides takes the familiar story of Odysseus' escape from the Cyclops Polyphemus and turns it to hilarious comic effect.

ROBIN WATERFIELD is a full-time writer and translator whose work includes translations, for Oxford World's Classics, of Euripides' *Orestes and Other Plays*, Plato's *Republic*, *Symposium*, *Gorgias*, and *Phaedrus*, Aristotle's *Physics*, Herodotus' *Histories*, Plutarch's *Greek Lives* and *Roman Lives*, and *The First Philosophers: The Presocratics and the Sophists*.

EDITH HALL is Leverhulme Professor of Greek Cultural History at the University of Durham and co-director of the Archive of Performances of Greek and Roman Drama at the University of Oxford. She has published widely on ancient Greek drama and society and has written introductions for the Oxford World's Classics editions of Euripides' *Medea and Other Plays*, *Bacchae and Other Plays*, *The Trojan Women and Other Plays*, and *Orestes and Other Plays*.

JAMES MORWOOD is Grocyn Lecturer in Classics and Fellow of Wadham College at Oxford University where he teaches Latin and Greek. He has translated Euripides' *Medea and Other Plays*, *Bacchae and Other Plays*, and *The Trojan Women and Other Plays* for Oxford World's Classics, and his other books include *The Plays of Euripides*, *A Dictionary of Latin Words and Phrases*, and works on Sheridan.

OXFORD WORLD'S CLASSICS

*For over 100 years Oxford World's Classics have brought
readers closer to the world's great literature. Now with over 700
titles—from the 4,000-year-old myths of Mesopotamia to the
twentieth century's greatest novels—the series makes available
lesser-known as well as celebrated writing.*

*The pocket-sized hardbacks of the early years contained
introductions by Virginia Woolf, T. S. Eliot, Graham Greene,
and other literary figures which enriched the experience of reading.
Today the series is recognized for its fine scholarship and
reliability in texts that span world literature, drama and poetry,
religion, philosophy and politics. Each edition includes perceptive
commentary and essential background information to meet the
changing needs of readers.*

OXFORD WORLD'S CLASSICS

EURIPIDES

Alcestis · Heracles Children of Heracles Cyclops

Translated by
ROBIN WATERFIELD

Introduction by
EDITH HALL

Notes by
JAMES MORWOOD

OXFORD
UNIVERSITY PRESS

OXFORD
UNIVERSITY PRESS

Great Clarendon Street, Oxford OX2 6DP

Oxford University Press is a department of the University of Oxford.
It furthers the University's objective of excellence in research, scholarship,
and education by publishing worldwide in

Oxford New York

Auckland Bangkok Buenos Aires Cape Town Chennai
Dar es Salaam Delhi Hong Kong Istanbul Karachi Kolkata
Kuala Lumpur Madrid Melbourne Mexico City Mumbai Nairobi
São Paulo Shanghai Taipei Tokyo Toronto

Oxford is a registered trade mark of Oxford University Press
in the UK and in certain other countries

Published in the United States
by Oxford University Press Inc., New York

Translations, Note on the Translation © Robin Waterfield 2003
Introduction, Select Bibliography © Edith Hall 2003
Explanatory Notes © James Morwood 2003
Chronology © 1997 James Morwood

British Library Cataloguing in Publication Data

Data available

Library of Congress Cataloging in Publication Data

Euripides.
Heracles and other plays / Euripides; translated by Robin Waterfield;
introduction by Edith Hall; notes by James Morwood.
p. cm.—(Oxford world's classics)
Includes bibliographical references.
Contents: Alcestis—Heracles—Children of Heracles—Cyclops.
1. Euripides—Translations into English. 2. Alcestis (Greek mythology)—Drama.
3. Heracles (Greek mythology)—Drama. 4. Heracles (Greek mythology)—Family—Drama.
5. Cyclopes (Greek mythology)—Drama. I. Waterfield, Robin, 1952– II. Title.
III. Oxford world's classics (Oxford University Press).
PA3975.A2.2003
882′.01—dc21
2002030374

ISBN 0–19–283259–X

3

Typeset in Ehrhardt
by RefineCatch Limited, Bungay, Suffolk
Printed in Great Britain by
Clays Ltd, St Ives plc

CONTENTS

ABBREVIATIONS

AJP	*American Journal of Philology*
BICS	*Bulletin of the Institute of Classical Studies*
CJ	*Classical Journal*
CP	*Classical Philology*
CQ	*Classical Quarterly*
CR	*Classical Review*
G&R	*Greece & Rome*
GRBS	*Greek, Roman, and Byzantine Studies*
HSCP	*Harvard Studies in Classical Philology*
JHS	*Journal of Hellenic Studies*
PCPS	*Proceedings of the Cambridge Philological Society*
TAPA	*Transactions and Proceedings of the American Philological Association*
YCS	*Yale Classical Studies*
s.d.	*stage direction*

INTRODUCTION

EURIPIDES AND HERACLES

IN the third century BCE a Greek champion boxer also pursued an alternative career on the stage. Although today the phenomenon of sportsmen who recreate themselves as actors is not unknown, their favoured medium tends to be popular cinema rather than tragedy. The ancient boxer, however, supplemented his victories in sports competitions with prize-winning performances as male heroes in tragedies, mostly by Euripides, which included the masterpiece *Heracles*.[1] This information is important to the study of Euripides' plays because it reminds us that the ancient theatre was as robust and spectacular as it was intellectual and emotional. The boxer-actor also reinforces the point that Heracles' physical stature was as crucial to his ancient popularity as to the most recent artwork with indisputable echoes of Euripides' *Heracles*, the Disney animated blockbuster *Hercules* (1997, directed by John Musker).

The plays in this volume date from the fifth century BCE, when all three great ancient Greek tragedians lived and worked in classical, democratic Athens. During that century alone Heracles appeared in scores of dramas, including Euripides' *Alcestis* and *Heracles*, Sophocles' *Women of Trachis* and *Philoctetes*, and Aristophanes' comedies *Birds* and *Frogs*. Yet the ancient theatre survived to dominate Greek and Roman cultural life not only until Hellenistic times, when the champion boxer starred in revivals of Euripidean classics, but for at least another millennium. The empires of the Macedonians and subsequently the Romans saw theatres built in almost every corner of the known world, from Austria to Turkey and Afghanistan, from Carthage to St Albans. Where there was a theatre there was always Heracles; in the first century CE an epigram dedicated to the tragic actor Apollophanes lists his props, giving primacy to Heracles' club (*Palatine Anthology* 11.169). To the same century belongs the most famous amateur actor of antiquity, the Emperor Nero, whose preferred tragic roles included the mad Heracles (Suetonius, *Nero* 21). But Heracles was also central to satyr play, to comedy, and to

---

[1] See G. M. Sifakis, *Studies in the History of Hellenistic Drama* (London, 1967), 84.

pantomime, a serious genre of musical theatre in which ballet dancers performed myths familiar from spoken tragedy. Episodes from Heracles' life were favourites: one dancer, when playing the mad Heracles, was famous for a stunt in which he aimed arrows into the audience (Macrobius 2.4).

The staying power of Heracles in the ancient theatre was a result of his complex ontological status, which allowed him to bridge, as no other figure in ancient myth could, the world of the gods and the world of human beings. Through Heracles the Greeks and Romans could explore almost every aspect of their condition and their relations to the inscrutable workings of the universe.[2] Heracles was worshipped in every corner of their world as both a god and a hero, but experienced his tribulations as a man. He is of course the most physically impressive of all ancient heroes (his boxing, wrestling, and archery render him more versatile than the hoplite warrior Achilles). His series of arduous physical labours, celebrated in all three tragedies in this volume, were and are some of the most well known and important of all myths from the ancient Mediterranean. His physicality is also reflected in his comic characterization (apparent in his portrayal in Euripides' tragicomic _Alcestis_), which always stressed his phenomenal appetites for food, wine, partying, and sex. Yet it cannot be sufficiently stressed that the red-blooded, carnal Heracles is also, paradoxically, found at the heart of the Greeks' exploration of more metaphysical concerns. In _Alcestis_ he cogently argues for the pursuit of happiness in the face of the transience of human existence (780–802), and in _Heracles_ he calls into question fundamental tenets of traditional theodicy, the system by which the Olympian gods were conceived as administering justice (1340–6).[3]

The cerebral Heracles of serious literature, whose heightened metaphysical consciousness arises from his dual divine and human status, allows humans, through him, to transcend the limitations of their mortal existence and adopt a perspective more than mortal. He also offers them the hope of life beyond the grave. For Heracles actually conquers death: his own return from the underworld, and his

---

[2] For an excellent general discussion of Heracles in both ancient and modern literature, see G. Karl Galinsky, _The Herakles Theme: The Adaptations of the Hero in Literature from Homer to the Twentieth Century_ (Oxford, 1972).

[3] References to Euripides' plays refer to the numeration of the Greek Oxford Classical Text of James Diggle.

miraculous ability to rescue others from it (Alcestis, Theseus), are connected with his role in mystery religion and its promise of a blessed afterlife; he was regarded as the first initiate of the most important of such cults to the ancient Athenians, the Eleusinian Mysteries. He was the mythical prototype of all who shared in their secret knowledge.[4]

Euripides' attraction to Heracles was not lost on his contemporaries. The most powerful evidence for the impression that Euripides made on his original public is Aristophanes' comedy *Frogs*, first produced in 405 BCE, just one year after Euripides' death. The protagonist of the comedy is Dionysus, the tutelary god of drama, who decides to retrieve Euripides from Hades and bring him back to Athens. In Euripides' *Heracles* the hero returns, alive, from the underworld: in order to brave the terrors of Hades the comic Dionysus knows that he must borrow this hero's costume and equipment. For Heracles was crucial to Euripides' confrontation of his audience with questions as different and as huge as the nature of genre, of virtue, of heroism, of mortality, immortality, and even of the divine. In *Heracles* the audience is not only asked whether Heracles is an international terrorist or saviour of the human race, but whether traditional gods exist at all, whether humans must ultimately take ethical decisions without divine guidance, whether murderers are really physically polluted, and whether adoptive parents can be better than biological ones. It would be wonderful to know to what uses Euripides put Heracles in the several other tragedies, now lost, in which this incomparable hero also featured, including *Alcmene* (in which Heracles may have been born), *Auge* (a scandalous piece during the course of which Auge gave birth in a temple to Heracles' son), and, more surprisingly, *Antigone*.[5]

The presence of Heracles in the three tragedies included in this volume (although that presence takes different forms) is one reason why they are grouped together. In *Alcestis* Heracles is both saviour and drunkard; in *Heracles* he is the saviour of Theseus and of his own family, but turns into the unwitting slayer of that same family; in *Children of Heracles* he is dead, but still acting as a saviour when

---

[4] Walter Burkert, *Greek Religion* (English trans., Oxford, 1985), 210–11.

[5] The lost tragedies of Euripides are discussed in T. B. L. Webster, *The Tragedies of Euripides* (London, 1967). In this Introduction references to the fragments of Euripides are cited from A. Nauck, *Tragicorum Graecorum Fragmenta*, 2nd edn., with supplement by B. Snell (Hildesheim, 1964).

he makes a mysterious meteoric offstage appearance; as the father of the play's asylum-seekers, he certainly still dominates the political and psychological landscape of Greece. *Cyclops* does not include Heracles. But, as a satyr play, it would originally have been performed at the end of a group of tragedies, and it thus belongs in the same volume as *Alcestis*, an experimental semi-jocular play which was performed in the same position. The comic dimension of *Alcestis* and *Cyclops* explains other features they share: an interest in drunkenness, a slightly 'folktale' atmosphere, and an upbeat ending in which a Greek hero triumphs over a villainous antagonist.

Another feature which unites all four plays is an interest in male violence—the struggle between Heracles and Death in *Alcestis*, the carnage of *Heracles*, the confrontations of *Children of Heracles*, and the blinding scene in *Cyclops*. But the tragedies are also connected by more psychological concerns, in particular as studies of the elderly. This feature of Euripidean tragedy used to inspire derision: critics throughout the nineteenth and early twentieth centuries recycled the influential A. W. von Schlegel's complaint that Euripides' 'aged persons are always complaining of the wants and helplessness of age, and crawl with trembling joints up the ascent from the orchestra to the stage . . . sighing over the misery of their situation'.[6] But this is to misunderstand Euripides' senior citizens, whose age compounds their tragic situations (Amphitryon in *Heracles*), or shows that experience does not decrease an individual's capacity for destructive moral agency (the selfish Pheres in *Alcestis*, the vindictive Alcmene in *Children of Heracles*).

EURIPIDES AND HIS TRADITION

The Greeks and Romans were passionate about the innovative and emotive Euripides. A character in a comedy announced that he would be prepared to hang himself for the sake of seeing this (by then dead) tragedian (Philemon fr. 118).[7] Aristotle's formalist discussion of tragedy complains about Euripides' use of the *deus ex machina*, his unintegrated choruses, and the 'unnecessary' villainy of some of his

---

[6] A. W. von Schlegel, *A Course of Lectures on Dramatic Art and Literature*, 2nd edn., trans. John Black (London, 1840), i. 149.

[7] Fragments of comedy are cited throughout from R. Kassel and C. Austin (eds.), *Poetae Comici Graeci* (Berlin, 1983–95).

characters. Yet even Aristotle conceded that Euripides was 'the most tragic of the poets', meaning that he was the best at eliciting fear and pity in his spectators (*Poetics* 56ª25–7, 54ᵇ1, 61ᵇ21, 53ª20).

In his *Rhetoric*, Aristotle also revealingly states that Euripides was the first tragic poet to make his characters speak naturally in everyday vocabulary (Aristotle, *Rhetoric* 3.1404ᵇ18–25). For the single most significant reason underlying Euripides' remarkable ancient popularity was probably the accessible, fluent, and memorable poetry in which his characters expressed themselves: even Alexander the Great, no professional actor, is supposed to have been able to perform a whole episode of a Euripidean tragedy off by heart as a party trick (Athenaeus, *Deipnosophists* 12.537d–e). The audiences adored the accessibility and psychological immediacy not only of the diction but of the *sentiments* Euripides attributed to his Bronze Age heroes: a good example is the concrete detail in a speech of Alcestis' widower Admetus reflecting on how desolate the house will seem without his wife: the empty chair, the floor uncleaned, the children crying for their mother (944–9). Thus Thessalian kings, Theban heroes, grandmothers who once mated with Zeus, children, slaves, and high priestesses, practitioners of human sacrifice, incest, and kin-killing: Euripides managed to make them all 'speak like human beings' (see Aristophanes, *Frogs* 1058).

Euripidean tragedy became 'classic' almost immediately after his death, was imitated by Roman tragedians—a version of *Heracles* is attributed to Seneca—and made a huge impact on the non-tragic literature of succeeding generations, especially Plato (who ostensibly objected to Euripidean drama but was partial to *Alcestis*), Menander, Virgil, Ovid, and the orators of both Greece and Rome. *Alcestis* survived because it was regarded as sufficiently important in the first or second century CE to be chosen among the ten Euripidean tragedies selected for study in the schools of the ancient world. Moreover, Euripides' plays are everywhere apparent in the *visual* culture of the Mediterranean. Homer apart, no author stimulated the arts more. The Romans painted Euripides' scenes on their walls and carved them on their sarcophagi (on which a popular choice, because of its soteriological associations, was a scene with Heracles leading Alcestis back from the dead); the Byzantines commissioned elaborate mosaics keeping his pagan myths alive in the visual imagination of Christendom.

The nineteenth-century scholar Benjamin Jowett said this tragedian was 'no Greek in the better sense of the term',[8] for after his
revivification in the Renaissance Euripides often suffered by comparison with the structural perfection, 'purity', and 'Hellenic' spirit
perceived in his rival Sophocles. This is, however, to simplify the complex and largely unwritten story of Euripidean reception and performance. *Alcestis* was translated into French and Latin in the early
1500s, lies behind the final scene of Shakespeare's *The Winter's Tale*
(1609), gave rise to dozens of operas by important composers including Lully, Handel, and Gluck, and has proved consistently important
to works by authors with deceased or discarded wives: Robert Brown-
ing's *Balaustion's Adventure* (1871), T. S. Eliot's *The Cocktail Party*, first
performed at the Edinburgh Festival in 1949, and Ted Hughes's
Alcestis, which premièred in Halifax, England, in September 2000.[9]
The influence of *Heracles* has been more subterranean; the Senecan
version, familiar in the Renaissance, lies behind several of the most
famous madmen of the Renaissance stage, including Hieronimo in
Thomas Kyd's *The Spanish Tragedy* (c.1587). The way that Euripides'
original play probes the nature of heroism, violence, and masculinity
has, however, attracted some interest in the more immediately recent
past.[10] *Children of Heracles* has been little performed, although it is an
influence on a bestselling American nineteenth-century novel, *Altars
of Sacrifice*, by Augusta Evans.[11] *Cyclops* has found some important
translators, including Percy Bysshe Shelley (1819), and has been
important to theorists of drama. In the Renaissance satyr drama was
(incorrectly) confused with satire, but was also (correctly) viewed as
a genre intermediate between tragedy and comedy, and *Cyclops*
played a role in discussions of mixed genres and as a model for
pastoral tragicomedy.[12]

The last hundred years have smiled on Euripides more than any
era since antiquity. One reason is his approach to myth, which has

[8] See A. N. Michelini, *Euripides and the Tragic Tradition* (Madison, 1987), 11 n. 40.
[9] For the performance reception of *Alcestis* and *Heracles* see Fiona Macintosh, 'Alcestis on the British Stage', *Cahiers du GITA*, 14 (2001), 281–308, E. Hall, 'Greek Plays in Georgian Reading', *G&R* 44 (1997), 59–81.
[10] Jan Kott, *The Eating of the Gods* (London, 1974), 78–124; Kathleen Riley, 'Heracles as Dr. Strangelove and GI Joe: Male Heroism Deconstructed', in E. Hall, F. Macintosh, and A. Wrigley (eds.), *Dionysus since 69* (Oxford, 2003).
[11] See E. Hall, 'Sophocles' *Electra* in Britain', in Jasper Griffin (ed.), *Sophocles Revisited: Essays Presented to Sir Hugh Lloyd-Jones* (Oxford, 1999), 261–306, p. 297.
[12] B. M. T. Herrick, *Tragicomedy* (Urbana, Ill., 1955), 7–14.

been characterized as subversive, experimental, playful, and eccentric in an identifiably modern way. Although he has occasionally been seen as a formalist or mannerist, the term 'irony' dominates criticism. 'Irony' is taken to describe Euripides' polytonality—his ability to write in two simultaneous keys. This 'irony', however, is conceived in more than one way: sometimes it describes the hypocritical gap between the rhetorical postures which Euripidean characters adopt and their true motives. Alternatively, 'irony' defines the confrontation of archaic myths with the values of democratic Athens, a process which deglamorizes violence, casting heroic stories of bloodshed and conflict—for example, myths explaining the origin of cults at the Athenians' sanctuary at Marathon in *Children of Heracles*—as sordid 'gangland killings'.[13]

Another reason for Euripides' modern popularity is that his supple and multifaceted works easily adapt to the agendas of different interpreters. Euripides has been an existentialist, a psychoanalyst, a proto-Christian with a passionate hunger for 'righteousness', an idealist and humanist, a mystic, a rationalist, an irrationalist, and an absurdist nihilist. But perhaps the most tenacious Euripides has been the pacifist feminist.

'Radical' Euripides was born in the first decade of this century with Gilbert Murray as midwife. This famous liberal scholar, later Chairman of the League of Nations, was himself a radical, and found his own restless intellect and interests mirrored in Euripides. The ancient dramatist, wrote the young Murray, was 'a man of extraordinary brain-power, dramatic craft, subtlety, sympathy, courage, imagination; he pried too close into the world and took things too rebelliously to produce calm and successful poetry.'[14] A few years later Murray initiated in Edwardian London a series of performances of Euripides in his own English translations. *Trojan Women* (1905) was interpreted by many as a retrospective indictment of the concentration camps in which the British had interned and starved Boer women and children during the Boer War; as a result of *Medea* (1907) the heroine's monologue on the plight of women (see below, 'Athenian

---

[13] This phrase is borrowed from W. G. Arnott's excellent article 'Double the Vision: A Reading of Euripides' *Electra*', *G&R* 28 (1981), 179–92.

[14] Gilbert Murray, *A History of Ancient Greek Literature* (London, 1897), 274. See Pat Easterling, 'Gilbert Murray's Readings of Euripides', *Colby Quarterly*, 33 (1997), 113–27.

Society') was recited at suffragette meetings.[15] Murray's political interpretations of Euripides, developed in performance, found academic expression in *Euripides and his Age* (1913). This book has fundamentally conditioned all subsequent interpretation, whether by imitation or reaction. A decade later Euripides' radicalism had become apocalyptic: 'not Ibsen, not Voltaire, not Tolstoi ever forged a keener weapon in defence of womanhood, in defiance of superstition, in denunciation of war, than the *Medea*, the *Ion*, the *Trojan Women*.'[16]

EURIPIDES THE ATHENIAN

What would Euripides have made of his modern incarnations? The reliable external biographical information amounts to practically nothing. No dependable account of Euripides' own views on politics, women, or war survives, unless we are arbitrarily to select speeches by characters in his plays as the cryptic 'voice of Euripides'. Aristophanes and the other contemporary Athenian comic poets, who wrote what is now known as 'Old Comedy', caricatured Euripides as a cuckold and a greengrocer's son, but their portrait offers little more truth value than a scurrilous cartoon.

The problem is not any dearth of evidence but a dearth of factual veracity. For the student of Euripides has access to a late antique 'Life' (*Vita*) and a fragmentary third-century biography by Satyrus. There are also the so-called 'Letters of Euripides', a collection of five dull epistles purporting to be addressed to individuals such as Archelaus (king of Macedon) and Sophocles, but actually written in the first or second century CE. Collectively these documents provide the first example in the European tradition of the portrait of an alienated artist seeking solace in solitude. This Euripides is a misogynist loner with facial blemishes who worked in a seaside cave on the island of Salamis, and retired to voluntary exile in Macedon as a result of his unpopularity. Unfortunately, however, this poignant portrait is demonstrably a fiction created out of simplistic inferences from Euripides' own works or from the jokes in Athenian comedy. Beyond what is briefly detailed below, the only aspect of the 'Euripides myth' almost certain to be true is that he possessed a large personal library (see Aristophanes, *Frogs* 943, 1049).

---

[15] See further Edith Hall, 'Medea and British Legislation before the First World War', *G&R* 46 (1999), 42–77.

[16] F. L. Lucas, *Euripides and his Influence* (London, 1924), 15.

Euripides' lifespan was almost exactly commensurate with that of democratic Athens' greatness. He was born in about 485 BCE, and was therefore a small boy when the city was evacuated and his compatriots thwarted the second Persian invasion in 480 BCE. He spent his youth and physical prime in the thriving atmosphere of the 460s and 450s, a period which saw the consolidation of Athens' empire and position as cultural centre of the Greek-speaking world. He was witness in 431 BCE to the outbreak of the Peloponnesian war, fought between Athens and her rival Sparta over hegemony in the Aegean. He lived through the turbulent 420s, having the opportunity to observe at first hand the ambition and brilliant oratory of Athenian leaders such as Pericles and Cleon; he lived through the Athenians' worst catastrophe ever, when in 413 the fleet and many thousands of men were lost at Syracuse in Sicily (the setting, as it happens, of his satyr play *Cyclops*) after an attempt to extend Athenian imperial influence westward. He witnessed the oligarchic coup of 411, which overturned the democracy for the first time in nearly a century; this was soon followed by the reinstatement of the democracy, marred by terrible factional struggles. But by dying in 406 BCE, Euripides did narrowly avoid the humiliating events of 404, when his city lost the war, her empire, and (briefly) her democracy and her pride.

The plays in this volume probably span the last three and a half decades of Euripides' life. *Alcestis* is the earliest of all Euripides' surviving plays. It was performed in 438 BCE, when it took the place of a satyr drama as last in a group of plays all by the same playwright, performed on the same day. It originally followed three lost tragedies, *Cretan Women*, *Alcmaeon in Psophis*, and *Telephus*. The other three plays in this volume are undated, but there are fairly good reasons for assigning *Children of Heracles* to around 430, *Heracles* to 416 or 414, and *Cyclops* to a few years later. It is almost certain, then, that they all date from the period of the Peloponnesian war, which broke out in 431 BCE and lasted until 404, a period during which conflict with Sparta or her allies was a semi-continuous fact of Athenian life.

It is tempting to speculate on Euripides' own reaction to the unfolding story of the war, and to ask whether it affected the evolution of his dramatic technique. It has been argued that Euripides' dramas, especially those on war themes, became increasingly pessimistic towards the end of his life, when tragedies like *Phoenician Women* (probably 409) and *Iphigenia at Aulis* (405) stress that amorality and atrocity are unavoidable by all warring nations and individuals. Yet such a notion of linear artistic and intellectual development is compromised by the survival of only nineteen plays attributed to Euripides, out of a total of at least eighty, and possibly ninety-two. The evolutionary model is also inconsistent with the production in the 420s of *Hecuba*, one of the bleakest war dramas ever written, and *Children of Heracles*, which enacts a terrible crime against an innocent young woman, and leaves questions about the conduct of foreign policy emphatically unanswered. Euripides' own plays must not be made to lend any substantial support to the widely held view that after initially supporting Athenian expansionism the poet despaired and retreated from the contemporary scene as the promoters of war became more powerful. It may be that truth lies behind the biographical tradition that he spent his last two years at the Macedonian court of Pella, supposedly writing plays including *Bacchae* and *Iphigenia at Aulis*; it may be that the very existence of the 'Macedonian exile' tradition reveals Euripides' anti-democratic (and therefore anti-imperialist) sympathies. On the other hand, the lack of evidence for a political career, in contrast with Sophocles' attested appointments to high office, may suggest a neutral emotional detachment from public affairs.

Yet Euripides was profoundly engaged with the intellectual and ethical questions which the war had asked and which underlay the policy debates in the Athenian assembly. For these appear in thin disguise in his tragedies, which repeatedly confront notions of patriotism, pragmatism, self-interest, expediency, and *force majeure* with the ideals of loyalty, equity, altruism, justice, and clemency. In *Alcestis* the debate between Admetus and his father Pheres, although centred on the implausible proposition that bargains with Death are negotiable, asks some painful questions about the value of individual human lives in a time of crisis. *Children of Heracles*, in enacting a diplomatic crisis in heroic Athens, examines some painful political choices. These theatrical disputes find parallels in the agonizing debates in Thucydides which decided the fates of rebels, hostages, prisoners of war, and also of wives and children, during the conflict between Athenian and Spartan empires.

Antiquity believed that Euripides studied moral philosophy with Socrates, but also that he studied physics with Anaxagoras and rhetoric with Prodicus (Aulus Gellius, *Noctes Atticae* 15.20.4); his tragedies reveal interest not only in ethics and political theory, but in every other significant field studied by the professional intellectuals ('sophists') in contemporary Athens: ontology, epistemology, philosophy of language, medicine, psychology, and cosmology. Euripidean characters certainly adopt the new philosophical and rhetorical *methods*: they subtly argue from probability and relativism, and formulate their points as antilogy, proof and refutation. In this they are patently influenced by the developing sophistic 'science' of rhetoric, or 'persuasion'. Euripides' flashiest orators appear in plays composed after the arrival in Athens in 427 BCE of the great Sicilian sophist and rhetorician Gorgias, famous for his verbal pyrotechnics and ability to make a tenuous argument appear overwhelmingly convincing, 'to make the weaker argument appear the stronger'. The plays in this volume contain some ostentatious verbal displays, especially in the so-called debate scenes (see below, 'Speech').

EURIPIDES IN PERFORMANCE

Most Euripidean tragedies were first performed at an annual festival in honour of Dionysus, the Greek god of wine, dancing, and theatrical illusion, who is the protagonist of Euripides' most obviously 'Dionysiac' tragedy, *Bacchae*. The Great Dionysia was held in the spring when sailing became feasible. It was opened by a religious procession in which a statue of Dionysus was installed in the theatre, along with sacrifices and libations. Yet the Dionysia was also a political event. It affirmed the Athenian citizenry's collective identity as a democratic body with imperial supremacy: front seats were reserved for distinguished citizens, and only Athenians could perform the prestigious benefaction of sponsorship (*chorēgia*). The spectators included representatives from Athens' allied states. The allies displayed their tribute in the theatre, where they also witnessed a 'patriotic' display by the city's war orphans—an aspect of the performance context which must be borne in mind when considering how the original audience might have reacted to 'war plays' such as *Children of Heracles*. The plays were expected to suit this audience: insulting Athens at the Dionysia may have been a prosecutable offence (Aristophanes, *Acharnians* 501–6). It is not certain whether women attended the drama competitions, although most scholars assume that if women were present at all it was in small numbers, perhaps consisting only of important priestesses.

The tragedies were performed over three successive days in groups by three poets: each poet offered three tragedies plus one satyr play.

In 431 BCE, for example, Euripides took third place with three traged-ies (*Medea, Philoctetes*, and *Dictys*), followed by a satyr play called *Theristai* (*Reapers*); the other two competitors were Euphorion (Aeschylus' son), who won first prize, and Sophocles, the runner-up. It seems, indeed, that Euripides only won three times: in 441, in 428 with the group including *Hippolytus*, and posthumously (probably in 405) with *Bacchae* and *Iphigenia at Aulis*. He came second to Sophocles with the group concluded by *Alcestis* in 438 BCE. The plays were judged by a panel of democratically selected citizens, and care was taken to avoid juror corruption, but the audience's noisy applause and heckling influenced the outcome (Plato, *Republic* 6.492b5–c1).

The performances took place in the Theatre of Dionysus on the south slope of the Athenian Acropolis. The theatre was in the open air: when Euripides' dying Alcestis addresses the sun, the daylight, and the clouds (244–6), the impact was consequently different from that which can be achieved in a darkened auditorium. Individual actors probably performed their speeches and songs most of the time on the stage (*skēnē*), while the chorus of twelve sang and danced to forgotten steps and gestures in the dancing arena (*orchēstra*). All the performers were male, and all were masked; little is known about the degree to which actors in female roles attempted to disguise their true gender. For performance conventions we have to rely on the characters' words, since the Greeks did not use stage directions. The last three decades have produced important work on the visual dimension and its contribution to the meaning of tragedy: scholar-ship has focused on physical contact, and on entrances and exits. The evidence for the material resources of the theatre as early as the fifth century is slight, although the poets had access to a machine which permitted the airborne epiphanies *ex machina*, such as Madness and Iris in the middle of *Heracles*. There was also the *ekkuklēma*, a con-traption allowing bodies to be wheeled out of the doors of the palace, temple, or tent forming the 'backdrop' to most surviving tragedies: in the case of *Heracles* the tableau which was 'rolled out' included the bound, sleeping hero in addition to his dead wife and children. Vase-paintings offer a stylized reflection of the costumes, masks, and scenery, and some are directly inspired by individual tragedies.[17]

---

[17] See A. D. Trendall and T. B. L. Webster, *Illustrations of Greek Drama* (London, 1971).

ALCESTIS

In antiquity, and from the Renaissance until the late nineteenth century, *Alcestis* enjoyed an extraordinarily high reputation. Its central attraction was its portrayal of a perfect mother and wife. Yet Euripides' self-abnegating exemplar of ideal femininity nearly disappeared from the public consciousness in the second half of the twentieth century, which could not tolerate the implicit assumption that a woman's life is worth less than a man's; it is only in recent years that the appearance of occasional revivals, notably Ted Hughes's *Alcestis* (2000), shows that it is once again possible to revisit this important text without our responses being intolerably distorted by contemporary sexual politics.

The action of *Alcestis* is simple. A Thessalian queen sacrifices her own life to save that of her husband Admetus; but his friend Heracles rescues her from Hades and restores her to Admetus alive. The play is little interested in its own mythical background, in the dealings between gods and men which produced the preposterous scenario in which Admetus could bargain with Death. It is rather more concerned with his outstanding performance as an employer (of Apollo) and as host (of Heracles); it is, indeed, the particular virtue of hospitality for which Admetus is so richly rewarded. Modern critics, for whom hospitality is no longer a fraught and potentially dangerous issue, need reminding that this play asks a serious practical question about competitive social obligations. The question counterposes duty to dead kin with duty to living friends. Although seeming now an odd theme for drama, the question must have arisen often enough in a pre-industrial society: is it right to offer a friend bed and board, however many days' distance he may be from alternative accommodation, when you are newly in mourning?

The answer might depend on the behaviour your guest was likely to exhibit. When the fun-loving Heracles appears in *Alcestis*, before the heroine has even been buried, he precipitates a violent clash of rites, sensibilities, and genres—symposium or funeral, hilarity or woe, comedy or tragedy. The fascinating tonal dislocations which ensue are connected with the play's position in its tetralogy. As the fourth and last, following three tragedies, *Alcestis* occupied the position which was normally taken by a satyr drama (see further below, '*Cyclops*'). Aware of its unusual status, scholars ancient and modern have applied the label 'pro-satyric', but such terminology can actually hamper appreciation of the play's distinctive qualities. Generic labelling occludes the play's intellectual sophistication, especially the sophistic wisecracking of Apollo and Death in the opening scene; more importantly, it obscures the prevalent melancholy of the emotional register, a melancholy little alleviated by the audience's knowledge, from the opening scene onwards, that Alcestis' life will be saved (65–71).

The sadness derives from the play's fascination with thanatology. It is the only ancient drama to portray Thanatos (Death) himself, a sarcastic, peevish, status-conscious god, wielding his sword to shear hair from his victims (74–6), and jealous of his prerogatives. Admetus longs for the 'tongue and music of Orpheus' in order to entrance Persephone and Hades and so recover his wife from the underworld (357–62), mythical references which draw attention to the play's nature as a 'return from the underworld' (*anodos*) myth-type familiar from other stories.[18] But before her sinister, silent resurrection in the closing scene, the action of the play is dominated first by a dying woman and then by her cadaver. The verse speaks of shrouds, of veils, of pyres, cortèges, and gravestones. It is an extended representation of the process of dying and a painful examination of the social repercussions and aesthetics of death. Indeed, the tightly scripted death scene remains unsurpassed in European theatre. Alcestis' entrance has been prepared by her maidservant's observations that she is wasted, limp, and has difficulty breathing (203–5); once on stage, she visibly undergoes increasing weakness. She hears Charon calling to her from his two-oared boat, sees Hades himself, winged and dark-browed, coming to take her 'to the halls of the dead', senses darkness shrouding her vision, and collapses as her legs fail her (253–7, 259–63, 267–90). But it is the deathbed presence of her children that renders this scene so compelling. Euripides used children more adventurously than Sophocles (Aeschylus, as far as we know, did not use them at all). By the time of *Medea* and *Trojan Women* he was extracting maximum pathos from the deaths of children, but in *Alcestis* the emotion is generated by a little boy's parting from his dying mother.

Euripides deftly explores the emotions inherent in this situation.

---

[18] See the excellent article by Helene Foley, 'Anodos Dramas: Euripides' *Alcestis* and *Helen*', in Ralph Hexter and Daniel Selden (eds.), *Innovations of Antiquity* (New York, 1992), 133–60 (revised version in Foley's *Female Acts in Greek Tragedy* (Princeton, 2001), 301–31).

Alcestis' death is premature (as Death gloats in the opening scene, 55); the early demise of young wives and mothers occurred much more frequently in Euripides' society than in our own, and many in his audience will have been in emotional situations identical to Alcestis and her family. She is bitter that Admetus' own parents refused to die in his place, and terrified that if he remarries his new wife will be unkind to her children (290–310). Her greatest anxiety is for her little daughter, who she believes will receive no help in finding a suitable husband, and (a typically Euripidean detail) will have to undergo labour deprived of the traditional support of her own birth mother (318–19).

Admetus imagines having a statue of his wife placed in the marital bed where he can embrace and address it (348–52). This morbid notion underlines the play's own status as a beautiful artwork memorializing a beautiful woman. Other ancient ideas about non-physical immortality are surveyed; death can be transcended by a lingering reputation (323–5). This theme is stressed in the dead queen's choral obituary; she will be remembered for time immemorial at festivals in both Sparta and Athens, 'For in dying you have bequeathed to poets a rich theme' (445–54). But the play suggests that the legacy of her death, although the death sentence itself is rescinded, will also be emotionally disturbing. The happy ending cannot erase Admetus' questionable earlier decision to allow his wife to die in his place. Euripidean tragedy is exceptionally attuned to the notion that certain traumas inevitably involve a life sentence of psychological suffering. Early in the play Alcestis' maidservant says that Admetus will suffer 'sorrow so great it will never leave his heart' (198). Neither Alcestis' fame, nor the superficially happy ending, can erase the uncomfortable atmosphere and the implication that there will be sorrow still in the heart and house of Admetus.

HERACLES

Heracles is a play about survival. Its superlative conclusion portrays the moral courage of a man whose life sentence of emotional pain is unbearable. He knows that the psychological torture awaiting him will be unremitting, like the physical pain suffered by Ixion, chained to a wheel throughout eternity (1298). For Euripides' Heracles, as for many perpetrators and victims of atrocity throughout history, the suicide he rejects would have been incomparably an easier option.

This bloody, inspiring tragedy pushes traditional beliefs about the nature of divine justice to their limits. Heracles suffers the worst imaginable fate for a parent—he kills his own beloved children. As the play presents his story, he has done absolutely nothing to deserve this. Heracles is hated by Hera because she is his stepmother, but that is the extent of the explanation offered for her attack on his sanity. The action thus articulates, in the most lucid manner, the problem of unmerited suffering. Euripides has gone out of his way to pose this ethical conundrum unambiguously. In some other tragedies, such as Sophocles' *Women of Trachis*, Heracles is an indifferent, even brutal father. But Euripides' Heracles is a loving and responsible parent.

Heracles has always been regarded as a work of an extreme nature. Antiquity recorded a tradition that Euripides was prosecuted by the fifth-century Athenian statesman Cleon for showing Heracles going mad in a play at the Dionysia.[19] The story, although probably untrue, reveals something of antiquity's shocked reaction to the drama. Euripides was interested in madness; in *Bacchae* he explored the mania associated with Dionysus, and in *Orestes* the psychotic obsession with reciprocal bloodletting caused by the Erinyes. But *Heracles* is the only Greek tragedy in which Madness herself appears. Here she takes the form the Greeks called *Lyssa*, a personification of the peculiarly male form of mental disorientation to which trained killers are vulnerable, the madness characteristic of soldiers who have gone berserk on the battlefield.

The perceived extremity of *Heracles* has produced extreme reactions in its more recent reception. Byron acknowledged its masculine potency when he laughed at an earnest bluestocking, 'That prodigy | Miss Araminta Smith | Who at sixteen translated *Hercules Furens* | Into as furious English' (*Don Juan* 11.52). Browning introduces his translation of the play in *Aristophanes' Apology* (1875) with explicit panegyric: it is 'the consummate tragedy', the test for 'true godship', even 'the perfect piece'. In 1905 an important Euripidean scholar, A. W. Verrall, announced that 'For power, for truth, for poignancy, for depth of penetration into the nature and history of man, this picture of the Hellenic hero may be matched against anything in art.'[20]

---

[19] *The Oxyrhynchus Papyri*, no. 2400 (vol. 24, 107–9), lines 10–14.
[20] *Four Plays of Euripides* (Cambridge, 1905), 134–5.

Many aesthetic reactions to *Heracles* have, however, been proportionately negative. Some Euripidean tragedies, such as *Trojan Women*, are 'spilt milk' dramas which begin with the 'reversal' and most if not all of the carnage. Others, such as *Medea*, keep the explosion of violence until near the end. *Heracles* places the turning point in its hero's fortunes at its precise centre. Since the eighteenth century complaints have been directed against the play's 'diptychal' or 'broken-backed' structure. There are different ways of addressing this alleged problem. One is to emphasize themes which are central to the whole play—hope, luck, salvation, excellence, reputation, violence, friendship. Another is to point to some of the more disturbing uses of language in the earlier references to Heracles, and argue that his madness is subtly prefigured in the first half. A third line of defence sees the unique structure as a response to the unique nature of Heracles: Euripides designed the bifurcated plot in order to explore his hero's ontological hybridity, his blurring of the margin between human and divine.

Yet discussions of the play's structure have not usually considered the impact of the play in *performance*. On stage the diction and action completely transcend the alleged dislocation. Only performance can demonstrate the aural impact of the poetry in the 'madness' panel; the remarkable range of verbal ambiguity, etymologies, repetition, punning, and jingles produces a sense of linguistic madness, a tornado of poetic diction through which meaning is revealed.[21] Furthermore, performance reveals that Heracles is omnipresent as a topic of discussion if not actually in person. The tragedy concludes by sending him to Athens to receive a hero cult, but in doing so asks what such a violent, anachronistic firebrand of a hero can offer a fifth-century democracy, in which the glorious exploits of brilliant individuals need to be subordinated to the welfare of the wider community. The play examines almost every aspect of the earlier mythical traditions surrounding Heracles. But ultimately it is only Athens and the Athenian genre of tragedy which 'can rescue Heracles from the "death" and anachronism with which he is threatened in the earlier scenes and create an untraditional spiritualized hero equal to the mutability of life and valuable for the Athenian *polis*'.[22]

---

[21] See the brilliant article by Christina Kraus, 'Dangerous Supplements: Etymology and Genealogy in Euripides' *Heracles*', *PCPS* 44 (1998), 137–56.

[22] Helene Foley, *Ritual Irony: Poetry and Sacrifice in Euripides* (1985), 150.

Finally, it is only performance that fully reveals the importance of Amphitryon's role. He is himself a profoundly tragic figure, who loses everything, but must live on alone in Thebes and organize the funerals of his daughter-in-law and grandchildren. Heracles' 'adoptive' father is on stage throughout almost the entire action (except only 348–450 and 733–1041), and his role demands a versatile actor. He delivers the prologue, which establishes his claim on the audience's sympathy (cf. Aristotle, *Politics* 7.1336^{b}27–31), and a major rhetorical speech in the 'archery' debate with Lycus (170–235). His voice utters the crucial offstage cries marking the death of the children (886–908); he is the only singing actor in the play, and performs a complex sung dialogue with the chorus (1042–88). To him belongs the terrible task of breaking the news to Heracles (1109–62). Above all, as a man who unswervingly and asexually loves another man to whom he is biologically unrelated, Amphitryon is the chief representative of the force of human affective ties—*philia*—and their power to transcend even the very worst that the gods can send.

In myth and cult Heracles was the universal Best Friend, the divine figure with whom the Greeks associated the advanced human capacity for loving non-kin.[23] In *Heracles* (as in *Alcestis*) his relationships with other humans exemplify this principle and prove that it alone can offer some protection against the gods' vindictiveness. Thus of all surviving Greek tragedies *Heracles* most demands the epithet 'humanist' in its truest sense. Although on one level a religious drama providing a mythical explanation for a traditional hero's place in Athenian cult, *Heracles* radically calls traditional religion into question and replaces it with more human-centred ethics. Euripides' contemporary Athenians associated such ideas with Protagoras, an agnostic thinker who denied that human attempts to intercede with the gods could shape events. Significantly, later antiquity believed that it was at Euripides' house that Protagoras read out his famous treatise on the gods, beginning 'Man is the measure of all things' (fr. 80 B 1 Diels-Kranz; Diogenes Laertius 9.8.5). Heracles denies that gods can be vindictive and calls myths mere poetic fictions; Amphitryon and Theseus ignore traditional pollution taboos in order to help the traumatized criminal. In *Heracles* Euripides forces his heroes, and thereby his audience, to leave heroic myth behind in the toy box, and to enter the more exacting adult world of moral responsibility, autonomy, and accountability.

---

[23] Burkert, *Greek Religion*, 211.

CHILDREN OF HERACLES

In one of the most extraordinary moments in Greek tragedy, a miracle near an Athenian sanctuary of Zeus transforms an old man into a muscular young warrior. The decrepit Iolaus, former companion and nephew of Heracles, is awarded this supernatural rejuvenation by Zeus and Hebe, goddess of youthfulness and consort of the now deified Heracles.[24] The renewed strength of Iolaus allows him finally to arrest Eurystheus, the villain who has been tormenting Heracles and his family for several decades. The miracle is without parallel in surviving Greek tragedy. Outside the genre-subverting *Alcestis*, Euripides' profoundly tragic humans, although interfered with and despotically governed by immortals, are not usually offered supernatural or miraculous opportunities to evade the misery of ageing and of death.

In myth Heracles fathered numerous children in addition to those by Megara whom he kills in *Heracles*. In *Children of Heracles* the sons and daughters who survived him are in mortal danger. Under the supervision of their senescent cousin Iolaus and grandmother Alcmene they have fled from Argos in order to escape death by stoning, a punishment decreed by their father's old persecutor, Eurystheus. They have now taken refuge at the temple of Zeus in Marathon, in Athenian territory on the eastern coast of Attica. This creates a religious and diplomatic crisis. The Athenians, led by their king Demophon (Theseus' son), decide to defend the suppliants, but events take a terrible turn when Persephone demands a human sacrifice as the Argives invade Attica. These problems are superficially resolved when the eldest daughter of Heracles heroically offers herself for sacrifice and the Athenians defeat the Argives in the offstage battle prior to which Iolaus is rejuvenated. Eurystheus, the arch-enemy of both Heracles' family and now of the Athenians, is captured and brought before Alcmene, Heracles' embittered old mother. The last scene revolves around the question of whether Eurystheus should be summarily executed, and, if so, what should be done with his body.

This potent dramatic situation reverberates loudly today. A family of asylum-seekers, with a valid case for being offered protection, nevertheless presents an increasingly onerous burden to their host country. The refugee family is already a liability in terms of foreign policy, but their own unpredictable behaviour exacerbates the

---

[24] The wedding of Hebe and the deified Heracles was a popular theme in the visual arts: see R. Vollkommer, *Heracles in the Art of Classical Greece* (Oxford, 1988), 37–9.

problem: their volatile leader allows one of his young charges to be slaughtered, demands to be allowed to fight when physically unfit, and strips a temple of dedicated war trophies; their senior female is revealed to be a voluble and vindictive embarrassment with scant regard for either local or international law. The apparently honourable course chosen by the host country, the protection of innocent refugees, turns out to involve thoroughly dishonourable abuses of human rights, including the sanctioning of human sacrifice and the execution of a prisoner of war.

Iolaus' sudden physical transformation, and the unpleasant developments in the ethical situation, are symptoms of the chimerical power of this unique drama. Nearly everyone involved in the action undergoes a sudden metamorphosis, whether in nature, status, or situation. Demophon seems to be a strong and decisive moral presence, but is helpless in the hands of the despised class of soothsayers. Even a lifelong slave, uniquely in Greek tragedy, is offered emancipation. Alcmene changes from victim into aggressor, object of pity into a pitiless avenger: only just released from captivity and the threat of death herself, the final scene depicts her arguing maliciously for the immediate and dishonourable execution of her newly captive enemy Eurystheus. But this villain, official enemy of the Athenians and instigator of an act of military aggression against them, at the last minute turns into their benefactor; he promises that his corpse will act as their talisman, a safeguard against any future aggression from the children of Heracles (i.e. the Spartans, who traced their descent from this hero). The theme of sudden reversal and transformation thus underlies the play's distinctive project. No other Greek tragedy offers a 'twist in the tail' quite as surprising as *Children of Heracles*.

Despite its special qualities, however, it is probably Euripides' least familiar tragedy today. One reason is that the text is certainly incomplete (although there is disagreement about the nature and extent of the difference between the Euripidean text used for the original performance and that found in the manuscript tradition). It is suspicious that no reference is made to Heracles' slaughtered daughter subsequent to the sacrifice scene; there can be no doubt that the ending of the tragedy as it stands is not just abrupt but actually lacunose. Yet these problems of transmission alone do not account for the neglect the play has suffered, since a large part of the ending of the hugely popular *Bacchae* is also missing. The real obstacle facing the modern reader of *Children of Heracles* is the play's strong interest in somewhat obscure religious aetiology. Several of the turns taken by events in this highly charged political drama meant a great deal more to the original audience than it is possible to reconstruct with any confidence today; the rejuvenation of Iolaus was almost certainly linked to his cultic connection with young people, for example, and the graves of the sacrificed maiden and of Eurystheus may actually have been visible in the Marathon area.[25] This aetiological dimension makes *Children of Heracles* a vital document for historians of ancient hero cult and Athenian religion, but prevents it from being fully appreciated as drama.

This is a pity, not only because of the dramatic finesse demonstrated in the radical reversals of expectation, but also because several speeches and episodes are individually striking: the shocking initial confrontation between the frail Iolaus and the thuggish herald, where physical violence explodes over one of the Athenians' most sacred sanctuaries; the human sacrifice sequence, where Euripidean irony expertly dissects the fictions on which young people are fed when they are asked to die in the name of high-sounding causes; the subtlety of the interchange where Iolaus is shown all too hastily licensing this outrage while insisting on his affection for the girl; the scene in which he demands to enter battle, which includes a Euripidean experiment with the essentially comic stereotypes of the belligerent old man and the cheeky slave; and above all Eurystheus' scandalous but disarmingly frank account of his descent into moral depravity. The strange, painful, immoral world of *Children of Heracles* combines a dark ethical realism similar to that in *Hecuba* with experiments in absurdity, comedy, and sudden surprise. The play may be an enactment of an episode important to the local myths and religious beliefs of Euripides' audience, but it is also emotionally complex, theatrically innovative, morally honest and psychologically penetrating. In a modern world all too familiar with the phenomena of asylum-seekers and naïve teenagers volunteering for patriotic suicide, *Children of Heracles* may yet prove to be a tragedy whose time has come.

---

[25] For information and bibliography see William Allan (ed.), *Euripides, The Children of Heracles* (Warminster, 2001), 22–35.

CYCLOPS

During the fifth century BCE hundreds of satyr plays were performed after tragedies in the Athenian Theatre of Dionysus. Satyr plays featured heroes like Odysseus in *Cyclops* and Heracles, whose physical appetites made him the most popular hero of the genre; he starred in numerous lost examples including Euripides' own *Reapers*, *Syleus*, and *Busiris*. These heroes interacted with the satyrs in humorous visitations of the same kind of myths that supplied the plots of tragedies. Favourite satyric plot motifs included servitude and escape, eating and drinking, sexual pursuit, hunting, athletics, and inventions. In *Cyclops* the theme of servitude and escape reaches a climax in the Sicilian rustic symposium as a result of which the one-eyed giant Polyphemus can be blinded. The ancient critic Demetrius defined satyr drama as 'tragedy at play' (*de Elocutione* 169), and this playful piece is of great interest to the history of theatre as the only fully extant example of an ancient satyr drama. It shows how in this genre the tragedians added a chorus of satyrs and their father Silenus to well-known mythical narratives: in an adaptation of one of the most famous of all Greek myths, Odysseus' escape from the Cyclops (familiar from *Odyssey* book 9), the satyrs help Odysseus to blind Polyphemus and escape the Cyclops' island along with him. In adding satyrs and a theatrical dimension to the old story Euripides supplies new dialogue, removes the other Cyclopes, truncates Odysseus' adventures in the cave, reduces the number of sailors eaten by Polyphemus to two, and extends the farcical baiting of the blinded giant at the end of the action. Instead of escaping by the ruse of tying themselves to the underbellies of sheep, Euripides imagines a Sicilian symposium, complete with homoerotic escapades: Polyphemus, a self-confessed homosexual (583–4), gets drunk and grabs Silenus, whom he mistakes for Ganymede, the boy Zeus loved. He charges into his cave to rape the ageing satyr, thus giving Odysseus the opportunity to blind him. The exclusively male plot therefore revolves around alcoholic intoxication and morally unquestioned violence enacted against an outright villain who happens to be a homosexual rapist. Such a plot is slight, cruel, and unedifying, but fortunately the plot is not the point: what is at issue is the satyrs' perspective on the world and satyr drama's relationship with its non-identical twin sister, tragedy.

The minor adjustments to the action of the Cyclops episode in

Odyssey book 9 are nothing in comparison with the intellectual transformation of the material that has been engineered by Euripides.
With the sole exception of the tragedy named *Rhesus* attributed to
Euripides (but almost certainly not by him), which is a dramatic
retelling of an episode in the *Iliad*, the accidents of transmission
mean that no surviving tragedy can be compared in detail with the
treatment of its story in a surviving epic prototype. This makes the
modernization of the Cyclops story, and in particular the transformation of Polyphemus from a primitive cannibal into a personification
of radical ideas propounded by some late fifth-century political theorists, all the more suggestive and fascinating. In Euripides Polyphemus
is more like a mortal and less like a fantastic giant. He is a slave-
owner, a cattle-rancher, and a man of some substance, like most
fifth-century Athenian gentlemen. He is also a careful, even culti-
vated, cook, whereas in Homer he eats men raw, like a mountain
lion. But, most importantly, he has a considerable intellect, and is
given an important debate with Odysseus which undoubtedly par-
odies some distinctive currents in contemporary philosophical cir-
cles. Odysseus articulates a broadly democratic Athenian perspective,
based on the rule of law; Polyphemus' position caricatures some
strains in contemporary anti-democratic ideology, especially his view
that riches (here taking the form of comestibles) can substitute for
divinity (316, 336), and that man-made rules and laws are redun-
dant (338–40). It has been pointed out that this Polyphemus is
strongly reminiscent of Callicles in Plato's *Gorgias*, who argues that
civic laws are devised by the weak majority: natural law dictates that
strong individuals should satisfy their desires at the expense of such
man-made legislation.[26]

It may be that its intellectual sophistication made Euripides'
Cyclops an unusual example of its genre. It certainly replays serious
controversies about human society identical to those explored in tragedy, albeit in a different and more boisterous key.[27] There is no evidence of quite such pointed parody of philosophical argumentation
in the other important evidence for satyr drama, the large fragment
of Sophocles' satyric *Trackers*, discovered on papyrus in 1907. This
fragment has now been incorporated, in English translation, into

[26] See Richard Seaford (ed.), *Euripides' Cyclops* (Oxford, 1984), 51–3.
[27] See F. Lissarrague, 'Why Satyrs are Good to Represent', in J. J. Winkler and F. I.
Zeitlin (eds.), *Nothing to do with Dionysos?* (Princeton, 1990), 228–36.

Tony Harrison's drama *The Trackers of Oxyrhynchus* (first performed in 1988).[28] It remains difficult to generalize about this nearly lost genre, but it seems that it is indeed the traditional world view of the satyrs that Euripides is exploiting when in *Cyclops* he uses them as representatives of a particular political philosophy: their pre-industrial, rustic communism is an important counterpoint to Odysseus the urban modern democrat and Polyphemus, who is (in Athenian terms) an oligarchic sympathizer, a monadic proponent of the view that only Might is Right.[29]

Yet viewing dramatic satyrs from an anthropological perspective, as representatives of an early stage in human social development, runs the risk of reducing the magic of these complex and charming creatures. Like their master Dionysus, satyrs confound many of the polarities by which the Greeks organized their perception of the world. They are nearly human, yet are touched with the divine and have tails, animal ears, and often hoofs. They are cowardly yet violent. They are often bald and yet always childlike. They are sly and knowing, but simultaneously naive and innocent. They are often involved in the gods' inventions of the arts of civilization (in *Trackers* the lyre), but live in remote, uncultivated countryside. The Roman architect Vitruvius recommends specifically that the scenery for satyr drama be decorated 'with trees, caves, mountains and other things associated with the countryside' (5.6.9).

The one boundary satyrs do not cross is that demarcating male from female. They are exaggeratedly male from the biological point of view (erections are a recurrent feature of satyr drama), and decidedly homosocial—they live with members of their own sex, and spend their time on collective male pursuits: hunting, athletics, drinking, and chasing nymphs. In the female-free environment of *Cyclops* the satyrs can only fantasize about rape, but in many other satyr plays the plot revolved around sexual aggression against females. It may be that it is the masculine and sexualized viewpoint of satyr drama that can help explain why it was deemed an aesthetically, socially, and psychologically important way of concluding a tragic performance. The other plays in this volume are quite exceptional in that their choruses are all male: far more tragedies had a female chorus. For the final play in a tetralogy, it seems it was

---

[28] Published by Faber & Faber (London, 1990).
[29] David Konstan, 'The Anthropology of Euripides' Kyklops', in Winkler and Zeitlin (ed.), *Nothing to do with Dionysos?*, 207–27.

conventional if not actually compulsory for the chorus-men to lay aside their tragic robes, so often feminine, and don the costume of a libidinous satyr, a graphic signifier of testosterone. Most critics since the first scholar to understand the genre at all, Isaac Casaubon in the early seventeenth century,[30] have seen that the satyr play must have functioned to create a sense of release or relief from the psychological tension of the foregoing tragedies. More recently it has been stressed that the satyrs bring drama closer than heroic tragedy can to its tutelary deity, Dionysus, and therefore to its performance context at the Athenian festival of Dionysus. Satyr drama also sends its spectator out to the festival not only laughing rather than crying, but reassured of his place in a joyous, sexualized, male collective.[31] Satyr drama is not only tragedy at play: it is also the collective male Athenian democratic citizenry defining itself, in a utopian register, during its worship of Dionysus.

ATHENIAN SOCIETY

Euripides' plays were first performed in Athens at a festival celebrating Athenian group identity, and consequently often reveal an 'Athenocentrism' manifested, for example, in the famous praise in *Medea* of the beauty of Athens' environment, the grace of its citizens, and its cultural distinction (824–45). The Athenian focus similarly affects the plays in this volume. The northern Greek chorus of *Alcestis* refer to the importance of poetry in the prosperous city of Athens (445–54); Heracles, the greatest Greek hero of all, but associated with Thebes and Argos, is nevertheless brought into Athens' mythical ambit by Theseus' offer of a permanent residence (*Heracles* 1326–35); the whole of *Children of Heracles* is an enactment (although a morally complicated one) of an episode in Athens' mythical past, complete with several explicit choral praises of the city.

The social fabric of Athens in Euripides' own time was heterogeneous. In 431 BCE an estimated 300,000 human beings lived in the city-state of Attica. But at least 25,000 were resident non-Athenians

---

[30] *De Satyrica Graecorum Poesi, & Romanorum Satira Libri Duo* (Paris, 1605); repr. with an introduction by P. E. Medine (Delmar, NY, 1973).

[31] See P. E. Easterling, 'A Show for Dionysos', in P. E. Easterling (ed.), *The Cambridge Companion to Greek Tragedy* (Cambridge, 1997), 36–53; E. Hall, 'Ithyphallic Males Behaving Badly: Satyr Drama as Gendered Tragic Ending', in Maria Wyke (ed.), *Parchments of Gender: Deciphering the Body in Antiquity* (Oxford, 1998), 13–37.

('metics'), including businessmen and professionals; a third were slaves, the majority of whom came from beyond Hellenic lands—from the Balkans, the Black Sea, Asia, or Africa. This ethnic pluralism perhaps finds expression in the 'multi-ethnic' casts of tragedy. It is only an accident of selection that the casts of the tragedies included in this volume, with their settings in the cities and shrines of central Greece, happen to be less ethnically varied than the Egyptians, Colchians, Thracians, Asiatics, Levantines, and Crimeans who appear in other works by Euripides.

Slavery was fundamental to Athenian economy and society, and tragedy reminds us of this unfortunate portion of the population. In *Acharnians* Aristophanes commented on the intelligence Euripides imputed to his slaves (400–1), and his plays include slaves with important roles as well as mute attendants: in *Children of Heracles* two household slaves connected with Hyllus and Alcmene are involved in significant and demanding scenes. Alcmene's slave, who delivers the fine 'messenger speech', claims that he has been promised manumission, a quite exceptional notion in Greek tragedy. It may be connected with the role played by manumitted slaves in the historical battle of Marathon.[32]

Both *Heracles* and *Children of Heracles* show how a family without powerful allies or means of support must fear degrading poverty and even starvation. The ethical dilemmas and emotional traumas in Euripides are never wholly inseparable from the decidedly unheroic pressures of finance and economics. Some Euripidean characters express lucid insights into the economic basis of society; the most famous example is Medea's first monologue in *Medea*, which clarifies the socio-economic imperatives underlying her own and other women's predicament:

Of everything that is alive and has a mind, we women are the most wretched creatures. First of all, we have to buy a husband with a vast outlay of money—we have to take a master for our body . . . divorce brings shame on a woman's reputation and we cannot refuse a husband his rights . . . I would rather stand three times in the battle line than bear one child. (*Medea* 230–51)

She trenchantly exposes the jeopardy in which marriage placed

---

[32] See E. Hall, 'The Sociology of Athenian Tragedy', in Easterling (ed.), *The Cambridge Companion to Greek Tragedy*, 93–126, p. 112; Allan, *Euripides, The Children of Heracles*.

women: besides the insulting dowry system, they were subject to
legalized rape in marriage, a hypocritical double standard in divorce,
and agonizing mortal danger in childbirth.

This kind of speech outraged the Christian writer Origen, who
criticized Euripides for inappropriately making women express argu-
mentative opinions (*Contra Celsum* 7.36.34–6). It is indeed a remarkable feature of Euripidean tragedy that many of his best thinkers and
talkers are women: although Euripides' finest female orators (Medea
and Hecuba) appear in plays not included in this volume, in *Alcestis*
the heroine delivers some cogent rhetoric, Megara holds her own in
the ethical debates with which *Heracles* opens, and some of the most
memorable passages in *Children of Heracles* are spoken by Heracles'
daughter or by her grandmother Alcmene.

Women are of course prominent in tragedy generally: patriarchal
cultures often use symbolic females to help them imagine abstrac-
tions and think about their social order. It is also relevant that
women were heavily involved in death rituals and performed the
laments at funerals, that Dionysus' cult (in reality as well as in Euripides' *Bacchae*) involved maenadism and transvestism, and that
women were perceived as more emotionally expressive (like Alcestis
in *Alcestis*), psychologically erratic (like Alcmene in *Children of
Heracles*), or susceptible to divine interference (like Heracles' daughter
in *Children of Heracles*). They were also regarded as lacking in moral
autonomy: Athenian men were obsessed with what happened in
their households behind their backs, and all the badly behaved
women in tragedy—including Alcmene—are permanently or tem-
porarily husbandless. There was, however, a feeling even in antiquity
that Euripides' focus on women was sharper than that of either
Aeschylus or Sophocles; until recently critics were debating whether
Euripides was a misogynist or a feminist. But the only certainties are
that he repeatedly chose to create strong and memorable female
characters, and that as a dramatist he had a relativist rhetorical
capacity for putting both sides of the argument in the sex war.

The position of women in the real world of Athens has itself long
been a contentious issue, especially the degree of confinement to
which citizen women were subject. But it is clear that most men
would have preferred their wives and daughters to stay indoors, to be
little discussed in public, to practise thrift, to possess unimpeachable
sexual fidelity, and serially to produce healthy children, especially
sons. Alcestis, as a beautiful, faithful, fertile, careful housekeeper,

who regards herself as unimportant in comparison with her husband, is probably near to the Athenian ideal. Women could not vote or participate in the assembly; nor could they speak for themselves in the courts of law or normally conduct financial transactions except through the agency of their male 'guardian' (*kyrios*)—father, husband, or nearest male relative. A woman known to articulate views in front of men might be regarded as a liability: Heracles' daughter apologizes for making a public appearance in *Children of Heracles* (474–83); her grandmother Alcmene is aware that her own assertive behaviour is likely to win disapproval (978–80). But women did of course negotiate with the existing power structures (we hear hints in the orators of the need for men to seek their womenfolk's approval), and were prominent in the central arena of public life constituted by religion. This is reflected especially in the figure of the dignified priestess of Apollo in *Ion* and in the chorus of hierodules in *Phoenician Women*. Other Euripidean tragedies feature important priestesses, such as Iphigenia, a priestess of Artemis in his *Iphigenia among the Taurians*, and the Egyptian priestess Theonoe in his *Helen*. In a lost play the wise woman Melanippe defended women against practitioners of misogynist rhetoric; one of her strategies was to list the Panhellenic cults which women administered (fr. 499):[33]

Men's criticism of women is worthless twanging of a bowstring and evil talk. Women are better than men, as I will show . . . Consider their role in religion, for that, in my opinion, comes first. We women play the most important part, because women prophesy the will of Zeus in the oracles of Phoebus. And at the holy site of Dodona near the sacred oak, females convey the will of Zeus to inquirers from Greece. As for the sacred rituals for the Fates and the Nameless Ones, none of these would be holy if performed by men, but they prosper in women's hands. In this way women have a rightful share in the service of the gods. Why is it, then, that women must have a bad reputation?

EURIPIDES AND RELIGION

Melanippe's words are a fitting introduction to the category of dramatis personae constituted by the gods. What is to be deduced about Euripides' religious beliefs from his onstage divinities in these plays (Apollo, Death, Madness, Iris), and the Aphrodite, Athena, Artemis,

---

[33] Translation taken from M. R. Lefkowitz and M. B. Fant, *Women's Life in Greece and Rome: A Source Book in Translation* (London, 1992), 14.

Dionysus, Dioscuri, Poseidon, and Thetis who physically appear in others? One function of Euripides' gods from the machine, such as Madness and Iris in *Heracles*, is certainly to provide a metatheatrical 'alienation' device drawing attention to the author's power over his dramatic narrative. But does that mean that he was an atheist?

Allegations that Euripides was a religious radical began in his lifetime. Aristophanes' caricature includes the charge that Euripides had persuaded people 'that the gods do not exist' (*Women at the Thesmophoria* 450–1), and portrays him praying to the Air ('Ether') and 'Intelligence' (*Frogs* 890–2). Some characters in Euripides undoubtedly articulate views which must have sounded radical, modern, and even 'scientific' to his audience. Heracles believes that a god, if truly divine, must be indestructible, self-sufficient, and certainly not involved in sexual indiscretions or intra-Olympian politics (*Heracles* 1307–8, 1341–6). Here Euripides, brilliantly, makes Heracles an intellectual radical who calls into question the veracity of his own myth, thus destabilizing the very subject-matter which has brought him into theatrical life. Other Euripidean characters depart from traditional theology by attributing the workings of the universe either to physical causes or to the power of the human mind. In *Orestes* Electra refers to the enthroning of 'Nature' (*Physis*) by contemporary natural scientists (126–7), and later hints at ideas associated with the cosmology of the pre-Socratic thinker Anaxagoras (982–5). In *Trojan Women* Hecuba wonders whether Zeus should be addressed as 'the necessity imposed by nature, or human intelligence' (884–6). In one lost play a character asserted that 'the mind that is in each of us is god'; in another the first principle of the cosmos was said to be Air, which 'sends forth the summer's light, and makes the winter marked with cloud, makes life and death'; in a third Air was explicitly equated with Zeus (frr. 1018, 330.3–5, 941).

It has consequently always been tempting to see Euripides as actually seeking to overturn traditional religion, especially belief in the arbitrary, partisan, and often malevolent anthropomorphic gods of the Homeric epics. It has been argued that in figures such as the vindictive Hera of *Heracles*, Euripides portrayed the most 'Homeric' of all Greek tragic gods precisely to undermine them. Thus his tragic divinities, the argument goes, can be seen as nothing more than a literary throwback to the old anthropomorphism, constituting a consciously reductive enactment of the commonly accepted personalities of the Olympians. Yet it is mistaken to confuse Euripidean characters'

more innovative theological opinions with his (unknown) personal
views. Moreover, many of the expressions of scepticism are more
complicated than they seem. One rhetorical function of scepticism is
to *affirm* the belief being doubted simply by raising it to consciousness.[34] Despite the radical nature of some of the views expressed in
Heracles, the overall impact of Euripidean tragedy does nothing to
disrupt the three fundamental tenets of Athenian religion as prac-
tised by its citizens: that gods exist, that they pay attention (welcome
or unwelcome) to the affairs of mortals, and that some kind of
reciprocal allegiance between gods and humans was in operation,
most visibly instantiated in sacrifice. The tragic performances were
framed by the rituals of the Dionysia, and ritual fundamentally
informs tragedy's imagery, plots, and songs: a study of wedding and
funeral motifs, for example, has shown how they become conflated
into sinister variations of the figure of the 'bride of death', a strik-
ingly important poetic figure in the case of the two heroines in this
volume who volunteer for death, Alcestis and Heracles' daughter in
Children of Heracles.[35]

The plays themselves frame accounts of rituals, including the
description in *Heracles* of the thanksgiving sacrifice at the family
hearth, complete with baskets of grain, sacred water, and circling
children (925–9). Some rituals are even staged, such as the heart-
breaking antiphonal lament performed by Alcestis' husband and citizens after her funeral (*Alcestis* 860–934). Indeed, *Alcestis* is an
important source on ancient Greek household and funeral customs:
the mistress's prayer to Hestia, goddess of the family hearth (163–9);
the spring-water and shorn hair to be expected at the doors of
bereaved households (98–103). The *history* of religion certainly
seems to have fascinated Euripides. *Heracles* contains information
about the cult of this hero (1332–5); *Children of Heracles* is a rich
source for other cults in Attica.

Euripidean plots are repeatedly driven by violations of the great
taboos and imperatives constituting popular Greek ethics, the
boundaries defining unacceptable behaviour which in *Children of
Heracles* are called 'the laws common to the Greeks' (1010). These
regulated human relationships at every level. They proscribed, for

[34] See T. C. W. Stinton, ' "Si credere dignum est": Some Expressions of Disbelief in
Euripides and Others', *PCPS* 22 (1976), 60–89.
[35] Rush Rehm, *Marriage to Death: The Conflation of Wedding and Funeral Rituals in
Greek Tragedy* (Princeton, 1994).

example, kin-killing and failure to bury the dead. The worst type of kin-killing, a triple filicide, is the central event of *Heracles*, and two scenes in *Children of Heracles* revolve around the correct treatment of corpses—Heracles' daughter is understandably concerned to ensure that her body is properly prepared for burial by someone well disposed towards her (560–70), and the tragedy closes with an unpleasant altercation about the treatment which should be meted out to Eurystheus' corpse, an altercation in which, shockingly, he is still alive to participate.

The 'common laws' ascribed to Zeus the protection of vulnerable groups such as recipients of oaths, guests and hosts, and suppliants. These groups are important to Euripidean tragedy. Alcestis makes her husband swear a formal oath not to remarry (299–310). Hospitality is also an issue in *Alcestis*, in *Heracles* (where Theseus repays his obligation to a friend by inviting him to reside in his city), and even in *Cyclops*, where Polyphemus demonstrates, with comic excess, how *not* to entertain visitors. Supplication is an inherently theatrical convention, but it also possessed strong religious significance. Supplication at an altar was supposed to offer inviolable protection against physical assault or arrest, which is why Heracles' endangered family are found clustered at altars in both *Heracles* and *Children of Heracles*. But supplication did not necessarily require an altar: it could also take the form of a formal entreaty, accompanied by ritualized touching of knees, hand, and chin, which is intended to put the recipient under a religious obligation to accede to the suppliant's requests. Supplication in Euripides characterizes numerous crucial scenes; Amphitryon supplicates his own son, Heracles, when trying to persuade him to uncover his head, respond to Theseus, and 'to behave less like a proud, fierce lion!' (1203–13).

MUSIC, CHORUS, SONG

We have lost the melodies to which the lyrics of tragedy were sung to the accompaniment of pipes (*auloi*). But it is possible partially to decipher what John Gould called 'strategies of poetic sensibility'[36] within the formal, conventional media open to the tragedian: besides the choral passages, which were danced and sung, the tragedian had

---

[36] John Gould, 'Dramatic Character and "Human Intelligibility" in Greek Tragedy', *PCPS* 24 (1978), 43–67, especially 54–8.

several modes of delivery to choose from for his individual actors. In
addition to set-piece speeches and line-by-line spoken dialogue
(*stichomythia*), they included solo song, duet, sung interchange with
the chorus, and an intermediate mode of delivery, probably chanting
to pipe accompaniment, signalled by the anapaestic rhythm (∪ ∪ –).
Euripides' songs were extremely popular: the ancients believed
that some Athenians in Sicily saved themselves after the disaster at
Syracuse in 413 BCE by singing his songs to their captors (Plutarch,
Life of Nicias 29). In a lost comedy named *Euripides-Lover* (Axionicus
fr. 3) a character discussed people who hate all but Euripidean lyrics.

In this edition the sung and chanted sections have been labelled
and laid out in shorter lines so that the reader can appreciate the
shifts between speech and musical passages. Awareness of the inter-
mittent use of the singing voice matters because it mattered in
antiquity. The musicologist Aristoxenus said that speech begins to
sound like song *when we are emotional* (*Elementa Harmonica* 1.9–10).
In *Alcestis* the dying mother and her distraught young son are linked
by their sad sung delivery of lyrics (247–72, 393–403, 406–15); in
Heracles the only solo voice to be heard in a musical passage uttering
lyrics is Amphitryon's, from inside the house, as the crisis erupts
(886–908).

The chorus, although it can also speak, and even function as an
'umpire' between warring parties in a debate (*Children of Heracles*
179–80), is, however, the primary lyric voice in Euripidean tragedy.
Sometimes the chorus's songs 'fill in' time while actors change roles
(*Alcestis* 435–76) or 'telescope' time while events happen offstage,
even a full-scale military encounter such as the battle in *Children of
Heracles* (748–83). Often the chorus sings forms of lyric song derived
from the world of collective ritual. Passages of choral song may have
their roots in lament, wedding song, or in hymns of praise to heroes
or gods. In this volume the extended chorus recounting the hero's
labours in *Heracles* (348–451) clearly overlaps with songs performed
in the actual hero cult. In *Children of Heracles* the chorus perform a
hymn to the gods of Marathon and of Athens, Zeus and Athena,
asking their help in the battle against the Argives (748–83).

Some choral odes allude to mythical narratives functioning as a
form of memory; in *Heracles* the chorus celebrate the liberation of
Thebes after the death of the tyrant Lycus by recalling the names of
its rivers and sacred places, its foundation myth, and the birth and
genealogy of its hero (763–814). Other odes are more philosophical

or contemplative in orientation, and meditate in general terms on the issues which have been explored in the concrete situation of the play's previous episode. Thus the chorus of *Alcestis*, faced with Admetus' apparently inconsolable grief, engage in some sophisticated metaphysical reflections on the workings of the universe and man's attempts to alter them, concluding that Necessity is the most powerful cosmic force of all (962–1005). In *Heracles* the chorus's reflections on old age, their temperate response to the reappearance of Heracles, form one of the saddest lyrics in Greek literature (639–700).

SPEECH

In Aristophanes' *Frogs*, a prominent feature of Euripidean tragedy is the 'programmatic' prologue delivered by a leading character, which is characterized in the comedy as predictable both in metrical form and in 'scene-setting' function. But the Aristophanic caricature is unfair: the prologue establishes expectations, themes, and images which will subsequently become central to the drama. Euripides, moreover, took care over his choice of speaker. Opening *Alcestis* with Apollo allows the audience a divine perspective on the crisis afflicting Admetus' previously happy family in Thessaly, and stresses the extent to which humans are innocent victims of divine infighting; both *Heracles* and *Children of Heracles* are introduced by sympathetic elderly men entrusted with the unenviable task of keeping Heracles' children alive in the face of persecution.

The Roman rhetorician Quintilian judged Euripides of more use than Sophocles to the trainee orator (10.1.67), and the modern reader will undoubtedly be struck by the peculiarly formal debates in these plays, especially Amphitryon versus Lycus on the status of archery relative to hoplite warfare in *Heracles* (140–235), and the rival foreign policies proposed to Demophon by the Argive herald and Iolaus in *Children of Heracles* (120–231). The debate (*agōn*) is one of the features which Athenian drama assimilated from the oral performances which characterized two other great institutions of the democracy: the lawcourts and the assembly. To meet the increasing need for polished public speaking and its assessment under the widened franchise, the study of the science of persuasion, or the art of rhetoric, developed rapidly around the middle of the fifth century (see also above, 'Euripides the Athenian'); this is reflected in tragedy's

increased use of formal rhetorical figures, tropes, 'common topics'
such as pragmatism and expediency, and hypothetical arguments
from probability. One form of exercise available to the trainee orator
was the 'double argument'—the construction or study of twin
speeches for and against a particular proposition, or for the defence
and prosecution in a hypothetical trial. As a character in Euripides'
lost *Antiope* averred, 'If one were clever at speaking, one could have a
competition between two arguments in every single case' (fr. 189). In
assessing Euripidean rhetoric it must be remembered that his audience had become accustomed to startling displays by litigants in law-
suits (Aristophanes, *Wasps* 562–86); by the 420s political oratory
sometimes descended into competitive exhibitionism in which the
medium had superseded the message (Thucydides 3.38).

Euripides' gift for narrative is perhaps clearest in his 'messenger
speeches', vivid mini-epics of important offstage action. Alcestis'
maidservant movingly recounts her mistress's farewell to her household (*Alcestis* 152–98), and the messenger in *Children of Heracles* has
to deliver a detailed account of an entire military operation complete
with the generals' exhortations to their troops, a battle, and a miracle
(799–866). The stunning messenger speech in *Heracles*, recounting
with an unusually strong visual sense the onset of madness and the
slaughter of his family, was famous in later antiquity: in the third
century CE its pictorial quality was reworked to remarkable effect by
Philostratus in his *Imagines*, a work describing scenes which purport
to derive from paintings (2.23). All Euripides' poetry is marked by
exquisite simile and metaphor, often traced thematically through a
play; in *Heracles*, for example, there is a complex cluster of terms and
images connected with physical compulsion and restraint: yoking,
towing, and chaining. Euripides' picturesque style was much
admired in antiquity ('Longinus', *On the Sublime* 15.1–4).

Euripides showed infinite versatility of register, and was capable of
selecting rare poetic words for special effect (Aristotle, *Poetics* 58^{b}19–
24). Yet he still revolutionized the diction of tragedy by making his
characters speak in his distinctively 'human way'. This ordinary
quality of the language spoken by Euripides' characters attracted
emulation by able poets even within his lifetime, yet in Aristophanes'
Frogs Dionysus dismisses them as insignificant 'chatterers' in comparison (89–95). For Euripides was really doing something extremely
difficult in making his unforgettable characters express themselves
plausibly and 'like human beings'. Thus the author of an encomium

to Euripides in the *Palatine Anthology* justifiably discourages the aspiring imitator (7.50):

> Poet, do not attempt to go down Euripides' road;
> It is hard for men to tread.
> It seems easy, but the man who tries to walk it
> Finds it rougher than if it were set with cruel stakes.
> If you even try to scratch the surface of Medea, daughter of Aeetes,
> You shall die forgotten. Leave Euripides' crowns alone.[37]

[37] Thanks to Paul Cartledge and Lindsay Hall for helpful comments on a previous version of this Introduction. Thanks are also due to the AHRB, whose funding of the research at the Archive of Performances of Greek and Roman Drama in Oxford has facilitated the writing of the material on the reception of Euripides.

NOTE ON THE TRANSLATION

My policy as regards translation has, as usual, been to try to combine, as much as possible, fluency with accuracy. I have not attempted a verse translation: they very rarely work. Of course, the most difficult passages are the choral odes and lyric passages. It is clear that a poetic English version of these passages can be achieved only by taking considerable liberties with the literal meaning of the original Greek; indeed, even apart from such distortion, many translators simply omit whole words or phrases. Therefore, since my policy included the desire to give a faithful translation, I had to ignore most poetic values in favour of accuracy. So other than a tendency to employ more poetic syntax and vocabulary in these passages, the most I have done towards rendering them as verse is to break them up into shorter lines, so that the reader can see at a glance that they are different from—more emotionally charged than—the surrounding material. I have not broken up all the lyric passages into shorter lines like this; occasionally it made better sense not to distinguish them from the surrounding material, for instance where one character is speaking in the usual iambic trimeters, while the other is using lyrics, or the tone is still rather colloquial, or the verses are intrinsically part of the action of the play. Although, then, in most respects I have chosen accuracy of translation over considerations such as the possible modern production of any of the plays, the only major liberty I have taken with the text is to add stage directions, which are lacking in the manuscripts of Greek plays. However, I believe that an intelligent and creative director could still use the following texts as the basis for modern productions, and would thereby come close to Euripides' original intentions.

Apart from places marked in the translations with an obelus (which refers the interested reader to the Textual Notes, pp. 157–61), I have translated the Oxford Classical Text of J. Diggle (3 vols., 1981, 1984, 1994). Marginal line numbers refer to these Greek texts.

James Morwood and I would like to take this opportunity once again to thank Christopher Collard immensely for generously sharing his enormous knowledge of Greek tragedy, and of Euripides in particular.

SELECT BIBLIOGRAPHY

GENERAL BOOKS ON GREEK TRAGEDY

P. E. Easterling (ed.), *The Cambridge Companion to Greek Tragedy* (Cambridge, 1987); Simon Goldhill, *Reading Greek Tragedy* (Cambridge, 1986); Rush Rehm, *Greek Tragic Theatre* (London, 1992); Charles Segal, *Interpreting Greek Tragedy: Myth, Poetry, Text* (Ithaca, NY, 1986); Oliver Taplin, *Greek Tragedy in Action* (London, 1978); J. P. Vernant and P. Vidal-Naquet, *Tragedy and Myth in Ancient Greece* (English trans., Brighton, 1981); John J. Winkler and F. I. Zeitlin (eds.), *Nothing to do with Dionysos? Athenian Drama in its Social Context* (Princeton, 1990).

GENERAL BOOKS ON EURIPIDES

P. Burian (ed.), *New Directions in Euripidean Criticism* (Durham, NC, 1985); Christopher Collard, *Euripides* (*Greece & Rome New Surveys in the Classics*, 24, Oxford, 1981); D. J. Conacher, *Euripidean Drama* (Toronto, 1967); *Euripide, Entretiens sur l'antiquité classique*, vi, published by the Fondation Hardt (Vandouvres-Geneva, 1960); Helene P. Foley, *Ritual Irony: Poetry and Sacrifice in Euripides* (Ithaca, NY, 1985); G. M. Grube, *The Drama of Euripides* (2nd edn., London, 1962); M. Halleran, *Stagecraft in Euripides* (London, 1985); A. N. Michelini, *Euripides and the Tragic Tradition* (Madison, 1987); James Morwood, *The Plays of Euripides* (Bristol, 2002); Judith Mossman (ed.), *Oxford Readings in Euripides* (Oxford, 2000); E. Segal (ed.), *Euripides: A Collection of Critical Essays* (Englewood Cliffs, NJ, 1968); P. Vellacott, *Ironic Drama: A Study of Euripides' Method and Meaning* (Cambridge, 1976); C. H. Whitman, *Euripides and the Full Circle of Myth* (Cambridge, Mass., 1974).

EURIPIDES' LIFE AND BIOGRAPHIES

Hans-Ulrich Gösswein, *Die Briefe des Euripides* (Meisenheim am Glan, 1975); J. Gregory, *Euripides and the Instruction of the Athenians* (Ann Arbor, 1991); P. T. Stevens, 'Euripides and the Athenians', *JHS* 76 (1956), 87–94; M. R. Lefkowitz, *The Lives of the Greek Poets* (London,

1981), 88–104, 163–9; R. E. Wycherley, 'Aristophanes and Euripides', *G&R* 15 (1946), 98–107.

OPINIONS AND INTERPRETATIONS

R. Aélion, 'La Technique dramatique d'Euripide et sa conception de la destinée humaine', in J. Duchemin and F. Jouan (eds.), *Visages du destin dans les mythologies* (Paris, 1983), 69–85; R. B. Appleton, *Euripides the Idealist* (London, 1927); Robert Eisner, 'Euripides' Use of Myth', *Arethusa*, 12 (1979), 153–74; for 'historicist' approaches see E. Delebecque, *Euripide et la guerre du Péloponnèse* (Paris, 1951), and V. Di Benedetto, *Euripide: teatro e societa* (Turin, 1971); E. R. Dodds, 'Euripides the Irrationalist', *CR* 43 (1929), 97–104; H. Reich, 'Euripides, der Mystiker', in *Festschrift zu C. F. Lehmann-Haupts sechzigsten Geburtstage* (Vienna, 1921), 89–93; K. Reinhardt, 'Die Sinneskrise bei Euripides', *Eranos*, 26 (1957), 279–317—Euripides as a nihilist; in his *Existentialism and Euripides* (Victoria, 1977) William Sale draws on both Heidegger and Freud; A. W. Verrall, *Euripides the Rationalist* (Cambridge, 1895).

RECEPTION OF EURIPIDEAN TRAGEDY

Peter Burian, 'Tragedy Adapted for Stages and Screens: The Renaissance to the Present', in Easterling (ed.), *The Cambridge Companion to Greek Tragedy* (see above), 228–83; Pat Easterling, 'Gilbert Murray's Readings of Euripides', *Colby Quarterly*, 33 (1997), 113–27; Stuart Gillespie, *The Poets on the Classics* (London, 1988), 90–4; Edith Hall, 'Talfourd's Ancient Greeks in the Theatre of Reform', *International Journal of the Classical Tradition*, 3 (1997), 283–407; Edith Hall, 'Medea and British Legislation before the First World War', *G&R* 46 (1999), 42–77; Edith Hall, 'Greek Tragedy and the British Stage', *Cahiers du GITA*, 12 (1999), 113–34; Edith Hall, Fiona Macintosh, and Oliver Taplin (eds.), *Medea in Performance 1500–2000* (Oxford, 2001); K. Mackinnon, *Greek Tragedy into Film* (London, 1986); Fiona Macintosh, 'Tragedy in Performance: Nineteenth- and Twentieth-Century Productions', in Easterling (ed.), *The Cambridge Companion to Greek Tragedy* (see above), 284–323; Fiona Macintosh, 'Alcestis on the British Stage', *Cahiers du GITA*, 14 (2001), 281–308; Martin Mueller, *Children of Oedipus and Other Essays on the Imitation of Greek Tragedy*

1550–1800 (Toronto, 1980), 46–63; F. L. Lucas, *Euripides and his Influence* (New York, 1928).

VISUAL ARTS

Vase-paintings illustrating scenes from Euripides are collected in A. D. Trendall and T. B. L. Webster, *Illustrations of Greek Drama* (London, 1971), 72–105, and supplemented in the articles under the names of each important mythical character (e.g. 'Theseus') in the multi-volume ongoing *Lexicon Iconographicum Mythologiae Classicae* (Zurich, 1984–). See also Richard Green, *Theatre in Ancient Greek Society* (London, 1994); Richard Green and Eric Handley, *Images of the Greek Theatre* (Austin, Tex., 1995); Oliver Taplin, 'The Pictorial Record', in Easterling, *Cambridge Companion to Greek Tragedy* (see above), 69–90; Kurt Weitzmann, 'Euripides Scenes in Byzantine Art', *Hesperia*, 18 (1949), 159–210.

PRODUCTION AND PERFORMANCE CONTEXT

Giovanni Comotti, *Music in Greek and Roman Culture* (English trans., Baltimore, 1989), 32–41; E. Csapo and W. J. Slater, *The Context of Ancient Drama* (Ann Arbor, 1995), 79–101; P. Easterling and Edith Hall (eds.), *Greek and Roman Actors: Aspects of an Ancient Profession* (Cambridge, 2002); S. Goldhill, 'The Great Dionysia and Civic Ideology', in J. Winkler and F. I. Zeitlin (eds.), *Nothing to do with Dionysos? Athenian Drama in its Social Context* (Princeton, 1990), 97–129; John Gould, 'Tragedy in Performance', in B. Knox and P. E. Easterling (eds.), *The Cambridge History of Classical Literature*, i (Cambridge, 1985), 258–81; John Gould, 'Dramatic Character and "human intelligibility" in Greek Tragedy', *PCPS* 24 (1978), 43–67; Edith Hall, 'Actor's Song in Tragedy', in Simon Goldhill and Robin Osborne (eds.), *Performance Culture and Athenian Democracy* (Cambridge, 1999), 96–122; Nicolaos C. Hourmouziades, *Production and Imagination in Euripides: Form and Function of the Scenic Space* (Athens, 1965); Maarit Kaimio, *Physical Contact in Greek Tragedy* (Helsinki, 1988); Solon Michaelides, *The Music of Ancient Greece: An Encyclopaedia* (London, 1978), 117–19; A. Pickard-Cambridge, *The Dramatic Festivals of Athens*[3], rev. by J. Gould and D. M. Lewis (Oxford, 1988); Erika Simon, *The Ancient Theater* (London, 1982); Oliver Taplin, *The Stagecraft of Aeschylus* (Oxford, 1977), and 'Did Greek Dramatists

Write Stage Instructions?', *PCPS* 23 (1977), 121–32; on satyr drama see below, '*Cyclops*'.

SOCIAL AND HISTORICAL CONTEXT

Paul Cartledge, *The Greeks* (Oxford, 1996) and (ed.), *The Cambridge Illustrated History of Ancient Greece* (Cambridge, 1997); John Gould, *Myth, Ritual, Memory, and Exchange* (Oxford, 2001); J. K. Davies, *Democracy and Classical Greece* (Glasgow, 1978), 63–128, and 'Athenian Citizenship: The Descent Group and the Alternatives', *CJ* 73 (1977–8), 105–21; Colin McLeod, 'Thucydides and Tragedy', in *Collected Essays* (Oxford, 1983), 140–58; Christopher Pelling (ed.), *Greek Tragedy and the Historian* (Oxford, 1997); Anton Powell, *Athens and Sparta: Constructing Greek Political and Social History from 478 BC* (London, 1988).

For an overview of the problems in reconstructing Athenian women's lives, see Josine Blok's review in J. Blok and H. Mason (eds.), *Sexual Asymmetry: Studies in Ancient Society* (Amsterdam, 1987), 1–57. For a recent range of views on gender issues see D. Cohen, *Law, Sexuality, and Society: The Enforcement of Morals in Classical Athens* (Cambridge, 1991); Elaine Fantham et al. (eds.), *Women in the Classical World* (New York, 1994); Helene Foley, *Female Acts in Greek Tragedy* (Princeton, 2001); John Gould, 'Law, Custom, and Myth: Aspects of the Social Position of Women in Classical Athens', *JHS* 100 (1980), 38–59; Virginia Hunter, *Policing Athens* (Princeton, 1994), 9–42; R. Just, *Women in Athenian Law and Life* (London, 1989); Froma Zeitlin, *Playing the Other: Gender and Society in Classical Greek Literature* (Chicago, 1996).

SPECIFIC ASPECTS OF EURIPIDEAN DRAMA

Rachel Aélion, *Euripide. Héritier d'Eschyle*, 2 vols. (Paris, 1983); Luigi Battezzatto, *Il monologo nel teatro di Euripide* (Pisa, 1995); Francis M. Dunn, *Tragedy's End: Closure and Innovation in Euripidean Drama* (New York, 1996); H. Erbse, *Studien zum Prolog der euripideischen Tragödie* (Berlin, 1984); M. Fusillo, 'Was ist eine romanhafte Tragödie? Überlegungen zu Euripides' Experimentalismus', *Poetica*, 24 (1992), 270–99; Richard Hamilton, 'Prologue, Prophecy and Plot in Four Plays of Euripides', *AJP* 99 (1978), 277–302, and 'Euripidean Priests', *HSCP* 89 (1985), 53–73; Rosemary Harriott, 'Aristophanes' Audience and the Plays of Euripides', *BICS* 9 (1962), 1–9; Martin Hose, *Studien zum Chor bei Euripides* (Berlin, 1990–1); E. O'Connor-Visser, *Aspects of Human Sacrifice in the Tragedies of Euripides* (Amsterdam, 1987); S. Said, 'Greeks and Barbarians in Euripides' Tragedies: The End of Difference?', in Thomas Harrison (ed.), *Greeks and Barbarians* (Edinburgh, 2002), 62–100; Bernd Seidensticker, 'Tragic Dialectic in Euripidean Tragedy', in M. S. Silk (ed.), *Tragedy and the Tragic: Greek Theatre and Beyond* (Oxford, 1996), 377–96; H. P. Stahl, 'On Extradramatic Communication of Characters in Euripides', *YCS* 25 (1977), 159–76; Sophie Trenkner, *The Greek Novella in the Classical Period* (Cambridge, 1958) 31–78; R. P. Winnington-Ingram, 'Euripides: *poiētēs sophos*', *Arethusa*, 2 (1969), 127–42; Froma Zeitlin, 'The Artful Eye: Vision, Ecphrasis and Spectacle in Euripidean Theatre', in S. Goldhill and R. Osborne (eds.), *Art and Text in Ancient Greek Culture* (Cambridge, 1994), 138–305.

For the lost plays of Euripides see C. Collard, M. J. Cropp, and K. H. Lee (eds.), *Euripides: Selected Fragmentary Plays*, i–ii (Warminster, 1995, 1999); T. B. L. Webster, *The Tragedies of Euripides* (London, 1967).

On slaves in Euripides see H. Kuch, *Kriegsgefangenschaft und Sklaverei bei Euripides* (Berlin, 1974); K. Synodinou, *On the Concept of Slavery in Euripides* (English trans., Ioannina, 1977); Edith Hall, *Inventing the Barbarian* (Oxford, 1989); Edith Hall, 'The Sociology of Athenian Tragedy', in Easterling, *The Cambridge Companion to Greek Tragedy* (see above), 93–126; D. P. Stanley-Porter, 'Mute Actors in the Tragedies of Euripides', *BICS* 20 (1973), 68–93. On children see G. Sifakis, 'Children in Greek Tragedy', *BICS* 26 (1979), 67–80. On women see H. Foley, 'The Conception of Women in Athenian Drama', in H. P. Foley (ed.), *Reflections of Women in Antiquity* (London, 1981), 127–67; Ruth Herder, *Die Frauenrolle bei Euripides* (Stuttgart, 1993); Nicole Loraux, *Tragic Ways of Killing a Woman* (English trans., Cambridge, Mass., 1987); Rush Rehm, *Marriage to Death: The Conflation of Wedding and Funeral Rituals in Greek Tragedy* (Princeton, 1994); Richard Seaford, 'The Structural Problems of Marriage in Euripides', in A. Powell (ed.), *Euripides, Women and Sexuality* (London, 1990), 151–76; Nancy Sorkin Rabinowitz, *Anxiety Veiled: Euripides and the Traffic in Women* (Ithaca, NY, 1993); Froma Zeitlin, *Playing the Other: Gender and Society in Classical Greek Literature* (Chicago, 1996).

For religion in Euripides see C. Sourvinou-Inwood, 'Tragedy and Religion: Constructs and Meanings', in Christopher Pelling (ed.),

Greek Tragedy and the Historian (Oxford, 1997), 161–86. For sceptical
discussions see M. R. Lefkowitz, 'Was Euripides an Atheist?', *Studi
italiani*, 5 (1987), 149–65, and ' "Atheism" and "Impiety" in Euripides' Dramas', *CQ* 39 (1989), 70–82; G. E. Dimock, *'God or Not God, or
between the Two': Euripides' Helen* (Northampton, Mass., 1977)—
Euripides' evangelism; T. C. W. Stinton, ' "Si credere dignum est":
Some Expressions of Disbelief in Euripides and Others', *PCPS* 22
(1976), 60–89; Harvey Yunis, *A New Creed: Fundamental Religious
Beliefs in the Athenian Polis and Euripidean Drama* (= *Hypomnemata*, 91,
Göttingen, 1988). On supplication scenes, see J. Gould, 'Hiketeia', *JHS*
93 (1973), 74–103.

On the sophists, philosophy, and the intellectual background see
D. J. Conacher, *Euripides and the Sophists: Some Dramatic Treatments
of Philosophical Ideas* (London, 1998); J. H. Finley, 'Euripides and
Thucydides', in *Three Essays on Thucydides* (Cambridge, Mass.,
1967), 1–24; S. Goldhill, *Reading Greek Tragedy* (Cambridge, 1986),
222–43; G. B. Kerferd, *The Sophistic Movement* (Cambridge, 1981);
W. Nestle, *Untersuchungen über die philosophischen Quellen des Euripides*, *Philologus* suppl. 8.4 (1901), 557–655, and *Euripides: Der Dichter
der griechischen Aufklärung* (Stuttgart, 1901); F. Solmsen, *Intellectual
Experiments of the Greek Enlightenment* (Princeton, 1975), 24–31,
132–41.

On rhetoric see V. Bers, 'Tragedy and Rhetoric', in I. Worthington
(ed.), *Greek Rhetoric in Action* (London, 1994), 176–95; Richard Buxton, *Persuasion in Greek Tragedy* (Cambridge, 1982); C. Collard, 'Formal Debates in Euripidean Drama', in I. McAuslan and P. Walcot,
Greek Tragedy (Oxford, 1993), 153–66; D. J. Conacher, 'Rhetoric and
Relevance in Euripidean Drama', *AJP* 102 (1981), 3–25; E. Hall, 'Law-
court Dramas: The Power of Performance in Greek Forensic Oratory',
BICS 40 (1995), 39–58; M. Lloyd, *The Agon in Euripides* (Oxford,
1992).

On characterization, see H. P. Stahl, 'On "Extra-dramatic" Communication in Euripides', *YCS* 25 (1977), 159–76; J. Griffin, 'Characterization in Euripides', in C. Pelling (ed.), *Characterization and
Individuality in Greek Literature* (Oxford, 1990), 128–49.

On speech, language, style, and imagery, see Shirley Barlow, *The
Imagery of Euripides* (London, 1971); I. J. F. de Jong, *Narrative in
Drama: The Art of the Euripidean Messenger-Speech* (Leiden, 1991);
Ewald Kurtz, *Die bildliche Ausdrucksweise in den Tragödien des Euripides*
(Amsterdam, 1985); P. T. Stevens, *Colloquial Expressions in Euripides*

(Wiesbaden, 1976); Ernst Schwinge, *Die Verwendung der Stichomythie in den Dramen des Euripides* (Heidelberg, 1968).

ALCESTIS

Editions

A. M. Dale (ed.), *Euripides' Alcestis* (Oxford, 1954); D. J. Conacher (ed.), *Euripides' Alcestis* (Warminster, 1988).

Studies

C. R. Beye, 'Alcestis and her Critics', *GRBS* 2 (1959), 109–27; E. M. Bradley, 'Admetus and the Triumph of Failure in Euripides' *Alcestis*', *Ramus*, 9 (1980), 112–27; A. P. Burnett, 'The Virtues of Admetus', *CP* 60 (1965), 240–55; R. G. A. Buxton, 'Euripides' Alkestis: Five Aspects of an Interpretation', in *Papers Given at a Colloquium in Honour of R. P. Winnington-Ingram* (London, 1987), 18–27; V. Castellani, 'Notes on the Structure of Euripides' *Alcestis*', *AJP* 100 (1979), 487–96; H. Erbse, 'Euripides' *Alkestis*', *Philologus*, 116 (1972), 32–52; Helene P. Foley, '*Anodos* Drama: Euripides' *Alcestis* and *Helen*', in Ralph Hexter and Daniel Selden (eds.), *Innovations of Antiquity* (New York, 1992), 133–60; R. Garner, 'Death and Victory in Euripides' *Alcestis*', *Classical Antiquity*, 7 (1988), 58–71; J. Gregory, 'Euripides' *Alcestis*', *Hermes*, 107 (1979), 259–70; M. Halleran, 'Text and Ceremony at the Close of Euripides' *Alkestis*', *Eranos*, 86 (1988), 123–9; A. Lesky, *Alkestis. Der Mythos und das Drama* (Vienna, 1925); M. Lloyd, 'Euripides' *Alcestis*', *G&R* 32 (1985), 119–31; R. M. Nielsen, 'Alcestis: A Paradox in Dying', *Ramus*, 5 (1976), 92–102; G. Paduano, *La formazione del mondo ideologico e poetico di Euripide* (Pisa, 1968); G. A. Seeck, *Unaristotelische Untersuchungen zu Euripides: Ein motivanalytischer Kommentar zur Alkestis* (Heidelberg, 1985); G. Smith, 'The *Alcestis* of Euripides: An Interpretation', *Rivista di filologia e di istruzione classica*, 111 (1983), 129–45; W. D. Smith, 'The Ironic Structure in *Alcestis*', *Phoenix*, 14 (1960), 127–45; K. von Fritz, 'Euripides' Alkestis und ihre modernen Nachahmer und Kritiker', in *Antike und moderne Tragödie* (Berlin, 1962), 256–321; J. R. Wilson (ed.), *Euripides' Alcestis* (Englewood Cliffs, NJ, 1968).

HERACLES

Editions

Godfrey Bond, *Euripides' Heracles* (Oxford, 1981); Shirley Barlow, *Euripides' Herakles* (Warminster, 1996).

Studies

Shirley Barlow, 'Structure and Dramatic Realism in Euripides' *Herakles*', *G&R* 29 (1982), 115–25, repr. in I. McAuslan and P. Walcott (eds.), *Greek Tragedy* (Oxford, 1993); Shirley Barlow, 'Sophocles' Ajax and Euripides' Heracles', *Ramus*, 10 (1981), 112–28; G. J. Baudy, 'Die Herrschaft des Wolfes. Das Thema des "verkehrten Welt" in Euripides' *Herakles*', *Hermes*, 121 (1993), 159–80; H. Chalk, '*Arete* and *bia* in Euripides' *Herakles*', *JHS* 82 (1962), 7–18; Martin Cropp, '*Heracles*, *Electra* and the *Odyssey*', in M. Cropp et al. (eds.), *Greek Tragedy and its Legacy* (Calgary, 1987), 187–99; G. Karl Galinsky, *The Herakles Theme* (Oxford, 1972), 40–80; J. C. Gibert, 'Euripides *Heracles* 1351 and the Hero's Encounter with Death', *CP* 92 (1997), 247–58; J. Gregory, 'Euripides' *Heracles*', *YCS* 25 (1977), 259–75; M. R. Halleran, 'Rhetoric, Irony, and the Ending of Euripides' *Herakles*', *Classical Antiquity*, 5 (1986), 171–81; R. Hamilton, 'Slings and Arrows: The Debate with Lycos in the *Heracles*', *TAPA* 115 (1985), 19–25; J. C. Kamerbeek, 'Unity and Meaning of Euripides' *Heracles*', *Mnemosyne*, 19 (1966), 1–16; Christina Kraus, 'Dangerous Supplements: Etymology and Genealogy in Euripides' *Heracles*', *PCPS* 44 (1998), 137–57; K. H. Lee, 'The Iris–Lyssa Scene in Euripides' *Heracles*', *Antichthon*, 16 (1982), 44–53; J. D. Mikalson, 'Zeus the Father and Heracles the Son in Tragedy', *TAPA* 116 (1986), 89–98; H. Parry, 'The Second Stasimon of Euripides' *Herakles*', *AJP* 86 (1965), 363–74; D. H. Porter, 'Only Connect: Euripides' *Heracles*', in *Only Connect: Three Studies in Greek Tragedy* (Laxham, 1987), 85–112; C. Ruck, 'Duality and the Madness of Herakles', *Arethusa*, 9 (1976), 53–75; J. T. Sheppard, 'The Formal Beauty of the *Hercules Furens*', *CQ* 10 (1916), 72–9; M. S. Silk, 'Heracles and Greek Tragedy', *G&R* 32 (1985), 1–22, repr. in I. McAuslan and P. Walcott (eds.), *Greek Tragedy* (Oxford, 1993); C. Willink, 'Sleep after Labour in Euripides' *Heracles*', *CQ* 38 (1988), 86–97; Froma Zeitlin, 'Thebes: Theater of Self and Society in Athenian Drama', in Winkler and Zeitlin, *Nothing to do with Dionysos?* (see above), 130–67.

CHILDREN OF HERACLES

Editions

John Wilkins, *Euripides' Heraclidae* (Oxford, 1993); William Allan, *Euripides: The Children of Heracles* (Warminster, 2001).

Studies

U. Albini, 'La falsa convenzionalità degli Eraclidi', *SIFC* 11 (1993), 106–11; H. C. Avery, 'Euripides' *Heraclidai*', *AJP* 92 (1971), 539–65; P. Burian, 'Euripides' *Heraclidae*: An Interpretation', *CP* 72 (1977), 1–21; A. P. Burnett, 'Tribe and City, Custom and Decree in *Children of Heracles*', *CP* 71 (1976), 4–26; J. Davidson, 'Two Notes on Euripides' *Heraclidae*', *Athenaeum*, 84 (1996), 243–7; T. M. Falkner, 'The wrath of Alcmene: Gender, Authority and Old Age in Euripides' *Children of Heracles*', in T. M. Falkner and J. de Luce (eds.), *Old Age in Greek and Latin Literature* (Albany, NY, 1989), 114–31; J. W. Fitton, 'The *Suppliant Women* and the *Heraklidai* of Euripides', *Hermes*, 89 (1961), 430–61; R. Guerrini, 'La morte di Euristeo e la implicazione eticopolitiche negli Eraclidi di Euripide', *Athenaeum*, 50 (1972), 45–67; Emily Kearns, *The Heroes of Attica* (*BICS* suppl. 57, London, 1989); E. Krummen, 'Athens and Attica: *Polis* and Countryside in Tragedy', in A. Sommerstein et al. (eds.), *Tragedy, Comedy and the Polis* (Bari, 1993), 191–217; A. Lesky, 'On the *Heraclidae* of Euripides', *YCS* 25 (1977), 272–38; J. McLean, 'The *Heraclidae* of Euripides', *AJP* 55 (1934), 197–224; Rush Rehm, 'The Staging of Suppliant Plays', *GRBS* 29 (1988), 263–307; J. A. Spranger, 'The Political Element in the *Heraclidae* of Euripides', *CQ* 19 (1925), 117–29; F. Stoessl, 'Die Herakliden des Euripides', *Philologus*, 100 (1956), 207–34; M. Visser, 'Worship your Enemy: Aspects of the Cult of Heroes in Ancient Greece', *Harvard Theological Review*, 75 (1982), 403–28; J. Wilkins, 'The Young of Athens: Religion and Society in the *Herakleidai* of Euripides', *CQ* 40 (1990), 329–39; 'The State and the Individual: Euripides' Plays of Voluntary Self-Sacrifice', in A. Powell (ed.), *Euripides, Women, and Sexuality* (London, 1990), 177–94; G. Zuntz, 'Is the *Heraclidae* Mutilated?', *CQ* 41 (1947), 46–52; G. Zuntz, *The Political Plays of Euripides* (2nd edn., Manchester, 1963).

CYCLOPS

Editions

Richard Seaford (ed.), *Euripides' Cyclops* (Oxford, 1984).

Studies

W. G. Arnott, 'Parody and Ambiguity in Euripides' *Cyclops*', in *Melanges W. Kraus* (Vienna, 1972), 21–30; W. Biehl, 'Die Funktion des Opfermotivs in Euripides' *Kyklops*', *Hermes*, 111 (1987), 283–99; F. Brommer, *Das Satyrspiel* (Berlin, 1959); L. Campo, *I drammi satireschi della Grecia antica* (Milan, 1940), 221–61; I. Chalkia, 'Fonctions narratives et substitutions dans le Cyclope d'Euripide', *Hellenica*, 31 (1979), 293–315; N. E. Collinge, 'Some Reflections on Satyr Plays', *PCPS* 185 (1958–9), 28–35; P. E. Easterling, 'A Show for Dionysos', in Easterling, *The Cambridge Companion to Greek Tragedy* (see above), 36–53; E. Hall, 'Ithyphallic Males Behaving Badly: Satyr Drama as Gendered Tragic Ending', in M. Wyke (ed.), *Parchments of Gender: Deciphering the Bodies of Antiquity* (Oxford, 1998), 13–37; R. Hamilton, 'Euripides' Cyclopean Symposium', *Phoenix*, 33 (1979), 287–92; D. Konstan, 'The Anthropology of Euripides' *Kyklops*', in Winkler and Zeitlin, *Nothing to do with Dionysos?* (see above), 207–27; F. Lissarrague, 'Why Satyrs are Good to Represent', in Winkler and Zeitlin, *Nothing to do with Dionysos?* (see above), 228–36; F. Lissarrague, 'The Sexual Life of Satyrs', in D. M. Halperin, J. J. Winkler, and F. I. Zeitlin (eds.), *Before Sexuality* (Princeton, 1990), 53–81; L. E. Rossi, 'Il Ciclope di Euripide come KOMOS mancato', *Maia*, 23 (1971), 10–38; B. Seidensticker, 'Das Satyrspiel', in G. A. Seeck (ed.), *Das griechische Drama* (Darmstadt, 1979); D. F. Sutton, *The Greek Satyr Play* (Meisenheim am Glan, 1980); R. G. Ussher, 'The *Cyclops* of Euripides', *G&R* 18 (1971), 166–79.

A CHRONOLOGY OF EURIPIDES'
WORK AND TIMES

Dates of productions of extant
plays (adapted from C. Collard,
Euripides (Oxford, 1981), 2)

Dates in the history of Athens

		462	Radical democracy established in Athens
455	first production		
		448	Building of Parthenon begun
441	first prize (play unknown)		
438	*Alcestis*—second prize		
431	*Medea*—third prize	431	Outbreak of Peloponnesian War between Athens and Sparta
430–428	*Heraclidae*	430	Outbreak of plague in Athens
428	*Hippolytus* (revised from earlier production)—first prize		
?425	*Andromache*		
before 423	*Hecuba*		
?423	*Supplices*		
?before 415	*Hercules Furens*		
before 415	*Electra*		
		416	Slaughter by the Athenians of the men of the island of Melos and the enslavement of its women and children
415	*Troades*—second prize	415–	Disastrous Athenian expedition
before 412	*Iphigenia at Tauris*	413	to Sicily
?before 412	*Ion*		
412	*Helen*		
?412	*Cyclops* (satyr play)		
411–408, ?409	*Phoenissae*—second prize	411	Oligarchic revolution in Athens
408	*Orestes*		
after 406	*Iphigenia at Aulis* and *Bacchae*—first prize		
		404	Defeat of Athens by Sparta in the Peloponnesian War

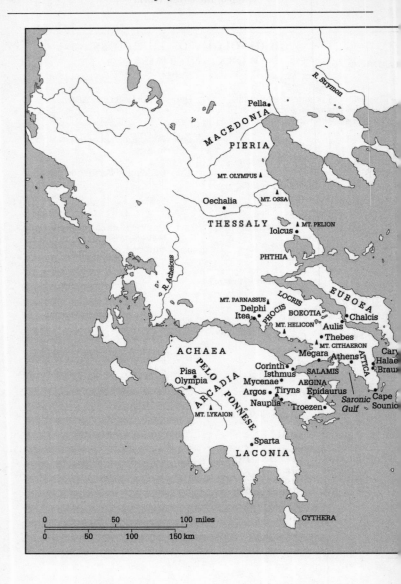

ALCESTIS

Characters

APOLLO
DEATH
MAIDSERVANT, Alcestis' slave
ADMETUS, king of Pherae
ALCESTIS, wife of Admetus
BOY, son of Alcestis and Admetus
HERACLES
PHERES, Admetus' father
MANSERVANT, Admetus' slave

CHORUS of elderly citizens of Pherae

Scene: in front of the palace of Admetus in Pherae, Thessaly.
APOLLO enters from the palace, carrying a bow and quiver.

APOLLO (*with regret*). Dear palace of Admetus, where, for all
that I am a god, I allowed myself to work and be fed as a hired
labourer. It was Zeus' doing: he killed my son Asclepius with a
fiery blast to the chest and in a fit of fury I killed the Cyclopes,
the forgers of Zeus' fire.* In requital for this my father forced
me to work as a hired labourer for a mortal man. I came to
this land and worked as a herdsman for my host,* and from
then until now I have kept his household safe. For in the son   10
of Pheres I found an honourable man, and I acted with honour too: I tricked the Fates and saved him from death.* The
divine Fates granted my request that Admetus might escape
Hades* for the time being, as long as he gave another life to
the powers below. He went in turn to all those who were close
to him† and sounded them out, but he found no one except
his wife who was willing to end her time on earth and die for
him. At this very moment she is breathing her last, supported
in his arms inside the palace, since this is the day on which   20
she is fated to die, to leave this life. In order to avoid the
taint of pollution in the house,* I am leaving this palace here
and its beloved halls.

But now I see Death approaching, the priest of the dead, to take her down to Hades' domain—a timely visit, because he has been watching out for today, when she must die.

Enter DEATH, carrying a sword.

DEATH (*catching sight of APOLLO*). Oh, no! You, by the palace! Why are you hanging around here, Phoebus?* Are you plan- 30
ning to do wrong again, to restrict and abolish the privileges of the dead once more? Aren't you content with having prevented Admetus' death by the cunning trick you devised to cheat the Fates? Are you now watching over her too (*pointing towards the palace*), bow in hand, when she—Pelias' daughter,* I mean—has promised to free her husband by dying herself in his place?

APOLLO. Don't worry.* I am armed only with justice and sound arguments.

DEATH. Why do you need a bow, then, if you have justice?

APOLLO. It is my custom always to carry this bow and these 40
arrows.*

DEATH. Yes, and to offer unjust help to this household.

APOLLO. That's because it upsets me to see a man who is dear to me suffer.

DEATH. Are you going to rob me of this second corpse?

APOLLO. But I didn't use force even in depriving you of the first one.

DEATH. Then why is he on earth and not down below the ground?

APOLLO. He changed places with his wife, for whom you've come now.

DEATH. Yes, and I *will* take her away with me to the underworld.

APOLLO. Go ahead, take her. I doubt I can persuade you.

DEATH. What? To kill those I must? That's my job.

APOLLO. No, to grant your intended victim a stay of death. 50

DEATH. Now I see your point; now I see your intentions.

APOLLO. Is there any way for Alcestis to reach old age?

DEATH. No. You should expect me too to enjoy my privileges.

APOLLO. Either way, it's still only one life you'd be getting.

DEATH. Early deaths win me greater honour.

APOLLO. If she dies in old age, she'll have a rich burial.

DEATH. The precedent you're trying to establish, Phoebus, would benefit the rich.

APOLLO. What do you mean? Can I have missed your sophistic side?

DEATH. Well-off people could buy late deaths.

APOLLO. Don't you think you might grant me this favour? 60

DEATH. Absolutely not. You know what I'm like.

APOLLO. Yes, you're hated by mortals and loathed by the gods.*

DEATH. You can't have everything you shouldn't.

APOLLO (*aside*). For all your savage nature, you will certainly be won over. The right man will come to Pheres' palace* on a mission from Eurystheus to bring a team of horses from the wintry regions of Thrace.* Lodged as a guest in Admetus' halls here, he will forcibly steal this woman from you. You will end up doing what I want anyway, but without earning 70 my gratitude,* and you will remain an object of loathing to me.

> *Exit* APOLLO.

DEATH. All these words of yours will get you nowhere: the woman will go down to Hades. I'm going to her now, to wield my sword in the preliminary rites of sacrifice. For anyone from whose head this sword of mine has consecrated some hair is sacred to the gods of the underworld.*

> *Exit* DEATH *into the palace. Enter the* CHORUS. *It divides into two Semichoruses.*

SEMICHORUS A. Why is no sound to be heard in front of the palace? Why is Admetus' house wrapped in silence?

SEMICHORUS B. Nor is there even any friend near by who might 80 tell us whether we should be mourning our queen in death, or whether she is still alive, and still sees the light of this day— Alcestis, I mean, the child of Pelias, thought by me and by all to have proved herself the best of wives to her husband.

SEMICHORUS A. Can anyone hear from inside tears or the sound of hands beating breasts, or wailing as if it were all over?

SEMICHORUS B. No, and neither is there any slave standing by 90 the doorway. O Paean,* appear, I beg you, and bring us relief from disaster.

SEMICHORUS A. If she were dead, there would not be silence,
I'm sure.

SEMICHORUS B. For her corpse has of course not been brought
from the house.†

SEMICHORUS A. How do you know? I'm not sure. Why are you
so certain?

SEMICHORUS B. There's no way that Admetus would have
conducted the burial of a wife as good as his without
mourners.

SEMICHORUS A. Look, there's no spring water in front of the
doorway, as is customary for the doors of the dead.   100

SEMICHORUS B. Nor are there any shorn locks of hair lying by
the door, as is fitting when grieving for the dead.†* Nor is
there the beating of the massed hands of women.

SEMICHORUS A. And yet this is the appointed day . . .

SEMICHORUS B. What is it you were going to say?†

SEMICHORUS A. . . . when she must go beneath the ground.

SEMICHORUS B. Your words pierce my heart, pierce me to the
core.

SEMICHORUS A. When the brave are in agony, those who from   110
childhood have been deemed loyal are bound to mourn.

The Semichoruses reunite and sing.

CHORUS. Nowhere on earth might one might send a ship,
not to Lycia nor to the waterless seat of Ammon,†*
to save the life of the wretched woman.
Inexorable fate draws near her, and I no longer know
of any god's altar to approach with sheep for slaughter.   120
Only† if the son of Phoebus* were alive to see
the light of this day might she have escaped
the murky realm and the gates of Hades.
For he raised those whom death had laid low,
until he was struck by the fiery bolt of thunder,
hurled by Zeus. And so what hope now   130
may I still entertain that she will live?†

The CHORUS stops singing, and the Chorus-leader continues alone.

But one of the serving-girls is coming out of the palace, in
floods of tears. What's happened? What is she going to tell
me?

Enter the MAIDSERVANT *in distress.*

(*To the* MAIDSERVANT) If something has happened to your mistress, I sympathize with your grief. But please tell me: is she   140
still alive or has she died?

MAIDSERVANT. You could say that she was alive—but also that
she was dead.

CHORUS. But how can the same person be both dead and alive?

MAIDSERVANT. Head bowed, she is already breathing her last.

CHORUS. Is there no longer any hope that she might be saved?

MAIDSERVANT. No, this is the day of her doom. Her death is
inevitable.

CHORUS. Are the appropriate rites being conducted over her?

MAIDSERVANT. Yes, the finery in which her husband will bury
her is ready and waiting.

CHORUS. Poor man, the wife you're losing was your equal in
nobility.

MAIDSERVANT. My master doesn't appreciate his loss yet, but
he will once he's suffered.

CHORUS. Well, she should at least know that she dies with a   150
glorious reputation as by far the best wife in the world.

MAIDSERVANT. She is indeed the best. Who will deny that she
is by far the noblest wife of all?† What greater proof could a
woman give of her love for her husband than by being prepared to die for him? This is public knowledge, but you'll be
astonished to hear what she did indoors. When she realized
that the appointed day had come, she washed her pale skin*
in river water, took clothing and jewellery from their homes   160
of cedar,* and dressed herself appropriately. Then she stood
before the altar of Hestia* and offered up a prayer: 'Mistress,
since I am about to go down to the underworld, I have one
final request to make of you: I implore you to look after my
children when I am gone.* Marry him to an affectionate wife,
and her to a noble husband. May my children not die before
their time, as their mother is, but live a complete and happy
life in the land of their birth.'

Next she went to all the altars inside Admetus' palace.   170
Plucking leaves off branches of myrtle,* she placed wreaths
on the altars and offered up prayers. She shed no tears and
made no complaints, and she retained the natural beauty of

her complexion even in the face of imminent doom. Finally she rushed into her chamber and fell upon her bed—and then at last she wept and spoke as follows: 'Dear bed, where I lost my youthful virginity to my husband—the husband for whom I am dying—farewell! I bear you no ill will, though you are entirely responsible for my death, since it is because I was not prepared to betray you and my husband that I am dying. Some other woman will possess you in my place*—a woman who may be more fortunate than I, but no more selfless.' 180

She hurled herself onto the bed and kissed it, and soaked it through with the tears flooding from her eyes. When, after a long while, she had wept all she could, she hurried from the bed with her head bowed. Over and over again she left the room only to turn around and fling herself back again onto the bed. Her children clung weeping to their mother's clothes. In awareness of her imminent death, she picked them up and kissed them one after another. All the slaves indoors began to cry out of pity for their mistress. She reached out her hand to each in turn, and none was so mean as to refuse to reply when she spoke to him. 190

This is the distressing news from Admetus' palace. If he had died, he would be no more, but in escaping death he has gained sorrow so great that it will never leave his heart.

CHORUS. I imagine that Admetus is heartbroken at the terrible prospect of having to lose such a noble wife? 200

MAIDSERVANT. Yes, with tears in his eyes he's holding his dear wife in his arms and begging her not to desert him. But this is a hopeless request, since she is fading away, wasted with illness. She lies limp in his arms, a pitiful burden, but while she is still breathing, however faintly, she wants to see the light of the sun.† But I shall go and announce your presence. There are plenty of people who are not well enough disposed towards their rulers to stand loyally by them in times of trouble, but your devotion to my master and mistress goes back a long way. 210

Exit the MAIDSERVANT *into the palace.*

The CHORUS *divide as before into two Semichoruses.*

SEMICHORUS A. Ah, Zeus, is there anywhere any escape from

these troubles, any way for our rulers to evade the misfortune that afflicts them?

SEMICHORUS B. Alas! Will someone come?† Am I truly to cut my hair now and dress myself in robes of black?

SEMICHORUS A. Her fate is clear, my friends, clear indeed†— and yet we shall pray to the gods, for there is no power greater   220 than that of the gods.

SEMICHORUS B. O lord Paean, devise some deliverance for Admetus from his troubles.

SEMICHORUS A. Help him, help him! For you found deliverance for him before.† So now too save him from death! Stop murderous Hades!

SEMICHORUS B. Oh woe! < . . . >† O son of Pheres, what a blow is the loss of your wife!

SEMICHORUS A. Alas! This demands death by cold steel, and is more than enough to make you put your neck in a noose hung on high!*

SEMICHORUS B. For on this very day you shall see the death of   230 your wife, a woman who was not just close, but closer to you than anyone.

Enter ADMETUS and ALCESTIS from the palace. A BOY, their son, is with them, and a daughter. Attendants accompany the royal family and carry a couch, which they place centre stage.

SEMICHORUS A. Look! Look! Here she comes out of the palace, along with her husband.

SEMICHORUS B. Cry out loud, O land of Pherae! Lament the best of women! Wasted by illness, she is going to Hades beneath the earth.

The CHORUS reunites.

CHORUS. Never will I say that marriage brings more joy than pain. This was clear to me before, but even more so when I   240 see the misfortune of the king, who, once he has lost this wife of his, will live for the rest of his days a life that is no life at all.

ALCESTIS (*passionately*). O Sun! O daylight! O clouds, swirling on your course in the sky!

ADMETUS. The Sun sees you and me, partners in misfortune, although we have done the gods no wrong for which you should die.

ALCESTIS. O Earth! O palace! O bridal chamber back home in
Iolcus!*

ADMETUS. Rouse yourself from your misery! Don't desert me!   250
Implore the gods in their power to have mercy on you!

ALCESTIS. I see the two-oared boat on the lake! I see it! The
ferryman of the dead, Charon,* has his hand on the quant
and calls to me now: 'Why delay? Hurry! You're holding me
up!' With these words he urgently bids me make haste.

ADMETUS. Oh, no! Bitter indeed to me is the voyage of which
you speak! Oh miserable wife, how we are suffering!

ALCESTIS. He's taking me! Someone is taking me away! Can't
you see? Someone is taking me to the halls of the dead. It's   260
winged Hades, frowning from beneath his dark-gleaming
brow. What are you doing? Let me go! What a terrible path I
must tread in utmost misery.

ADMETUS. This path of yours brings sorrow to your friends, but
especially to me and your children, who share this grief
together.

ALCESTIS (*to the attendants. In the course of this speech she sinks
down onto the couch*). Let go of me, let go of me now! Lay me
down! My legs are weak. Hades is near, dark night slides over
my eyes. Children, oh my children, your mother is no more,   270
no more! Farewell, children, and may you both continue to
look on the light with joy!

ADMETUS. Oh, no! This is hard for me to hear, harder to bear
than death. I beg you in the name of the gods, and of these
children, whom you will leave motherless, don't cruelly desert
me! Up! Find the inner strength to get up! For if you die my life
will be no more. We depend on you; whether we live or die is
in your hands. For we value the love you can give us.

ALCESTIS (*recovering somewhat*). Admetus, you can see what's   280
happening to me: I'm going to die, but first I'd like to tell you
my wishes. As far as I am concerned, I am dying because of
my high regard for you, and because at the cost of my life I see
to it that you remain alive. I am dying for you when I did not
have to die. No, I could have married any man in Thessaly I
chose and lived in a king's rich palace. But I did not want a life
in which you had been taken from me and my children had
lost their father, nor did I mind the loss of my youth, even
though I was blessed with things which gave me pleasure.

Your father and your mother let you down, however,   290
although they had reached an age when death would have
been fine for them, and it would have been fine to save
their child and die a glorious death. For you were their
only son, and there was no chance of their producing
other children after your death. Then you and I would
have lived for the remainder of our days, and you would not
now be lamenting the loss of your wife and looking after
motherless children. But one of the gods arranged things in
this way.

So be it. As for you, please remember what you owe me in
return. The favour I am going to ask is not the equivalent of
what I'm doing, since life is uniquely valuable, but it is fair.   300
I'm sure you'll agree that it's fair, because you love these
children just as much as I do, if your heart is in the right
place. Please let them have the house where I have lived as
their own domain—that is, don't marry again and find a
stepmother for these children.* She could not be a better wife
than I, and so out of spite she would raise her hand against
our children—yours and mine. The favour I ask of you, then,
is not to do this, whatever else you might do. A stepmother
comes with hatred for the children who are already there; she   310
is as fierce as a viper.

A male child has his father as a tower of strength,† but
you (*turning to her daughter*), my precious daughter, how will
you grow to proper womanhood? What kind of stepmother
will you get? I worry that she might drag your name through
the mud and ruin your marriage prospects while you are in
your youthful prime. You won't have a mother to see you
married, child, or to attend you and reassure you when
you're giving birth, when there is nothing more reassuring
than a mother. For I am bound to die, and this evil is not   320
due tomorrow or the day after,† but very shortly I shall be
numbered among the dead.

And so farewell to you all, and may you be happy. Husband,
you may boast that you married the best of wives, and,
children, that the best of mothers gave you birth.

CHORUS. You can rest assured that—since I do not hesitate to
speak my mind in front of the king—he'll do as you say, if he
has the sense to act correctly.

ADMETUS. I will, I will, don't worry. During your lifetime you
were my wife, and after your death you alone shall still be   330
known as my wife. No Thessalian bride will ever address me
as her husband in your place. No woman has a father as
noble as yours or such remarkable beauty either. As for children, I am content with the ones I already have, and I pray
that the gods may let me benefit from them, as I didn't in your
case. I shall bear my grief for you not just for a year, Alcestis,
but for as long as I live—just as I shall continue to hate my
mother and loathe my father. Their love for me turned out to
be no more than words, not real, whereas you saved me by   340
giving all you love for my life.

    Don't I have good reason to grieve, when I am losing the
kind of wife I had in you? There'll be no more parties and
symposia for me; away with garlands and the music that used
to fill my palace. Never again shall I take my lyre in hand or
cheer my heart by singing to the Libyan pipes.* For you take
with you all the joys of my life. On my bed will lie an image of
your body, fashioned by skilled craftsmen; as I kneel before it   350
and embrace it, I shall call your name and imagine that in my
arms I have what I will not have—my own dear wife. It will be
cold comfort, I suppose, but all the same it might lighten my
heavy heart. But you will haunt my dreams and I'll
enjoy that: it's pleasant to see those one loves even in dreams,
however brief their visit.

    If I had the tongue and music of Orpheus, so that I could
entrance Demeter's daughter or her husband with songs and
recover you from Hades,* I'd have gone down there, and nei-   360
ther Pluto's hound* nor the boatman Charon, guide of souls,
would have stopped me, until I had restored your life and
brought you back up to the light of the sun. But start expect-
ing me there when I die, and make ready a house for us to
share. I will instruct these children to put me in the same
cedarwood coffin as you, and to lay me close by your side. For
not even after death do I want to be apart from you, my one
true friend.

CHORUS. You should know that, as one friend to another, I
share the burden of your grief and distress for this woman.   370
She is entitled to it.

ALCESTIS. Children, you are witnesses to your father's promise

that he will never take another wife and set her over you
—that he will never treat me with such disrespect.

ADMETUS. Yes, and I hereby repeat the promise, which I shall
keep.

ALCESTIS. Under these circumstances, then, I release the children from my arms into your care.

She releases the children from her embrace and they run over to
ADMETUS.

ADMETUS. I accept them, a gift I shall cherish from arms that I
cherish.

ALCESTIS. You will have to be the mother of these children
instead of me.

ADMETUS. I must, I really must, since they have lost you.

ALCESTIS. Children, at a time when life should be mine, the
underworld is my destination.

ADMETUS. Oh, what on earth shall I do without you?   380

ALCESTIS. Time will ease your pain. A dead person is nothing.

ADMETUS. Take me with you, I beg you: take me down with you.

ALCESTIS. No, it is enough that I am dying for you.

ADMETUS. O Fate, what a noble wife you are taking from me!

ALCESTIS. Now a weight of darkness presses on my eyes.

ADMETUS. There is no hope for me if you leave me, Alcestis!

ALCESTIS. You can speak of me now as one no longer in the
land of the living.

She slumps back on the couch.

ADMETUS. Lift up your head! Don't leave your children!

ALCESTIS. Not willingly, to be sure! But farewell, my children!

ADMETUS. Look at them! Look at them!   390

ALCESTIS. My life is at an end.

ADMETUS. What are you doing? Are you going?

ALCESTIS. Farewell, Admetus.

*She sinks back and dies.**

ADMETUS. Oh, no! There's no hope for me!

CHORUS. She has gone. Admetus' wife is no more.

BOY (*sings*). Alas for my misfortune! My mother has gone down
below,

no more to live under the light of the sun, father,
and she has left me to a wretched life, deprived of a parent.
Look! Look at her eyes† and her outstretched arms!
Listen to me, mother, I beg you. Can't you hear me?   400
Mother, it is I, it is I, mother, your little one
who falls on your lips and calls your name!†

ADMETUS. She can't hear you or see you. This is a heavy
burden of misfortune for us to bear.

BOY (*sings*). I have been left alone, father, robbed in my youth
of my own dear mother. Oh, this is a hard fate for me
— and for you, sister, since you suffer just as much as I.   410
< . . . >†
Vain, father, vain was your marriage: you have not reached
the end of your life with her by your side. She has died first.
Mother, your death is a disaster for the whole house!

CHORUS. Admetus, you must endure this tragedy. You are by no
means the first, nor will you be the last person to have lost a
noble wife. You should recognize that death is our common lot.

ADMETUS. I know, and it's not as if this disaster suddenly   420
swooped down on me out of the blue: I have long been tor-
mented by the knowledge of it. While I go and make
arrangements for the burial of this body of hers, you stay
here and sing the verses of a paean, unaccompanied by any
libation, to the god below.* I command every Thessalian subject of mine to join in the mourning for this woman by cutting his hair short and wearing dark clothes. Any of you who
owns horses—whether it's a team harnessed for his chariot
or a single horse for riding—is to take a knife to their manes
and cut them short.* And for twelve complete lunar cycles no   430
pipes or lyres are to be played in the town. For I will never
bury anyone else who was dearer or better to me. She
deserves to be honoured by me, for she was the only one who
chose to die in my place.

Exeunt ADMETUS *and the children into the palace, followed by the*
attendants who carry ALCESTIS' *body on the couch. One or two*
attendants remain.

CHORUS (*sings*). Dear daughter of Pelias, farewell. I hope you
find joy

as you dwell in your sunless home in Hades' domain.
Hades, that dark-locked god, should be aware,
and the old man who guides the dead, sitting at oar   440
and tiller, should know that in his two-oared skiff
he has ferried across the waters of Lake Acheron*
she who is by far, by far indeed the best of women.

You will be the subject of many a minstrel's song;
on the seven-stringed shell of the hill-dwelling tortoise*
and in songs unaccompanied by the lyre they will celebrate
    you,
in Sparta when the circling season of the Carnean month
comes round and the moon is aloft all night long,*   450
and in Athens too, glowing with prosperity. For in dying
you have bequeathed to poets a rich theme for their songs.

Would that I had the power! I would guide you to the light
away from Hades' halls and the waters of Cocytus,*
rowing across the river, rowing through the underworld.
For you, you alone, beloved woman, had the courage,   460
the resolve, to redeem your own husband from Hades,
though it cost you your life. May the earth fall lightly
on you, lady.* And if your husband marries again,
finds another partner for his bed, he will indeed
be an object of loathing to me and to your children.

Neither mother nor aged father were prepared
to be buried in the ground for their son. < . . . >†
They gave him life, but they did not have the courage
to save him, the wretches, for all their advanced years.   470
But you went to your death in the bloom of your youth,
dying for a husband who was also still young.
May I find such affection in my wife and partner—
but it is rarely found in life. Truly with such a woman
by my side throughout my life I would feel no pain.

Enter HERACLES, *instantly recognizable by his lionskin and massive
club.*

HERACLES. Strangers, citizens of this land of Pherae, will I find
    Admetus at home?
CHORUS. Yes, the son of Pheres is inside the palace, Heracles.
    (*They signal to an attendant to go into the palace and fetch*

ADMETUS) But tell us what purpose has brought you to Thessaly, and why you have come here to Pherae.   480

HERACLES. I am carrying out a task for Eurystheus of Tiryns.*

CHORUS. And what is your destination? What journey are you engaged on?

HERACLES. I'm going to fetch the four-horse chariot of Diomedes of Thrace.

CHORUS. How will you manage that? Don't you know how he treats visitors?*

HERACLES. No, I know nothing about him. I've never been to the land of the Bistonians.*

CHORUS. He won't let you master the horses without a fight.

HERACLES. But neither can I refuse any of my labours.

CHORUS. Then you'll either kill him and make it home, or die and stay there.

HERACLES. This won't be the first such contest I'll have faced.

CHORUS. What will you gain by defeating the horses' master?   490

HERACLES. I'll take the horses back to the king of Tiryns.

CHORUS. It won't be easy to insert a bit inside their mouths.

HERACLES. I'll manage—unless they breathe fire from their nostrils!

CHORUS. They don't do that, but they tear men to pieces with their darting jaws.

HERACLES. It sounds as though they eat like wild beasts in the mountains, not like horses.

CHORUS. You'll see their feeding-troughs; they're drenched with blood.

HERACLES. Whose son does their owner claim to be?

CHORUS. He is master of the golden Thracian shield, and his father is Ares.*

HERACLES. The task you describe is typical of my fate, which is always tough and arduous. It looks as though I am bound to   500 fight sons of Ares. First there was Lycaon, then Cycnus,* and now I am approaching a third such contest, in which I'll take on both the horses and their master. But no one will ever see Alcmene's son* frightened of an opponent, however strong.

CHORUS. Look! Admetus, the king of this land, is coming out of the palace.

Enter ADMETUS, accompanied by the attendant who fetched him. He is wearing black and his hair has been cut short, the traditional signs of mourning.

ADMETUS. Greetings, son of Zeus and descendant of Perseus.

HERACLES. And greetings to you too, Admetus, lord of the 510 Thessalians. I hope I find you well.

ADMETUS. I wish that you had. But I realize that you meant well.

HERACLES. I can't help noticing that you have your hair cut short in mourning. Why is that?

ADMETUS. Today is the day when I am to bury someone.

HERACLES. May the god keep this disaster from your children!

ADMETUS. My children are alive and indoors.

HERACLES. Well, if it's your father who has died, he was old enough.

ADMETUS (*bitterly*). He too is still alive, Heracles, as is my mother.

HERACLES. Surely it isn't your wife Alcestis who has died?

ADMETUS. Anything I could say about her would be ambiguous.

HERACLES. Do you mean that she's still alive, or is she dead? 520

ADMETUS. She both is and is not alive.* That's why I'm upset.

HERACLES. I'm none the wiser. I can't make sense of what you're saying.

ADMETUS. Don't you know what is fated to happen to her?

HERACLES. Yes, she has undertaken to die instead of you.

ADMETUS. Then how can she still be truly alive, since she has made that promise?

HERACLES. Ah, don't weep too soon for your wife. Wait until it's real.

ADMETUS. A person about to die is already dead, and no longer exists on this earth.

HERACLES. But existence and non-existence are two entirely different things.

ADMETUS. That's your view, Heracles; I disagree.

HERACLES. So why are you in mourning? Which of your 530 friends or family has died?

ADMETUS. A woman. It was a woman I spoke of just now.

HERACLES. Was she a relative, or from outside the family?

ADMETUS. She wasn't a blood relative, but you could say she had close ties with my household.

HERACLES (*looking again at* ADMETUS' *shorn hair*). So how did she come to die in your house?

ADMETUS. After her father's death she was looked after here.

HERACLES. Oh, how I wish I hadn't found you in mourning, Admetus.

ADMETUS. Why? What's the meaning behind your words?

HERACLES. I shall be on my way and look for lodging elsewhere.

ADMETUS. No, my lord! Such a gross impropriety must not be allowed to happen!

HERACLES. Mourners find the arrival of a visitor a nuisance.   540

ADMETUS. The dead are dead. Come inside.

HERACLES. It's not right for guests to feast when mourners are around.

ADMETUS. The rooms I'll show you to are out of the way.

HERACLES. I'd really appreciate it if you'd let me go on my way.

ADMETUS. No, you can't go to someone else's house. (*To the attendant*) Show him the way, and once you've opened up the guest-rooms—the ones which are separate from the main building—tell those whose job it is to lay on plenty of food,* and you should all make sure that the doorway to the court-yard is securely closed. It would be wrong for guest-friends at dinner to hear the distressing cries of mourners.   550

            Exeunt HERACLES *and attendant into the palace.*

CHORUS. What are you doing? How can you think of entertaining guests, Admetus, under the present tragic circumstances? How can you be so stupid?

ADMETUS. Would you have approved more had I driven him away from my home and this city when he had come looking for lodging? Of course not: the catastrophe would not thereby have been diminished, while my rudeness would have increased. It would have been one more misfortune, on top of those we already have, for my household to gain a reputation for turning away guest-friends. And whenever I pay a visit to thirsty Argos, I myself find him the best of hosts.*   560

CHORUS. Why did you keep your present misfortune secret, then, if the man who has arrived is a friend, as you say?

ADMETUS. He'd have refused to enter the house if he had the slightest inkling of my troubles. I imagine that some people would regard my behaviour as unwise and would not think well of me for it; but these halls of mine do not know how to repel and scorn guest-friends.

Exit ADMETUS.

CHORUS (*sings*). O house! You have always welcomed guests,
always reflected the generosity of your master.
Even Pythian Apollo of the sweet-sounding lyre*   570
chose you as his dwelling-place, and deigned
to serve as a herdsman in your meadows,
over winding slopes playing on his pipes
pastoral mating-songs for your flocks.

Enchanted by his singing, spotted lynxes
helped him herd his flocks, and a tawny pride
of lions joined him from the glades of Othrys.*   580
To the music of your lyre, Phoebus Apollo,
there came lightly dancing the dappled fawn,
leaving the shelter of lofty pines,
enchanted by your joyful minstrelsy.

And so Admetus dwells in a house rich in sheep
by the fair waters of Lake Boebeis.*
To his plough-lands and his level fields
in the region of the sun's dark stables*   590
he sets as his border the sky over the Molossians,†*
while towards the sea-swept, harbourless coast
of the Aegean, Mount Pelion* falls under his sway.

And now he opens up his house to welcome a guest,
with his eye damp from mourning over the body
of his beloved wife, newly dead in the palace.
For in his nobility he is selfless to a fault.   600
Good men lack no virtuous qualities, and
I admire their wisdom. In my heart I remain
confident that a god-fearing man will fare well.

*Enter ADMETUS from the palace, with attendants carrying ALCESTIS
on a bier. They are all dressed in mourning clothes.*

ADMETUS. Men of Pherae, loyal band! Now, on a bier raised

high off the ground, attendants are bringing the corpse, in
full array, for her funeral and the pyre. As is customary, you
must pay your respects to the dead woman, as she departs on   610
her final journey.

CHORUS. But look! I can see your aged father making his way
here, and servants with finery—the ritual adornments for the
dead—in their arms for your wife.

Enter PHERES, with attendants carrying clothes, jewellery, etc.

PHERES. I've come out of sympathy with your troubles, my son.
No one will deny that the wife you've lost was noble and
selfless, but though the burden is heavy, you must bear it. I've
brought all this finery here for you: let it go with her to the
underworld. Her corpse deserves these honours, because she
died to save your life, my son, and made it possible for me not   620
to waste away, grieving in my old age, childless and lacking
your support. Moreover, by the nobility of the deed she was
brave enough to do, she has enhanced the good reputation of
all women. (*Turning to the corpse*) And so farewell! Thank you
for saving my son and preventing the collapse of our house. I
pray that things may go well for you in Hades' halls. In my
opinion, the kind of marriage you two had does men good,
while all others are worthless.

ADMETUS (*angrily*). First, you have not come to this funeral at
my invitation and, second, I do not count your presence here   630
as that of a friend. Alcestis shall never wear this finery of
yours; she needs nothing you can give for her funeral. You
should have been sympathetic before, when I was dying, but
you steered clear of the whole business and, despite your age,
you let a young person die instead. So will you now mourn for
her? I don't see how you can really be my father, or how the
woman who claims to have given birth to me and is called my
mother can really be my mother. I was born a slave's child
and surreptitiously introduced to your wife's breast. You
showed your true colours when you were put to the test, and I   640
no longer consider myself your son. You turned out, in fact,
to show a truly remarkable cowardice: you are old, you have
reached the end of your life, and yet you lacked both the will
and the courage to die for your own son. Instead, you let this
woman die, when she was no blood relative of mine. As far as

I'm concerned, she is the only person
as both mother and father. And yet, h
own son, you'd have left the field covered
case you had only a short time left to live.†

You have had as happy and successful a
could expect. You spent the prime of your life a
had a son—me—to inherit your estate, so that y
die childless and leave the royal house bereft
others to plunder. And you certainly can't excuse your giving
me up to die on the grounds that I scorned you in your old
age, because I have always been particularly respectful   660
towards you. And look at the thanks I got from you and my
mother in return for my respect! There's no time to waste,
then: you had better produce other sons to look after you in
your old age, array you in finery when you're dead, and lay
out your corpse,* because *I* shall not see to your funeral. I'll
have nothing to do with it. As far as you're concerned, I'm
dead. Since the fact that I'm alive now is due to my finding
someone else to save my life, I count myself that person's son,
and there's no one else I'll care for and look after in their old
age. There's no point in old people cursing old age and the   670
weary length of their life, and praying for death: when death
draws near, no one wants to die, and old age stops being a
burden.

CHORUS. Stop! What's already happened is tragedy enough! My
son, don't provoke your father to anger.

PHERES (*angrily*). My son, who do you think you're threatening?
Some Lydian or Phrygian slave you've bought? Don't you
realize that I am Thessalian, and was born a free man, the
true son of a Thessalian? Your abuse is outrageous, and you
won't get away with hurling brash insults at me like this. I   680
gave you life and brought you up to be master of my house,
but I'm not obliged to die for you. My *ancestors have not
handed down to* me the rule that fathers should die for their
sons, and this is not a Greek tradition either.* You were born
for yourself alone, whether your fate is good or bad. You have
already gained from me the things you should have got: you
are a king with plenty of subjects, and you'll inherit from me
many plethra* of farmland, just as I did from my father. So
how have I wronged you? What have I denied you? Don't die   690

nd I won't die for you. You enjoy being alive—do you
k your father doesn't? By my calculations, we spend a
good long time down below, while life is short but sweet. At
any rate, you fought shamelessly against death, and you're
living now beyond your appointed time because you condemned her (*pointing to* ALCESTIS) to death. And do you then
accuse *me* of cowardice—you, the ultimate coward, who
proved worse than the woman who died for you, her fine
young husband? You've discovered a cunning way to keep
avoiding death, if every time you can persuade your current   700
wife to die for you! How can you criticize your friends and
family for not being prepared to do what she did, when you
yourself hardly occupy the moral high ground? Just shut up!
You should appreciate that everyone loves their life,* just as
you love yours, and so anything bad you say about me will be
said about you many times over, and truthfully.

CHORUS. Too many insults have been spoken, now and before.
Please stop abusing your son, old man.

ADMETUS. No, go on. I stand by what I've said. But if it hurts
you to hear the truth, you'd better stop doing me wrong.

PHERES. I'd be making an even worse mistake if I died for you.   710

ADMETUS. Really? Is it the same for a man in his prime and for
an old man to die?

PHERES. We are obliged to live life with the one soul we have;
there's no extra one to be had.

ADMETUS. Then I hope you live to be older than even Zeus!*

PHERES. Do you curse your father when he's done you no
wrong?

ADMETUS. Yes, because it's plain that you lust after a long
life.

PHERES. But isn't it you who are burying this woman who died
so that you might live?

ADMETUS. She is proof of *your* weakness, you coward!

PHERES. It wasn't me who killed her. You can't say it was.

ADMETUS. Ah! I hope that one day you might come to need my
help!

PHERES. You'd better try to find many wives, so that more of   720
them can die.

ADMETUS. You're no better than me: you refused to die too.

PHERES. The light of this sun is precious, very precious.

ADMETUS. You have a coward's temperament; you're not a real
   man.
PHERES. If it was my old corpse you were carrying for burial,
   you'd be crowing—but it's not.
ADMETUS. But when you die you'll die disdained.
PHERES. A bad reputation won't bother me when I'm dead.*
ADMETUS. I can't believe it! The utter shamelessness of old age!
PHERES (*pointing to* ALCESTIS). Shamelessness wasn't her problem, but in her you found a stupid one.
ADMETUS. Go away! Leave me to bury her corpse.
PHERES. All right, I'm off—and she'll be buried by you, her   730
   murderer. One day you'll pay the penalty to her relatives. I
   can tell you that Acastus* is no true man if he lets you get
   away with killing his sister.
ADMETUS. Damn you and that wife of yours! The two of you
   can go and grow old childless, as you deserve, even though
   your child is living. For you will never again enter any building where I live. And if I'd had to get town-criers to announce
   my rejection of your hearth, my ancestral home, I'd have
   done so.

                         Exit PHERES, *followed by his attendants.*

(ADMETUS *continues to the* CHORUS *and his attendants*) As for us,
we must bear the troubles facing us, so let's go and place the   740
body on the funeral pyre.

CHORUS (*sings*). O farewell, woman of resolute courage,
   of nobility and perfect virtue.
   May Hermes of the underworld*
   and Hades receive you kindly.
   If virtue is rewarded there,
   you'll find a place by Hades' bride*
   and a share in these rewards.
Exit ADMETUS *and the* CHORUS,* *followed by the attendants solemnly
                                              carrying the bier.*

            Enter the MANSERVANT *from the palace.*

MANSERVANT. Before now, I've known many men, from all
   over the place, come as guest-friends to Admetus' palace, and
   I've served them their food. But I've never received at this   750
   hearth a worse guest than this one. First of all, he could see

that my master was in mourning, but he still had the cheek to
pass over the threshold and come inside. Second, although he
knew our situation, he was rude when he was served a pot-
luck meal—in fact, he insisted on being brought everything
we failed to bring. He took in his hands an ivy-wood cup and
drank undiluted wine,* pressed from dark grapes, until the
heat of the wine's flame infused his body. Then he put a
garland of myrtle twigs on his head and began a cacophon-   760
ous braying. There were two kinds of singing to be heard: he
was singing away without the slightest respect for the
troubles in Admetus' palace, and we slaves were mourning
our mistress. But we never appeared in front of the guest with
tears in our eyes, because Admetus told us not to. And so I'm
stuck inside the palace, entertaining a guest who's some kind
of thief or brigand, while my mistress has left the palace,
without me escorting her or reaching out my hand and lamenting her. She was like a mother to me and to all of us slaves,
because time and time again she got us out of trouble by   770
soothing her husband's anger.* Don't I have good reason to
hate this guest-friend, then, who has come when we are
afflicted by misfortune?

*Enter HERACLES, tipsy, from the palace. He is carrying a large cup of
wine and has a myrtle garland on his head.*

HERACLES. Hey, you! Why are you looking so serious and
thoughtful? A slave shouldn't frown when there are guests
around, but should receive them in an affable state of mind.
But although the man you see before you is a companion of
your master's, you're receiving him with a sullen and disapproving look, preoccupied by grief which doesn't even per-
sonally concern you. Come here, and I'll tell you something.
Do you know what the human condition is? I shouldn't think   780
so. How could you? Well, listen to me.

   All human beings are bound for death, and no one knows
whether his last breath will be taken on the following day, for
we cannot clearly see fortune's way:* it's not something that
can be taught, and it's not liable to skill either. So now that
you've listened to this lesson from me, cheer up, have a drink,
consider your life day by day as yours, and leave the rest to
fortune! And honour the goddess who gives mortal men the   790

very greatest pleasure, Cypris.* She is a kind goddess. Leave everything else and do as I say, if you think I'm right. I think I am, anyway. So why don't you shed this excessive grief of yours and have a drink with me? I'm sure that when the waves of wine from a cup fall on you, they'll carry you away from this gloomy, frowning state of mind. (*He offers the cup to the* MANSERVANT, *who refuses it*) Since we are mortal we should adopt a mortal state of mind. If you want my view,   800 people who are solemn and disapproving don't have what you could properly call a life at all, but a tragedy!

MANSERVANT. I know, but at the moment our situation doesn't call for revelry and laughter.

HERACLES. The woman who died was no personal concern of yours. Don't overdo your grief. The mistress of this house is still alive.

MANSERVANT. What do you mean, still alive? Don't you realize the disaster the house has suffered?

HERACLES (*with some hesitation*). Yes, unless perhaps your master told me a lie.

MANSERVANT. He's just too hospitable, far too hospitable.

HERACLES. Is the death of someone who's not a blood relative   810 of the house any reason why I shouldn't be treated well?

MANSERVANT (*sarcastically*). Oh, yes, right! Of course she was no blood relative!

HERACLES. Has something happened which he didn't tell me about?

MANSERVANT. Don't worry about it; just go. The troubles that afflict our master are only our concern.

HERACLES. What you've just said indicates personal involvement in the calamity.

MANSERVANT. Exactly. Otherwise I wouldn't be upset to see you partying.

HERACLES. So in actual fact, then, I've been treated badly by my host, have I?

MANSERVANT. You didn't come at a good time for the house to receive you.†

HERACLES. Could it be that one of his children has passed   820 away, or his aged father?

MANSERVANT. No, it's Admetus' wife who has died, sir.

HERACLES. What? And even so you all entertained me?

MANSERVANT. Yes, because he couldn't bear to turn you away from this house.

HERACLES. Oh, you poor man! What a paragon of a wife you have lost!

MANSERVANT. It is the end of all of us, not just of her.

HERACLES. You know, I did notice tears in his eyes, and then there was his hair and his expression. But he persuaded me that the body he was taking off to its funeral was not that of a relative, and so, however reluctantly, I crossed the threshold and set about drinking in the house of a man who welcomed   830
me as a guest-friend, even though he was in this state. And am I still equipped for a party, with a garland adorning my head? (*He hurls the cup and the garland away in disgust*) But you—you who kept quiet when the house was suffering under such a terrible disaster! Where exactly is he burying her? Where can I go and find him?

MANSERVANT. If you go straight along the road to Larisa* you'll see a tomb of polished stone just beyond the outskirts of the town.

Exit the MANSERVANT.

HERACLES. O my heart and hand, that have endured many trials! Now is the time for you to show what sort of a son Alcmene of Tiryns, the daughter of Electryon, bore for Zeus.* For I must save Alcestis, the woman who has just died,   840
and restore her to this house. That will be my way of thanking Admetus. I shall go and look out for Death, the dark-winged lord of the dead. I expect to find him quenching his thirst on the sacrificial offerings near the the tomb. If I wait for him in ambush, and then dash out and grab him, with my arms holding him tight in a rib-crushing grip,* no one will be able to break him free, until he gives the woman up to me. But if I miss my quarry—that is, if he doesn't come for his bloody   850
gobbets—I shall go to the sunless halls of Kore* and the lord of the underworld and demand Alcestis back. I'm sure I'll restore her to the upper world. Then I shall place her in the arms of my guest-friend, who took me into his home and didn't send me away, despite the heavy burden of sorrow with which he had been afflicted. In his nobility, and out of respect for me, he kept it secret. There's no one in Thessaly—no one

in all Greece—who is kinder to guest-friends. And so he will
not say that his nobility was not matched by the man he   860
helped.

Exit HERACLES.

Enter ADMETUS, *his attendants, and the* CHORUS, *returning from the
funeral.* ADMETUS *and the attendants are still dressed in mourning
clothes.*

ADMETUS (*in great distress*). Oh, how I hate to approach, how I
hate to see these bereaved halls! Oh, alas! Alas! Woe is me!
Where am I to go? Where am I to stay? What am I to say?
How can I keep silent? How can I make an end of life? It was
indeed a hideous fate my mother bore me for. I envy the dead,
I long to join them, I desire to dwell with them in their halls.
For it brings me no joy to see the sunlight, or to walk upon
this earth. What a woman Death took as my replacement and   870
handed over to Hades!

In what follows, ADMETUS' *cries of pain mingle with the* CHORUS's
emotional words. This whole scene is highly charged emotionally.

CHORUS. Go on, go on! Hide yourself inside the palace!
ADMETUS. Alas!
CHORUS. Your suffering calls for tears.
ADMETUS. Ah, misery!
CHORUS. Your path has been one of pain, I know.
ADMETUS. Oh, no!
CHORUS. You are not helping the one below.
ADMETUS. Ah, woe is me!
CHORUS. It is horrible that you will never again look directly
upon your dear wife's face.
ADMETUS. You've touched on what has rent my heart. For
what greater evil can there be for a man than for him to lose a
loyal wife? I wish I'd never married and lived with her in these   880
halls. I envy those men who are wifeless and childless. For
they have just the one heart, and it's not too hard to bear its
pain. But the sight of children ill and bridal beds ravaged by
death is not to be endured, when one could spend one's whole
life with wife or children.

In what follows, ADMETUS' *cries of pain again mingle with the*
CHORUS's *words.*

CHORUS. The fate you have met is an irresisitible fate.

ADMETUS. Alas!

CHORUS. But you are going too far in your grief.   890

ADMETUS. Ah, misery!

CHORUS. It's hard to bear, but all the same . . .

ADMETUS. Oh, no!

CHORUS. . . . you must endure. Others before have lost . . .

ADMETUS. Ah, woe is me!

CHORUS. . . . their wives. You are not the first to be oppressed
by misfortune.

ADMETUS. On and on it goes, the pain and grief for loved ones
under the ground. Why did you stop me from throwing
myself into the tomb's hollow trench, and lying there dead
with her, my perfect wife? Then Hades would have held not   900
just one but two souls, bound together by loyalty, together
crossing the underworld lake.

CHORUS. A relative of mine had a son who died at home. He
was his parents' only child and his death demanded tears, but
still he bore the pain with moderation, even though he had no
other children, his hair was already turning white with age,
and he was getting on in years.   910

ADMETUS. How am I to enter this familiar house? How live
there, after this change to my fortune? Alas! So much has
happened in between. Once I entered to the light of pine
torches* from Pelion and to the sound of wedding songs. I
held the hand of my beloved wife in my hand, and a noisy
band of revellers followed us, congratulating me and the
woman now dead on our marriage, which joined people of   920
noble blood, descended on both sides from the best families.
But now laments instead of wedding songs, and black clothing instead of white robes, escort me inside to a deserted
marriage bed.

CHORUS. Good fortune was yours until this grief assailed you:
you had never known pain. But you saved your life and
remained alive. Your wife has died, she has dissolved the bond   930
of affection between you. But this is nothing new: before now
Death has parted many men from their wives.

ADMETUS (*slightly calmer*). My friends, I regard my wife's lot as
happier than my own, despite appearances. She will never
again be touched by pain, and she has left behind all the

tribulations of life in glory, whereas I, who should not be alive
and have escaped my fate, will live a miserable life. I see this   940
now. Every time I go into the house, for instance, how shall I
endure it? Whom might I greet, and by whom might I be
greeted, to make my entrance pleasant? Whatever shall I do?
The emptiness indoors will drive me outside, when I see my
wife's bed and the chairs on which she used to sit unoccupied,
and the floors dirty, and the children throwing themselves at
my knees and crying for their mother, and the slaves weeping
for the excellent mistress they no longer have in the house.
That's what things will be like inside; but then I shall be   950
driven home from outside by gatherings full of women, such
as weddings between fellow Thessalians, because I won't be
able to bear the sight of women the same age as my wife. And
any enemy I happen to have will say, 'Look at him! It's disgraceful that he's alive! He didn't have the guts to die, but in a
cowardly fashion gave his wife instead so that he could escape
Hades. Does he still take himself to be a man? And he hates
his parents, even though he himself was not prepared to die
either.' As if I didn't have troubles enough, that's the kind of
reputation I shall have. So, my friends, why is it better for me   960
to live, with a bad reputation and a bad situation?

CHORUS (*sings*). Though I have explored the poets,
　raced on high through the heavens,*
　and studied countless doctrines,
　I have found that there is nothing
　more powerful than Necessity,
　nor have I found any remedy for it
　in the Thracian books recording
　Orphic hymns,* nor among all the herbs
　which Phoebus cut and gave the Asclepiads*   970
　to cure suffering humanity.

　For this goddess alone there are
　no altars and no images to approach,
　nor does she pay attention to sacrifices.
　Lady, I pray that you may not enter
　my life with any more force than before.
　For even Zeus cannot bring to pass
　any of his wishes without your help.

You master even the iron of the Chalybes*   980
with your power, and your spirit
is pitiless and inexorable.

(*To* ADMETUS)
You have been caught in the unbreakable chains
of the goddess's arms, but you must endure.
For your tears will not bring the dead back to earth
from down below. Even the sons of gods
fade in the darkness of death. We loved her   990
when she was with us, and even after death
we will love her still—the most noble of all wives,
whom you married and brought to your nuptial bed.

May your wife's tomb be held as no mere mound
over the remains of the dead, but may she find regard
as high as the gods, and be an object of reverence
to travellers who, walking the winding road, will say: 1000
'This woman here once died for her husband,
and now she is one of the blessed spirits.
Greetings, lady, and grant us your favour.'
With words such as these will she be addressed.

The CHORUS *stops singing, and the Chorus-leader continues alone.*

But look! Here comes Alcmene's son, apparently, walking
towards your home, Admetus.

Enter HERACLES *with a veiled woman.*

HERACLES. One should speak candidly to a friend, Admetus,
and not cherish secret grievances in one's heart. I decided to   1010
stand by you in your time of trouble and demonstrate my
friendship. But you didn't tell me that the body you were
preparing for funeral was that of your wife. You entertained
me in your palace as if you were preoccupied by grief which
was not of personal concern to you. And so I put a garland on
my head and poured libations to the gods in your home when
it was afflicted by misfortune. I do find fault with the treatment I received from you—yes, I do. But I don't want to cause
you pain in your time of trouble.

I'll tell you why I turned round and came back here. Please   1020
take this woman and keep her safe until I've killed the Biston-

ian king and returned with the Thracian mares. If something untoward should happen to me, as I hope it won't (for I
pray I may return), I give her to you as a domestic servant. It
took a great deal of effort for me to acquire her. What happened was that I came across some people holding a competition, which was open to all comers and good enough for
athletes to exert themselves over. I collected her as my prize
from these games. Those who came first in the light events*
took away horses as their prize, while those who won the 1030
major events—boxing and wrestling—got a herd of cattle,
and a woman along with them too. As I happened to be there,
it would have been disgraceful for me to have let this opportunity for glory and gain pass by. Anyway, as I said, you must look
after the woman. She's not stolen property; it took hard work
to get her. Here she is. In time even you will probably thank me.

ADMETUS. I assure you that my keeping the wretched truth
about what had happened to my wife secret was not meant as
a slight; it does not mean that I count you as someone con-
temptible. It's just that if you had left and looked for hospitality elsewhere, it would only have increased my pain. It was 1040
enough that I should mourn what is, after all, my own loss.

As for the woman, I wonder whether it is possible, my lord,
for you to ask one of my fellow Thessalians, someone who has
not suffered as I have, to look after her. You've got many
guest-friends here in Pherae. Please don't remind me of my
loss. You see, I wouldn't be able to stop the tears flowing if I
saw her in my house. Please don't make things worse for me
than they are. I'm burdened with enough troubles already.
Besides, I can tell from her clothes and jewellery that she's
young, and where would I keep a young woman in the house? 1050
Is she to live in the men's quarters? But how could she remain
pure if she was constantly in the company of young men? It's
not easy to restrain a young man in his prime, Heracles. I'm
showing consideration for you here. Alternatively, am I to put
her into my dead wife's room and keep her there? But how
could I let her use my wife's bed? I'm worried about incurring
criticism from two sources: from my fellow citizens, who
might accuse me of betraying my benefactress by falling into
bed with another young woman; and I must also give careful 1060
consideration to my dead wife, who deserves my respect.

(*To the veiled woman*) As for you, young woman, whoever
you are, you should know that you have the same build as
Alcestis, and a similar figure. (*To* HERACLES) Ah! I beg you,
take her away out of my sight! Don't kick a man when he's
down! When I look at her I seem to see my wife. She confuses
my heart, and tears spring from my eyes. Oh, the pain! Only
now do I really taste how bitter this grief is.

CHORUS. I can hardly say that what has happened is good, 1070
but you have to put up with the god's gifts, whatever they
are.

HERACLES. If only I were strong enough to bring your wife
back to the world of light from the domain of the dead! If only
I could do you this favour!

ADMETUS. I'm sure you would if you could. But how could you?
It's impossible for the dead to return to the light.

HERACLES. Don't go too far. Exercise restraint and bear your
pain.

ADMETUS. It's easier to give advice than to endure suffering.

HERACLES. But what good will it do you, if all you want to do is
mourn?

ADMETUS. I know this myself, but a kind of longing is leading 1080
me on.

HERACLES. Yes, loving someone who's dead does lead to tears.

ADMETUS. Her death has devastated me even more than I can
say.

HERACLES. You have lost an excellent wife. Who will deny it?

ADMETUS. And so I shall never again find joy in life.

HERACLES. Time will ease your pain, but at the moment it's still
fresh.

ADMETUS. Yes, you can say that time will do it, if 'time' means
'death'.

HERACLES. A wife and remarriage will stop you missing her.

ADMETUS. Be quiet! What a thing to suggest! I'd never have
thought it of you.

HERACLES. Why? Are you not going to marry? Will you stay a
widower?

ADMETUS. No woman will ever share my bed. 1090

HERACLES. Do you think this will do the dead woman any
good?

ADMETUS. Wherever she is, she deserves my respect.

HERACLES. That's commendable indeed—but you're making a fool of yourself.†

ADMETUS. May I die if I ever betray her, even though she is dead.

HERACLES. Just out of the kindness of your heart, then, won't you take this woman into your home?

ADMETUS. No, don't ask this of me, I beg you in the name of Zeus, your father!

HERACLES. But you'll be making a mistake if you don't.

ADMETUS. But if I do, my heart will be racked with pain.   1100

HERACLES. You should do as I say. Doing me this favour might coincide with what you need.

ADMETUS. Oh, how I wish you'd never brought her from the games!

HERACLES. But my victory is your victory too.*

ADMETUS. You're right—but send the woman away.

HERACLES. She'll go if she has to, but first make sure that she has to.

ADMETUS. Yes, she must—except I don't want to make you angry with me.

HERACLES. I too have my reasons for being so determined.

ADMETUS. All right, you win! But I don't like what you're doing.

HERACLES. But you'll thank me later. Just do as I say.

ADMETUS (*to the attendants*). Show her inside, since I have to   1110
take her into my house.

HERACLES. I'm not going to release the woman to your servants.

ADMETUS. You can take her in yourself, if you want.

HERACLES. No, as far as I'm concerned, I'll put her in *your* hands.

ADMETUS. I'm not going to lay a finger on her. She can just go inside.

HERACLES. I trust only you and your right hand.

ADMETUS. My lord, you're forcing me to do this against my will.

HERACLES. Go on! Reach out your hand and touch the stranger.

ADMETUS (*averting his gaze*). All right, I am reaching out, as if I were cutting off the Gorgon's head.†*

HERACLES (*throwing back the veil*). Look at her! Don't you think

she looks like your wife? Change your mood from sorrow to
happiness!

ADMETUS (*turning round and looking at* ALCESTIS). O gods, what
can I say? This is a miracle! I never expected to see this! Am I
really looking at my wife, or is it a hallucination, sent by some
god to drive me out of my wits with joy?

HERACLES. No, the woman you see here is your wife.

ADMETUS. Are you sure it's not a ghost?

HERACLES. The man you made your guest-friend is no conjuror
of spirits.

ADMETUS. But am I really seeing my wife, the woman I buried?

HERACLES. Absolutely. But I'm not surprised you can't believe 1130
what has happened.

ADMETUS. Can I touch her? Can I speak to her as if she were
my wife, alive?

HERACLES. Yes, speak to her. You have everything you wanted.

ADMETUS. O beloved wife! Dear face, dear body! Here you are,
when I never expected to have you back, never expected to see
you again!

HERACLES. You have her. May the gods withhold their
resentment!*

ADMETUS. O noble son of great Zeus, may you prosper and may
your father protect you! You have single-handedly made
things better for me. How did you bring her back up here to
the light from the underworld?

HERACLES. By joining battle with the spirit who had her in his 1140
control.

ADMETUS. You say you fought with Death? Where did this
happen?

HERACLES. Right by her tomb. I ambushed him and seized him.

ADMETUS. But why does my wife just stand there without
saying anything?*

HERACLES. You are not yet allowed to hear her speak to you.
You have to wait two more days, until she has been purified
from her consecration to the gods below. But take her inside
now—and, Admetus, do continue to act with justice and
respect towards your guest-friends. Farewell, now. I must go
and carry out my assigned task for the royal son of 1150
Sthenelus.*

ADMETUS. Please, stay here with us as our guest.

HERACLES. Another time, but now I must make haste.

Exit HERACLES.

ADMETUS. Well, bless you, and I hope you make it home again.
But I order the city and the whole surrounding province* to
celebrate my good fortune with a choral festival and with
supplicatory sacrifices of oxen until the altars drip with fat!
For now my life has changed for the better. I will not deny that
good fortune has come my way.

*Exit ADMETUS, taking ALCESTIS inside the palace. They are followed
by the attendants. The CHORUS process out, chanting the following
lines.*

CHORUS. Many are the guises of things divine;
Many things the gods achieve in surprising ways.   1160
Things we expect never come to pass,
while the god finds ways to make the unexpected happen.
That was certainly the way this affair turned out.*

HERACLES

Characters

AMPHITRYON, Heracles' human father
MEGARA, Heracles' wife
HERACLES
LYCUS, tyrant of Thebes
IRIS, messenger of the gods
MADNESS
MESSENGER
THESEUS, king of Athens

CHORUS of elderly male citizens of Thebes

Scene: in front of the house of HERACLES *in Thebes. There is an altar dedicated to Zeus the Saviour, on the steps of which* AMPHITRYON, MEGARA, *and the three sons she has borne* HERACLES *sit as suppliants, in obvious distress.*

AMPHITRYON. Is there anyone on earth who has not heard of me, Amphitryon of Argos, who shared his wife with Zeus?* My father was Alcaeus, the son of Perseus,* and I am the father of Heracles. I settled here in Thebes, where the crop of Sown Men grew from the soil.* Only a few of their kind were spared by Ares, and they peopled Cadmus' city with their children's children. Creon, the son of Menoeceus,* who ruled over this land, was one of their descendants. And Creon is the father of Megara here (*he points to her*), whom all the citizens   10
of Thebes once celebrated with wedding-songs, accompanied by pipes, when glorious Heracles brought her to my house as his bride.

But my son left Thebes, which I had made my home, and abandoned Megara and his relatives, out of a desire to live in fortified Argos and the city built by the Cyclopes,* from which I was banished for killing Electryon. In an attempt to lighten the burden of my troubles, and because he wanted to live in the land of his ancestors, he offered Eurystheus* a huge bribe to let me return, which was that he would clear the earth of   20

its wild elements.* Perhaps he was under the influence of
Hera's goad, or perhaps it was ordained. He completed all the
rest of his labours, and is now engaged on the last one: he has
gone down to Hades, through the entrance at Taenarum,* to
bring the triple-bodied hound* up to the world. He has not yet
returned from this mission.

Now, it's long been said in Thebes that in days gone by
Lycus, the husband of Dirce, used to be lord of this seven-
towered city, before the white-horsed pair, Amphion and
Zethus, the sons of Zeus, became the land's rulers.* Lycus'   30
son (also called Lycus), who is not a native of Thebes, but
came from Euboea,* killed Creon and, having done so, now
rules over the land. He attacked the city when it was rotten
with feuding. The fact that we are related to Creon by marriage is proving to be a terrible affliction. While my son is
somewhere in the recesses of the earth, this upstart ruler of
Thebes, Lycus, wants to get rid of Heracles' sons by killing
them and Heracles' wife—as if he could erase blood with   40
blood—and me too, if even a useless old thing like me ought
to be counted a man. He's frightened that when these boys
here have grown up they might one day exact payment for
the murder of members of their mother's family.

When my son was about to enter the black night of the
underworld, he left me at home here with the house and the
children in my care, and so, to prevent Heracles' sons being
killed, I've seated them, along with their mother, at this altar
of Zeus the Saviour. It was my noble son who set it up to
commemorate his glorious victory in war when he defeated   50
the Minyans.* We keep to our places here, though we lack all
the necessities of life, such as food and drink and a change of
clothes, and when we lie on the ground we have no bedding.*
For the doors of the house have been sealed against us,* and
here we sit, helpless to save ourselves. I see now that some of
our friends are not reliable friends, while those who are true
friends are unable to help us.* This is typical of what happens
when things go wrong for people. I pray that everyone who is
even moderately well disposed towards me may never meet
misfortune, which is the most revealing test of friends!

MEGARA. Old friend, who once led the Theban army to glory   60
when you destroyed the city of the Taphians,* how true it is

that nothing the gods do is comprehensible to humans. Take
my case, for instance. I was not excluded from good fortune,
first, where my father was concerned. Once he was famed far
and wide as a happy man: he had a kingdom, which makes
the bodies of those who prosper targets for long spears hurled
in lust for power, and he had offspring. And in giving me to
your son Heracles, he arranged a notable marriage for me.
But now all this has perished, melted into thin air. You and I   70
are about to be put to death, old friend, and so are Heracles'
sons, whom I protect under my wing as a bird shelters her
cowering brood. They come at me from all sides with their
questions: 'Mother, tell me, where in the world has father
gone?' 'What is he doing?' 'When will he come back?' In the
delusion of their youth they look for their father, while I try to
distract them with stories. Whenever the door creaks they all
jump up in wonder to rush to their father's knees. So can you   80
now relieve us with any hope or means of survival, old friend?
For I look to you for help. We cannot sneak across the border,
because there are guards on the roads who are stronger than
us, and we can no longer expect our friends to rescue us. So
please share your thoughts on the matter with us, or else our
death is certain.

AMPHITRYON. Dear daughter, in a situation like this it's not
easy just to toss out advice in a hurry, without effort. We are
weak; we should take our time.

MEGARA. Do you need any more pain?* Are you so in love with   90
life?

AMPHITRYON. Yes, I do enjoy life, and I love having hope.

MEGARA. So do I. But one shouldn't hope where there is no
hope, old friend.

AMPHITRYON. But postponing evil does offer relief.

MEGARA. But time spent waiting is a hideous torment.

AMPHITRYON. Well, daughter, you and I may yet run with a
fair wind behind us and escape the troubles currently afflicting us: my son, your husband, may yet return. But calm
down now, put an end to your children's floods of tears, and
talk to them to soothe their distress. Deceive them with the   100
poor deceit of stories. For even the disasters of life die down;
in time gale-force winds abate, and those who prosper do not
remain prosperous. Everything separates from everything

else.* The best man is the one who always puts his trust in hope; helplessness is the sign of a bad man.

MEGARA attends to her children. The CHORUS enter, hobbling with the help of sticks, and sing as they struggle over to and up the steps of the altar.

CHORUS (*sings*). Forth I went, leaning on my stick, an old
     singer of laments, like the white-plumed bird,*   110
to this imposing house and the old man in his bed.
Nothing but words am I now, a night-time
vision seen in dreams after dark. And here I am,
feeble but still eager, children—oh, you poor
fatherless children—and you, old friend, and you,
the poor mother of these children, who mourn
your husband in the domain of Hades.

(*each addressing himself*)
Don't let those feet and leaden legs grow tired,†
like a yoked horse labouring up a rocky slope,   120
bearing the weight of a wheeled cart.† Take hold
of the hands and clothes of anyone who falters
with uncertain step. Though you are old, support
an old man by whose side you once fought,
long ago, in the battles of your youth,
when you and he both were young. No disgrace
you were to the great glory of your country.

(*addressing one another, and reaching the group of suppliants*)
See how the eyes of these boys gleam   130
with savagery, just like their father's.
His bad luck has been passed down to them,
but they have his readiness to help too.
O Greece, what allies, what fierce allies
you will lose if you are robbed of these boys!

The CHORUS stop singing, and the Chorus-leader continues alone.

But here comes Lycus, the king of this land. I can see him drawing near the house.

Enter LYCUS with attendants.

LYCUS. I have some questions I'd like to ask Heracles' father and   140

his wife—and, since I am now your master, I suppose I may
ask what I like. For how long are you trying to extend your
life? Can you see any hope of finding some way to ward off
death? Do you really believe that these children's father, who
lies dead in Hades, is going to return? Since you are bound to
die, you're trying to stir up grief beyond what you deserve, by
spreading inane boasts—you (*pointing to* AMPHITRYON) that
Zeus was also your wife's partner and co-father of your child,
and you (*to* MEGARA) that you are famed as the wife of a great   150
hero.

Well, how splendid was your husband's achievement in
killing a marsh snake or even the Nemean beast, which,
according to him, he caught in a noose and strangled with his
bare hands?* Are these the exploits on which you base your
contention? Is it because of them that Heracles' sons ought to
be spared? For all his nullity, Heracles has acquired a specious
reputation for courage by fighting wild beasts, but in other
respects he is not brave at all. He has never put a shield on his
left arm or come within range of a spear. He carried a bow, a   160
weapon of extreme cowardice,* and was always ready to run
away. A bow is no test of a man's courage: a brave man is one
who, without flinching, keeps his place in the ranks while
facing squarely a spear-cut furrow racing towards him.

I am not prompted by ruthlessness, old man, but by cau-
tion. I am well aware that I owe my possession of the throne
to the fact that I killed Creon, this woman's father. I don't
want to leave these boys here to grow up and punish me for
what I did by settling the score.

AMPHITRYON (*pointedly ignoring* LYCUS). I shall leave Zeus to   170
defend that part of his son which is from Zeus. But in so far as
I am able, Heracles, it is my job to use arguments to demonstrate this man's ignorance about you. I cannot let him get
away with abusing you.

First, I must acquit you, with the gods as my witnesses, of
the unspeakable charge*—for I count the accusation of cowardice in your case, Heracles, as an unspeakable charge. I
hereby call to witness the thunderbolt of Zeus,* and the chariot on which he stood and planted his flighted missiles into
the bodies of the earth-born Giants,* before celebrating his   180
glorious victory with the company of the gods. (*Turning now*

to LYCUS) Why don't you go to Phol
kings, and ask those four-legged mo
whom they judge to be a man of unpa
my son, whose reputation for bravery
And if you were to ask Dirphys, home
place where you grew up,* it would not p
way that the land of your birth would at
since you have never done a single noble

Now, you criticize that supremely cle
bowman's weapon. Listen to what I have to   , then, and you
will learn something. A man in heavy armour is a slave to his   190
weapons, in the sense that if he breaks his spear he cannot
protect his body against a deadly assault, since he has just the
one means of defence. And if the others in his line of battle
lack courage, the cowardice of his neighbours causes his
death.* But those who take up the straight-shooting bow have
one outstanding advantage: they can shoot countless arrows
and still have others with which to protect themselves from
death. A bowman stands far away to defend himself against
the enemy, wounding them with arrows which go unseen by
their eyes, and he does not expose his body to his opponents,   200
but keeps himself safe. In a battle, there's nothing more clever
than harming the enemy while keeping yourself safe, and
detached from the element of luck. The thrust of this argument contradicts your views on the issue between us.

Next, why do you want to kill these boys? What harm have
they done you? There's only one respect in which I think you
are being clever, and that is because, as a coward yourself, the
children of a hero fill you with fear. All the same, it's hard for
us to bear the idea that we shall be put to death because of   210
your cowardice. Since we are better than you, it should be us
killing you, if Zeus was disposed to be just towards us. If you
really want to keep the rulership of this land without us
around, let us leave the country and go into exile. But
don't act with violence or you will suffer violence when the
god-sent winds happen to change against you.

(*Turning away from* LYCUS) Oh, land of Cadmus—for I'm not
going to miss you out either as I distribute my reproaches—is
this any way to protect Heracles and his sons,† when it was   220
he who single-handedly engaged all the Minyans* in battle

possible for Thebes to look out on the world with
in her eye? Nor have I anything to thank Greece
—I can't bear to keep this reproach to myself either—since
I find that she has treated my son terribly. She should have
come with fire, spears, and armour to help these little ones, in
repayment for the cleansing of the sea and the land which he
achieved by his own efforts and strength.†

For it is true, children, that neither Thebes nor Greece is
helping you. You look to me for support, but I am weak,
nothing but a tongue and its noise. The strength I once had   230
has deserted me, my limbs shake with age, my powers are
feeble. If I were young and still in control of my body, I would
have taken a spear and bloodied those golden locks of his,*
and at the sight of my spear he would have run like the
coward he is beyond the bounds of Atlas.*

CHORUS. Brave men find material for their arguments, don't
they, even when they are not particularly eloquent?

LYCUS. You're so proud of the words you use to speak ill of me,
but I shall repay them with such deeds that it will *go* ill for you.
(*To the attendants*) Go—some of you to Helicon, others to the   240
glens of Parnassus.* When you arrive there, get foresters to cut
logs of timber. Once they've been brought into the city, pack
the logs up around the altar, set fire to them, and reduce their
bodies to ashes, all of them! Then they will appreciate that now
it is I who rule this land, not the dead man. (*Some attendants
depart. LYCUS turns to the CHORUS*) As for you, old men, for your
opposition to my decisions you will mourn not only Heracles'
sons, but also the misfortune that will afflict your houses.   250
You will remember that you are slaves and I am your king!

*The CHORUS divide.† They attempt to raise their sticks and shake
them, but the effort tires them.*

SEMICHORUS A. Offspring of the earth, sown once by Ares after
he had stripped the fierce jaw of the dragon of its teeth,* will
you not raise the sticks on which you lean your right arms?
Will you not bloody the impious head of this man who rules
over us despite being no Theban but a craven foreigner?

SEMICHORUS B. No, you will never be *my* master and get away
with it! You will never take possession of all that I laboured
and toiled so hard to get. Take your high-handed ways back   260

where you came from, with my curses! As long as I'm alive
you shall never kill Heracles' sons. He may not be here with
his children, but he's not buried so deep in the earth below.

SEMICHORUS A. For you have grasped and destroyed this land,
while its benefactor is mistreated. (*Sarcastically*) So is it really
interference for me to help dead friends of mine, which is when
they are most in need of friends? O right hand of mine, how
you long to take up a spear! But your weakness confounds
this longing.

SEMICHORUS B. Then I'd have stopped you calling me 'slave'!   270
Then I'd have won glory helping this city of Thebes, which
you are exploiting for your own pleasure. A city which is
rotten with feuding and bad advice cannot think straight;
otherwise she would never have gained you as her master.

MEGARA. Old friends, thank you. It is proper for friends to feel
righteous indignation on behalf of friends. But I don't want
to see you come to any harm as a result of getting angry at
your master on our account. (*Turning to* AMPHITRYON) Listen
to my view, Amphitryon, and see if you think there's anything to it. I love my children. How could I not love them   280
when I gave birth to them and worked so hard over them?
Moreover, I am frightened of dying. But I think that anyone
who resists the course of necessity is stupid. In our case, we
are bound to die, but we don't have to die in the agony of the
fire, with our enemies taunting us. This, to me, is worse than
dying, because there must be nobility in the way we repay our
great debts to our house. Not only is it intolerable that you,
with your glorious reputation as a fighter, should die at the
hands of a coward, but my husband, whose glory needs no   290
witnesses, would not want to save these children if that
meant their gaining a reputation for cowardice. After all,
noble parents are hurt by their children's disgrace. And
besides, I must not reject my husband's example.

Here's my considered opinion about the hopes you entertain. Do you think your son will return from under the earth?
Did any of the dead ever come back from Hades?* Or perhaps
you hope that arguments of ours might get this man here
(*pointing to* LYCUS) to relent. There's no chance at all of
that. One should simply avoid a stupid enemy, and make
concessions only to those who are wise and well bred. It's   300

easier to win them over to your side by submitting to their
sense of fair play. I did wonder before whether we should ask
for these children to be allowed to go into exile, but it's no
happier an option for them to gain safety with miserable
poverty. They say that faces smile in welcome of exiled friends
only for a single day.

Bravely, by my side, face the death that awaits you anyway.
I appeal to your nobility, old friend. Those who keep on struggling against the fortune sent them by the gods show
resolution—but a foolish resolution. No one can ever un-   310
ordain that which is ordained.*

CHORUS (*to* MEGARA). If you'd been treated this arrogantly while
I still had strength in my arms, I'd easily have stopped it. But
now I am nothing. (*To* AMPHITRYON) And so it's up to you,
Amphitryon: find the best way through this awful situation.

AMPHITRYON. It's not cowardice or clinging to life that makes
me reluctant to die; I just want to save my son's children. But
I seem to be entertaining a vain desire for the impossible. (*He
leaves the protection of the altar, and the other suppliants slowly
follow him. He stands close to* LYCUS *and pulls aside his clothing*)
See, here is my neck for your sword: you can stab me, murder   320
me, and hurl my body from a cliff. But there's one favour we
beg of you, lord: kill me and this poor woman here before you
murder the children, so that we don't have to witness the
hideous sight of them breathing their last and calling on their
mother and grandfather. Go ahead and do everything else
you are so determined to do. We have no way to defend
ourselves against death.

MEGARA. I've got one more favour to beg of you; then you'll be
doing a double service at once, something for both of us.
Please let me dress the boys in their funeral clothes. You'll
have to open the door first, because at the moment we're   330
locked out. Then they will have inherited at least that much
of their father's estate.

LYCUS. All right. You servants, open the doors. (*To the suppliants
again*) Go inside and dress them. I don't mind letting you have
the clothes. But after you've dressed them in their finery, I
shall return to consign you to the underworld.

Exit LYCUS, *followed by his attendants once they have opened the
doors of the house.*

MEGARA. Children, follow your mother in her sorrow into your
    father's house, where the property is in others' hands, and all
    we have left is the name.

> *Exit MEGARA and the children into the house.*

AMPHITRYON. Zeus, it turns out that there was no point in my
    having you as my wife's partner, no point in my calling you   340
    co-father of my son. It turns out that you were less of a friend
    than you seemed. Though I am a man and you a great god, I
    am the better person, because I did not betray Heracles' sons.
    You are a past master at sneaking into others' beds and tak-
    ing other men's wives without their permission, but you don't
    know how to save members of your own family. Either you
    are an unfeeling god, or there is no justice in you.*

> *Exit AMPHITRYON into the house.*

CHORUS (*sings*). Beside a song of success Phoebus sings a
        lament,
    striking his dulcet-toned lyre with golden plectrum.*
    So I want to celebrate with praise, as a garland
    to his labours, the one who has gone down
    into the dark of the earth, down to the underworld,
    whether I should call him son of Zeus
    or scion of Amphitryon.* Great deeds
    performed with noble effort glorify the dead.

First he cleared Zeus' grove of the lion,   360
    and covered his golden hair with the tawny jaws
    of the terrible creature, drawing it over his back.*

Then the wild hill-dwellers, the tribe of Centaurs,
    he laid low with his deadly arrows, killing them
    with his flighted shafts. This deed was witnessed
    by the Peneus river with its fair, swirling waters,
    by the broad, barren flatlands, by the farms of Pelion,   370
    and by the huts of the pastures of Homole,*
    from where the Centaurs filled their arms with pines
    and galloped over their domain, the land of Thessaly.

Then, to the delight of the goddess of Oenoë,
    slayer of wild beasts, he killed the hind, of golden horns
    and dappled back, despoiler of the farmers' land.*

Then he mounted the chariot with its team of four   380
and tamed to the harness the mares of Diomedes,*
which in blood-drenched mangers used to dispatch
with unbridled zest their bloody food with their jaws,
foul diners delighting in the flesh of men.
He crossed to the further bank of the silvery waters
of the Hebrus,* a labourer for the king of Mycenae.*

On the coast near Pelion,† by Anaurus' streams,
he slew with his arrows Cycnus, cleaver of visitors,   390
the brutal inhabitant of Amphanae.*

Then to the maiden singers he went, to their home
in the west, to pluck with his hand the golden fruit
from the apple-laden leafy boughs, and he killed
the monstrous tawny-backed dragon which kept watch
over the fruit with its coils wrapped tightly round.*
Then he entered the depths of the salty sea   400
and made it calm for the oars of mortal men.*

Then to Atlas' halls he went, drove his hands
under the middle of heaven's seat, and kept steady
the starry home of the gods with his strength.*

Then across the inhospitable surge of the sea* he went
against the host of the horse-riding Amazons   410
near Maeotis, fed by many rivers. Which of his comrades
did he not form into a band and take with him, when he
    sailed
on the deadly quest for the girdle of the gold-decked robe†
of the warrior maid?* Greece took from the barbarian maid
the famous spoil, which is now kept safe in Mycenae.

Then with fire he destroyed the murderous, many-headed   420
hydra-hound of Lerna,* and smeared with its venom the
    arrows
with which he killed the triple-bodied herdsman of Erytheia.*

Then, after the glory and success with which he completed
his other journeys, for his final task he sailed to mournful
    Hades.
But there, to his misfortune, his life ended and he failed to
    return.

His friends have abandoned his house, and Charon's oar-   430
    blade*
waits at the end of the path of his children's life—
a path without return, without gods, without justice.
Your house looks for your strength, but you are not here.

If I were young and strong and could wield a spear in battle
with my fellow Thebans, I'd have championed these children,
defended them. But the glory days of my youth are now past.   440

The CHORUS *stops singing, and the Chorus-leader continues alone.*

But here I can see, wearing their funeral clothes, the children
of Heracles, who was once great and now is dead, and his
beloved wife pulling them along in a string† at her tender feet,
and Heracles' old father. Oh, misery! I can no longer stop the
tears welling from my aged eyes.   450

Enter MEGARA, AMPHITRYON, *and the children, who are dressed for
burial, with wreaths on their heads, and cling to* MEGARA's *legs.*

MEGARA. Well, then, who is going to act as priest and perform
    the ritual slaughter of the wretched victims?† Here they are,
    ready for him to take to Hades. Children, we are being taken
    away! What an unattractive team of corpses we make, an old
    man and children and their mother all harnessed together. O
    how wretched is the fate I and these children here suffer—
    these children I now look on for the very last time! I gave you
    birth, but what did I rear you for? To be abused, taunted,
    destroyed by your enemies!
       Oh, how thoroughly all my hopes have been dashed—all   460
    the expectations I held before as a result of things your father
    used to say! (*To the first son*) To you, for instance, your father,
    now dead, was going to assign Argos: you were to live in
    Eurystheus' palace and rule over fertile Pelasgia,* and he used
    to drape your head with the lionskin which was all his
    armour. (*To the second son*) And you were the lord of Thebes
    with its chariots: the plains of my country were the inherit-
    ance you wheedled out of your father, and for your defence   470
    he would put into your right hand his cunningly wrought
    club, and pretend it was a gift to you. (*To the third son*) And
    he promised you Oechalia,* which he once sacked with his

far-reaching arrows. Proud of his courage, your father wanted
to raise the three of you high with three kingships, while I
was selecting brides for you, forging alliances with Athens,
Sparta, and Thebes, to assure you of a happy life and the
security of a firm mooring. But there's no chance of any of   480
this now: your luck has changed and given you demons for
brides,* and the only water I shall bear for you in my misery
will be tears.* Your grandfather here is in charge of the cele-
brations for a wedding which forms a bitter alliance, because
he recognizes Hades as your father-in-law. (*She embraces the
three boys in turn*) Ah! Which of you shall I take first in my
arms? Which last? Who gets the first kiss, the first clasp? How
I wish that I could imitate a bee with its buzzing wings! I
would gather the grief from you all and condense it into a
single tear before giving it back.

O my darling Heracles, if the sound of any mortal voice   490
can be heard in Hades, I tell you that your father and children are being put to death, and that I too am to die—I
whom people used to congratulate because of you. Come,
save us! Let me see you even as a ghost! It would be enough
even if you were to come in a dream, for your children's
killers are cowards.

AMPHITRYON. Carry on trying to conciliate the powers below,
woman, while I call on you, Zeus, with my arms raised
towards heaven! If you are planning to do anything for these
children, protect them now, because before long they will be   500
quite beyond your help. But why do I bother? We have
appealed to you often before now. Our deaths are inevitable, it
seems.

(*He lowers his arms and turns to the* CHORUS) Well, old
friends, life is a thing of little significance. Get through it as
pleasantly as you can—that is, by avoiding pain morning,
noon, and night. For time is useless at preserving hopes; it
just flits along, busy about its own affairs. Look at me! Once
I was an object of admiration for my glorious achievements,
but now fortune has taken this from me in a single day, like   510
a feather blown skyward. I cannot think of anyone who
gains great wealth and fame and holds them securely. Farewell! This is the last time, comrades, you will ever see your
friend!

AMPHITRYON veils his head. Enter HERACLES, *recognizable from his lionskin and club.*

MEGARA. Wait! Old friend, is this my beloved husband I can see or what?

AMPHITRYON (*unveiling his head*). I don't know, daughter. I am struck dumb.

MEGARA. Here is the man we were told was in the underworld, unless this is a dream we're seeing in broad daylight. I don't know what to say. Am I deranged? Is this some kind of hallucination? It's none other than your son, old friend. Come here, children! Grab hold of your father's clothes! Go, quickly, and don't let go! He is just as much your saviour as Zeus the Saviour!* 520

The children are too frightened to approach their father yet, but at some point during the following scene they crowd around HERACLES *and take hold of his cloak.*

HERACLES. I welcome the sight of my house and the doorway to my hearth. How glad I am to return to the upper light and see you! (*To himself*) But what's this? I see my children in front of the house with their heads wreathed and arrayed for burial! And there, in a crowd of men, is my wife—and there's my father, weeping! What disaster can have happened? Come, I must draw near and find out. (*To* MEGARA) Wife, what news? 530 What has happened to my household?

MEGARA. My darling husband . . .

AMPHITRYON. Here you are, a beacon of hope for your father . . .

MEGARA. . . . have you really come? Are you really here, safe and sound, at this moment of crisis for your family?

HERACLES. What do you mean? Father, what upheaval have I arrived to find?

MEGARA. We were being killed. (*To* AMPHITRYON) Old friend, forgive me for interrupting and saying what you should by rights be telling him. Women are somehow more emotional than men, and it was my children who were being put to death, I who was being killed.

HERACLES. Apollo!* This is quite a beginning to your tale.

MEGARA. My brothers and my old father are dead.

HERACLES. What do you mean? What did he do? Or how did   540
death come upon him?

MEGARA. Lycus, the new lord of this land, killed him.

HERACLES. Did he meet them in battle? Or was there some
unsoundness in the land?

MEGARA. The country was rotten with feuding, and now he
rules over seven-gated Thebes.

HERACLES. But what reason do you and the old man have to be
afraid?

MEGARA. He was going to kill your father, me, and the
children.

HERACLES. What? Why was he afraid of my children in their
orphaned state?

MEGARA. He thought they might punish him one day for
Creon's death.*

HERACLES. Why are the children dressed like this, in a manner
fit for corpses?

MEGARA. We've already dressed in funeral clothes, as you can
see.

HERACLES. And you were being forced to die? Oh, what I have   550
to endure!

MEGARA. Yes, and our friends abandoned us. But we were told
that you were dead.

HERACLES. That must have disheartened you. What made you
think so?

MEGARA. That was the news we kept getting from Eurystheus'
messengers.

HERACLES. But why did you leave the safety of my hearth and
home?

MEGARA. We were forced out, with your father being thrown
out of his bed and . . .

HERACLES. Did a sense of shame not stop him treating an old
man so brutally?

MEGARA. Shame? He's moved well away from that goddess's
vicinity.

HERACLES. Was I so short of friends while I was away?

MEGARA. What friends does a man have when things go badly
for him?

HERACLES. Do they hold the battles I endured against the   560
Minyans in such contempt?

MEGARA. I repeat: misfortune is a friendless condition.

HERACLES. Tear from your hair these wreaths of Hades! Let the light shine once more from your eyes, with a look that is a welcome exchange for the darkness below! Now there's work for my hands. First I shall go and raze the palace of the new king to the ground. I shall cut off his sacrilegious head and throw it to the dogs. They can rip it to pieces. Any Thebans I discover to have repaid my benevolence with cowardice I shall overcome with this all-conquering club of mine, while I shall rip into others with my flighted arrows, until I fill the whole Ismenus with slaughtered bodies and redden with blood the clear waters of Dirce.* After all, who else should I defend, if not my wife, children, and aged father? Enough of my labours! They were pointless accomplishments compared with what needs to be done here. It is indeed my duty to risk death fighting for these children, since they were to die for their father. How could I count it admirable to fight a hydra and a lion on Eurystheus' orders, and then not do all I can to keep death from my own children?* People would stop calling me Heracles, glorious in victory, as they did before.

CHORUS. It is right for a father to help his children, his aged father, and his partner in marriage.

AMPHITRYON. It's typical of you, my son, to love those who are dear to you and to loathe your enemies.* But you shouldn't be in too much of a hurry.

HERACLES. Which of my suggestions was over-hasty, father?

AMPHITRYON. The king has on his side many men who, for all that they are thought to be well off, are actually poor. It was they who started the feuding and brought the city to ruin so that they could steal from their neighbours, since their own inheritance has been squandered, and has slipped through their fingers as a result of their laziness. Moreover, you were seen entering the city. And since you were seen, you have to be careful in case, having given your enemies time to group, you take an unexpected fall.

HERACLES. I don't care if the whole city saw me. But in fact I saw a bird on an inauspicious perch,* and so, realizing that my family had met with some trouble or other, I entered the land surreptitiously.

AMPHITRYON. Well done. Why don't you go inside now, where

570

580

590

you can pray to Hestia* and let your ancestral home see your 600
face? The king will come in person to take your wife, your
children, and me off for slaughter. If you wait here everything will fall into your lap and you will have the advantage
of safety. Don't disrupt your fellow citizens until you've sorted
things out here, my son.

HERACLES. I'll do as you suggest. It's a good idea. I shall go
inside. Since at last I've returned from the sunless depths of
Hades and Kore,* prompt prayers to the gods in my home is
the correct way to show my respect for them.

AMPHITRYON. Did you really enter Hades' halls, my son? 610

HERACLES. Yes, and I brought the three-headed beast up to the
light of day.

AMPHITRYON. Did you defeat it in a fight, or did the goddess
hand it over to you?

HERACLES. I had to fight it, but since I had witnessed the rites
of the Mysteries I was lucky.*

AMPHITRYON. And is the creature now in Eurystheus' palace?

HERACLES. It's being kept in the grove of Demeter Chthonia in
the town of Hermion.*

AMPHITRYON. Doesn't Eurystheus know that you have
returned to the upper world?

HERACLES. No, he doesn't. I wanted to come here first and find
out what was happening.

AMPHITRYON. Why did you spend so long in the underworld?

HERACLES. I brought Theseus back from Hades, father, and
that took time.*

AMPHITRYON. Where is he? Has he gone back to the country of 620
his birth?

HERACLES. Yes, he's gone to Athens, delighted to have escaped
the underworld. (*To his sons*) Well now, children, come with
your father into the house. It looks as though your going in
will be better than your coming out! Cheer up, and stop these
floods of tears. (*To MEGARA*) And you, wife, pull yourself
together and stop trembling—and let go of my cloak, all of
you! I have no wings; I'm not about to flee from my loved
ones. Oh, they're not letting go of my cloak, but are clinging
to it even harder. Was your situation so precarious? Well, I 630
shall take hold of these tenders and tow them along as if I
were a ship. I'm not above looking after my children. Human

beings are all the same: nobles and nobodies alike love their children. Money makes them different—some have it and some don't—but all humans love their children.

Exeunt HERACLES, MEGARA, AMPHITRYON *and the children into the house.*

CHORUS (*sings*). Youth is dear to me, but old age is a constant burden
   that lies heavier on the head than the crags of Etna,*   640
   and casts a veil of darkness over the eyes.
   Rather than the riches of an Asian king, rather than
   a palace filled with gold, I would have youth.
   For nothing is fairer than youth, whether one is rich or poor.
   I loathe old age, which is hideous and deadly.
   May it vanish beneath the ocean waves!   650
   I wish it had never visited the homes and cities of men.
   No, may it spend all time aloft in the air on wings.

   If the gods had understanding and wisdom as men do,
   good men would have won a second youth
   as a clear sign of their virtue, and after dying   660
   they would return once more to the sunlight in a second
      lap,
   while immoral men would have kept just the one life.
   We would then have a way to tell the bad from the
      good,
   even as among the clouds a constellation appears to sailors.
   But as things are the gods give us no sure way
   of distinguishing the good and the bad.   670
   As a man's life unfurls, it only increases his wealth.

   Never shall I stop blending the Graces* and the Muses!
   What a delightful pairing they make! I would not have life
   without the Muses, without garlands always on my head!
   I may be an aged singer, but still I shall celebrate
   Memory,* still sing of Heracles' glorious victories,   680
   to the accompaniment of Bromius,* giver of wine,
   and accompanied by the tunes of the seven-stringed lyre,
   made of tortoise shell, and by the Libyan pipes.
   Never shall I restrain the Muses who stirred me to dance!

   At the gates of the temple the women of Delos sing a paean

to the blessed son of Leto,* unfurling their fair dance.   690
But I, aged singer that I am, shall like a swan
sing a paean from grizzled mouth by your house.
For my songs have a fund of excellence to draw on.
He is the son of Zeus, but even this high birth
is eclipsed by his courage and virtue.
By his labours—in destroying fearsome beasts—
he has made life calm for mortal men.   700

*Enter LYCUS, with attendants, just as AMPHITRYON is coming out of
the house. He leaves the doors of the house open.*

LYCUS. It's about time for you to be coming out of the house,
Amphitryon. You've already spent a long time arraying yourselves with the clothing and ornaments of the dead. Now,
come on: tell Heracles' children and his wife to show themselves outside the house, to keep your promise to die
voluntarily.

AMPHITRYON (*obsequiously*). My lord, you're hounding me
when I'm already in a wretched state. This is brutal treatment, when I'm faced with the deaths of members of my own
family. Even though you're the ruler, you should pursue your
interests with moderation. But since you are compelling us to   710
die, we must put up with it. We must go along with your
wishes.

LYCUS. So where's Megara? Where are Heracles' sons?

AMPHITRYON (*peering indoors*). As far as I can tell from out here,
it seems to me that she's . . .

LYCUS. What? What do you 'seem' to know?

AMPHITRYON. . . . sitting as a suppliant at the sacred altar of
Hestia . . .

LYCUS. Yes, begging pointlessly for her life to be saved.

AMPHITRYON. . . . and making a vain attempt to call up her
dead husband.

LYCUS. Who's not here and will certainly never come.

AMPHITRYON. No, unless some god brings him back to life
again.

LYCUS. Go to her and bring her out of the house.   720

AMPHITRYON. But then I'd be an accomplice to her murder.

LYCUS. Since you have scruples about doing so, I shall go and
fetch the children and their mother. I have no such supersti-

tious fears. (*To his attendants*) Follow me, men! Then we'll be able to take a welcome break from our labours.

Exit LYCUS and attendants into the house.

AMPHITRYON. Yes, go! Your destiny awaits you there. Someone else will presumably take care of what remains. As an evil-doer, you should expect to meet with evil. (*To the CHORUS*) Old friends, he's going into the house! That's perfect! He'll be caught in a trap ringed with swords, the evil coward who 730 thought he would kill his neighbours. I shall go to watch him die. There is pleasure in the death of an enemy as he is punished for what he has done.

Exit AMPHITRYON into the house.

The CHORUS divides for the following lines.

SEMICHORUS A. Here is an end to our troubles! Great Heracles, once our lord, has wheeled the chariot of his life back from Hades. Hurray for justice and the ebb and flow of fate from the gods!

SEMICHORUS B. At last you have reached the place where you 740 will pay with your life for the brutal way you treated those who are better than you.

SEMICHORUS A. I weep for pleasure. He has returned, the lord of this land. Never before would I have expected to experience such feelings!

SEMICHORUS B. Well, old friends, let's also see what's happening indoors. I wonder whether a certain person is faring as I hope.

LYCUS (*from within*). Oh, no! No! 750

SEMICHORUS A. Here begins within the house the song I love to hear. Death is near by! The king's cries of pain herald his murder.

LYCUS (*from within*). I call out to the whole of Thebes! I am being treacherously killed!

SEMICHORUS B. Yes, because you are a killer yourself! Prepare to pay the penalty, as you are punished for what you have done.

SEMICHORUS A. Who, for all that he was a mere mortal, attributed lawlessness to the gods and spread the stupid idea that the blessed gods of heaven are weak and feeble?†

SEMICHORUS B. Old friends, the godless man is dead. There's no   760
  sound from the house. Let's turn to dancing.†

  The CHORUS reunites and sings and dances as usual.

CHORUS. Dancing, dancing and feasting, are the only concern
  in the sacred city of Thebes. For the end of tears,
  the end of misfortune, has bred new† songs.
  Gone is the usurper, and the old king rules,
  having left the harbour of Acheron.*   770
  My hopes have been unexpectedly fulfilled.

  The gods, the gods are concerned for the unjust
  and the just and notice their ways. Gold and success
  derange mortal men and involve unjust power.
  For no one who neglects the laws and indulges
  his lawlessness dares look to time's future.†
  And so he smashes the dark chariot of prosperity.   780

  O Ismenus,* deck yourself with garlands!
  O hewn* streets of the seven-gated city
  and fair-flowing Dirce, break into dance!
  And come too, maiden daughters of Asopus,*
  fair Nymphs, leave your father's waters
  and add your voices to the song in celebration
  of Heracles' glorious victory in the struggle.
  O wooded crags of the Pythian god,*   790
  O homes of the Muses of Helicon,*
  honour with joyful song my city, my walls,
  where there appeared the clan of Sown Men,
  a band of warriors with bronze shields,
  a sacred beacon for Thebes, who bequeath
  the land to the children of their children.

  O twofold liaison, begetting one child,
  of a mortal and of Zeus, who came to the bed   800
  of the young bride, descended from Perseus!*
  How that liaison of yours now long ago, Zeus,
  has turned out, against my hopes,
  to be credible! For time has revealed
  your glorious strength, Heracles.†
  You emerged from the chambers of the earth,

leaving behind the underworld halls of Pluto.*
You make a better ruler, as it seems to me,
than Lycus in his base immorality,   810
which now shows anyone who witnesses
the sword-bearing contest whether or not
justice still finds favour with the gods.

The two goddesses MADNESS *and* IRIS *appear. They fly through the air
(on the crane) and land above the backdrop.* The CHORUS *divides as
before.*

SEMICHORUS A. Aaaah! Old friends, are we feeling again that
    same fit of fear? What terrible apparition is this I see above
    the house?
SEMICHORUS B. Raise those heavy feet up off the ground! Flee,
    flee! Let's get away from here!
CHORUS (*as a whole*). O lord Paean,* keep us safe from disaster!   820

They attempt to run away, but stop when IRIS *begins to speak.*

IRIS. Courage, old men! Here you see Madness, the daughter of
    Night, and me, Iris, the servant of the gods. We have not
    come to hurt the city; our target is the house of just one man,
    who they say is the son of Zeus and Alcmene. While his bitter
    struggles remained unfinished, Fate kept him safe and father
    Zeus would not allow either Hera or me ever to do him
    harm. But now that he has completed the labours set him by   830
    Eurystheus, Hera wants to impose kindred murder on him
    by having him kill his sons, and that is my wish too.
       But come now, unwedded daughter of dark Night, brace
    your implacable heart! Visit madness upon this man, and the
    mental confusion necessary for killing children, and stir his
    feet to frenzied dancing. Let out your sail for bloodshed, so
    that once he has committed murder within his family and
    conveyed across the strait of Acheron his fair sons, the crown
    of his life, he may realize how furious Hera is with him, and   840
    recognize my anger too. Otherwise, if he remains un-
    punished, the gods count for nothing and mortal affairs
    take precedence.
MADNESS. I have noble blood on both sides, since my father
    was Heaven and my mother Night. The office I have to dis-
    charge here is unwelcome to my friends,† and indeed I take

no pleasure in visiting those mortals I hold dear. I'd like to
give Hera some advice, before I see her make a mistake, and
(*to* IRIS) I offer the advice to you too, if the two of you will
listen to what I have to say. This man here, whose house you
are having me enter, has a high reputation among both men   850
and gods. He tamed the trackless land and the fierce sea, and
was single-handedly responsible for restoring the worship of
the gods when it had been cast into the dust by sacrilegious
men.* And so my advice to you is that you shouldn't conspire
to do him serious harm.

IRIS. How dare you criticize Hera's and my plans!

MADNESS. I'm trying to guide your steps towards a better
course of action.

IRIS. Zeus' wife did not send you here to act with moderation.

MADNESS. I call on the Sun-god to witness that what I do here I
do with reluctance!* But if I must perform this service for
Hera and you,† I shall go about my business. The savage
power of the sea with its thundering waves, of the earth-
quake, and of the thunderbolt's pain-blasting shaft† is
nothing compared to the force with which I shall race into
Heracles' heart. I shall shatter his house and bring the roof
down on his head—once I've caused the death of his children. But their killer will not know that he has murdered his
own sons until he is free of my madness. Look! The race is on!
He's tossing his head, with his eyes rolling around furiously,
but uttering not a word. He's panting wildly, like a bull poised
to charge, and his terrible bellowing summons the Fates from   870
Tartarus* to rush screeching† and follow him as hounds follow a hunter. Soon I shall stir you to more violent dancing
and possess you with pipes of fear. (*To* IRIS) Fly, Iris—leave the
ground and make your way to Olympus. I shall slip unseen
into Heracles' house.

> IRIS *leaves on the crane, while* MADNESS *climbs down*
> *behind the backdrop, as if into* HERACLES' *house.*

CHORUS (*sings*). Oh, woe! Raise the lament! Wretched Greece,
your city-flower,* the son of Zeus, is being cut down!
You shall lose your benefactor; he will be gone,
made to dance by the raving madness of pipes.
Gone in her chariot is she who brings many woes,   880

and she goads on her horses, intent to cause harm.
She is Madness, Gorgon daughter of Night,*
with a hundred hissing snake-heads and a petrifying gaze.
Swiftly has Fate overturned him in his success.
Swiftly the children will die at their father's hand.

The CHORUS *continues to sing or chant, with* AMPHITRYON's *cries*
breaking in from within.

AMPHITRYON. Oh, misery!

CHORUS. Oh, Zeus, in no time at all the spirits of vengeance
in their savage, unjust madness will crush your family
with disasters and deprive it of its sons.

AMPHITRYON. Alas for the house!

CHORUS. The dancing begins, unaccompanied by drums,
distasteful to Bromius with his thyrsus* . . .   890

AMPHITRYON. Alas for my family!

CHORUS. . . . and designed for the shedding of blood,
not the pouring of wine pressed from Dionysus' grapes.

AMPHITRYON. Flee, children! Get away from here!

CHORUS. Murderous, murderous is the tune that is piped here.
His children are the quarry of his hunt! In her frenzy
against the house, Madness will surely have her way.

AMPHITRYON. Ah, what evil has been done here!

CHORUS. Well may you lament! What sorrow I feel for his aged   900
    father,
and for the mother whose children were born for nothing!
Look, look! A storm is shaking the house! The roof is caving
    in!

AMPHITRYON. Aaaah! Daughter of Zeus, what are you doing to
the house? Pallas, you are sending the turmoil of hell against
my family, as you once did in the case of Enceladus.*

Enter the MESSENGER, *a servant, from the house.*

MESSENGER (*loudly, to attract the attention of the* CHORUS, *who are*   910
scattered with emotion). Old sirs, white with age . . .

CHORUS. What is it? Why are you calling out to me?

MESSENGER. . . . appalling things have been going on indoors!

CHORUS. I shall summon no diviner other than myself.*

MESSENGER. The children are dead.

CHORUS. Alas!

MESSENGER. Well may you lament for these terrible deeds.

CHORUS. Murderous slaughter! Murderous were the father's hands!

MESSENGER. Words cannot encompass our suffering.

CHORUS. How did the father bring about the terrible death and destruction of his sons? Can you explain? Tell us how this horror, sent by the gods, struck the house, and about the wretched fate of the children.   920

MESSENGER. There were victims in front of Zeus' altar to purify the house, since Heracles had killed the king and thrown his corpse out of this house here.* His children were standing close by, forming a beautiful chorus, along with his father and Megara. The ritual basket had already been passed around the altar* and we were keeping a solemn silence. Heracles, who was due to fetch a brand in his right hand and dip it into the holy water, stood without saying a word. The children   930 glanced at him, surprised at the delay. He was no longer himself; his features were distorted. His pupils were rolling around in eyes that were suddenly bloodshot, and foam was dripping onto his bushy beard. With a manic laugh he said, 'Father, why am I purifying myself with fire before I've killed Eurystheus? I'm just doubling my labour. I can sort all of this out at a single stroke. When I've brought Eurystheus' head here, I shall cleanse my hands of all the recent deaths. Pour   940 away the water, let the basket fall from your hands. Who will give me my bow? Who will put my club in my hand? I'm off to Mycenae. I must take crowbars and pick-axes to smash the Cyclopean foundations, well laid with the help of red chalk-line* and cold chisels, and level them to the ground with iron hooks.' Then, saying that he had a chariot (which he didn't), he made as if to leave: he set about mounting the chariot and made jabbing motions with his hand, as if he were using a goad.

We slaves were unsure whether to feel amusement or fear.   950
We looked at one another, and someone said, 'Is our master

teasing us or is he crazy?' Meanwhile, Heracles was going
here and there in the house, and when he burst into the
middle of the dining room he claimed to have reached the city
of Nisus.* When he entered the main body of the house he
lay down on the ground without further ado and got ready
for a banquet. After a short stay there he claimed to be
approaching the wooded plains of the Isthmus. At this point
he undid the clasp fastening his clothes, stripped, and pro-
ceeded to wrestle with a non-existent opponent. He then   960
called for silence and unilaterally proclaimed himself the
winner of his bout against no one.

Roaring out curses against Eurystheus he came, or so he
said, to Mycenae. His father grasped his mighty hand in his
and said, 'My son, what's the matter with you? What kind of
insanity is this? Has the blood of the men you recently killed
driven you out of your wits?'* But Heracles thought it was
Eurystheus' father seizing his hand as a suppliant out of fear
for his son, so he pushed him away, and prepared to use his
bow and arrows, which were ready in their quiver, on his own   970
children, thinking he was killing Eurystheus' children. They
dashed to and fro in terror, one to seize his poor mother's
clothing, another to hide behind a pillar, and the third to go
and crouch like a bird under the shelter of the altar. Their
mother cried out: 'What are you doing? You're their father.
Are you going to kill your children?' The old man and the
assembled slaves shouted out to him as well.

But he, whirling horribly round and round, chased one of
the boys around the pillar, and then stood opposite him and
shot him deep in the belly. Sprawled on the ground, the boy
breathed his last, drenching the stone columns with his   980
blood. Heracles shouted out in triumph and cried out boast-
fully, 'That's one of Eurystheus' young brood dead! He has
paid with his life for his father's hostility towards me!' Then
he aimed his bow at another of his sons, the one who had
hoped to hide by crouching at the base of the altar. But before
his father could shoot, the wretched child fell at his father's
knees, thrust his hand towards his chin and neck,* and said,
'Dearest father, don't kill me! I am yours, your son! This is no
child of Eurystheus you're going to slay.' But Heracles turned   990
his eyes on him, with a look as savage as a Gorgon's, and

since the boy was too close for his death-dealing bow, he
raised his club over his head, like a smith at a forge, brought it
down on the boy's blond head, and smashed his skull. Having
dispatched the second child, he went to slaughter a third victim in addition to the other two. The children's poor mother
quickly snatched the child away into the house and locked the
door, but, just as if he were really attacking the Cyclopean
walls, he dug under the door panels and prised them up. Once
he had torn the door-posts out of their sockets, with a single
arrow he laid low both his wife and his son.   1000

Then he galloped off to kill the old man. But suddenly a
figure came—Pallas as it seemed to the eye—wielding a
spear.† She hurled a boulder at Heracles' chest, which
checked his furious bloodlust and put him to sleep. As he fell
to the ground, his back hit one the pillars which was lying on
the floor, broken in two when the house collapsed. Freeing   1010
our feet from their flight, we helped the old man tie Heracles
securely to the pillar with knotted loops of horse-trace, so
that when he wakes up he won't be able to do anything else.
The wretched man is fast asleep, but it is no happy state to be
in, since he has killed his sons and his wife. I, at any rate,
cannot think of anyone worse off than him.

Exit MESSENGER.

CHORUS (*sings*). Once the murder which the rock of Argos
    knows,
committed by the daughters of Danaus,*
was the outstanding, unbelievable crime of Greece.
But it is overtaken and surpassed by the horrors here,
which have afflicted the wretched son of Zeus.   1020
I could speak of Procne's murder of her only child,
sacrificed to the Muses.* But in your fated madness,
you murderer, you killed the *three* children you fathered.
Alas! What lamentation, what tears of grief,
what song for the dead or dance of Hades shall I sound?

HERACLES *is wheeled out of the house on the ekkyklēma.* He is tied to
  a pillar and surrounded by the bodies of his sons and of MEGARA.

Ah! See the doors of the high-gated house swing apart!   1030
Oh! See the wretched children lying before their poor father!

He is sleeping a terrible sleep after murdering his sons,
his body bound and wound around with knots and ropes,
Heracles' body tied to one of the house's stone pillars.

*AMPHITRYON enters from the house. The CHORUS stops singing, and
the Chorus-leader continues alone.*

And here, lagging behind and treading a bitter path, comes 1040
the old man, grieving like a bird for the unfledged young it
toiled over.

AMPHITRYON. Quiet, old men of Thebes, quiet!* Let him stay
relaxed in sleep and oblivious of his troubles.

CHORUS. Old man, I grieve and weep for you, for the children,
and for the conquering hero.

AMPHITRYON. Keep well away! No harsh noises, no raised
voices, don't wake the sleeper from his bed, from his peaceful 1050
rest.

CHORUS. Oh, how much blood there is . . .

AMHITRYON. Stop! You will destroy me!

CHORUS. . . . spilled on the ground and yet rising into the air!*

AMPHITRYON. Old friends, voice your grief quietly, please! Or
else he will wake up, unloose his bonds, destroy the city and
his father, and break up the house.

CHORUS. I can't! I can't!

AMPHITRYON. Quiet! I want to listen to his breathing. Come, let 1060
me put my ear close to him.

AMPHITRYON bends over HERACLES' face to listen.

CHORUS. Is he asleep?

AMPHITRYON. Yes, he's asleep. But his sleep is no real sleep, an
accursed thing, since he has killed his wife and children with
his twanging bow.

CHORUS. Let yourself grieve now . . .

AMPHITRYON. I do.

CHORUS. . . . for the death of the children . . .

AMPHITRYON. Oh, misery!

CHORUS. . . . and the ruin of your son . . .

AMPHITRYON. Alas!

CHORUS. . . . old man.

HERACLES stirs in his sleep.

AMPHITRYON. Quiet! Quiet! He's tossing and turning. He's waking up. Come, let me hide myself away in the house.   1070

CHORUS. No, don't worry. Darkness still fills your son's eyes.

AMPHITRYON. Beware, beware! In my misery, after all my suffering, it is not death I fear, but I worry that he might kill me, his father: he might contrive further evil and have yet more kindred blood on his already accursed hands.*

CHORUS. You should have died earlier, when you returned after sacking the sea-washed city of the Taphians, in revenge for   1080 the murder of your wife's brothers.*

HERACLES starts to wake up.

AMPHITRYON. Take to your heels, old men! Run from the house! He's waking up! Run from the madman! Or else he will soon shed more blood and rave anew through Thebes.

CHORUS. O Zeus, why do you feel such violent hatred for your son? Why did you bring him to this ocean of trouble?

AMPHITRYON and the CHORUS hide in the lee of the house, visible to the audience, but not to HERACLES in his bound state.

HERACLES. So I am alive, at least. I am seeing what I should see, the sky and the earth, and shafts of sunlight. What† a terrible   1090 state of mental turmoil and confusion I have fallen into! My breathing is hot and shallow, not a steady stream from my lungs. But look, why am I sitting by half-broken stonework, moored, like a ship, with ropes around my strong chest and arms? And why are the places all around me occupied by dead bodies? Scattered on the ground lie my bow and arrows, which in times past were my comrades-in-arms, protecting my   1100 side as I protected them. Surely I can't have gone back down again to Hades. I've only just come from there, on the return journey ordered by Eurystheus. No, I don't see Sisyphus' rock or Pluto and his queen, the daughter of Demeter.* I'm totally confused. Where am I that I should be so helpless? (*Calling out*) Hello! Is anyone there, close or far away? Can one of my friends or relatives cure this ignorance of mine? I can't see any familiar sights.

AMPHITRYON (*to the CHORUS*). Old friends, shall I approach the source of my suffering?

CHORUS. Yes, and I'll go with you. I won't desert you in your 1110 time of trouble.

AMPHITRYON and the CHORUS *come forward until* HERACLES *can see them.*

HERACLES. Father, why are you weeping? Why are you veiling your eyes and keeping your distance from your own dear son?

AMPHITRYON. My son—for even in your misfortune you are mine.

HERACLES. What has happened to me that is awful enough to make you cry?

AMPHITRYON. Things that would make even a god grieve, if he was aware of them.

HERACLES. That's a bold statement, but you haven't yet said what has happened.

AMPHITRYON. That's because you can see for yourself, if you've come to your senses.

HERACLES. Tell me what these hints of yours mean. Is there some new horror in my life?

AMPHITRYON. I'll tell you, as long as your hellish frenzy has finished.

HERACLES. Aaargh! Another disturbing riddle from you! 1120

AMPHITRYON. I'm trying to find out whether you're now stable and in possession of your senses.

HERACLES. I haven't got the slightest recollection of being in a frenzied state of mind.

AMPHITRYON (*to the* CHORUS). Shall I untie my son, old friends? What do you think?

HERACLES. Yes, and tell me who tied me up. I feel humiliated.

AMPHITRYON undoes HERACLES' *bonds.*

AMPHITRYON. I'll tell you something of your troubles, and I advise you to leave the rest alone.

But then AMPHITRYON *hesitates.*

HERACLES. Will silence serve to tell me what I want to know?

AMPHITRYON (*looking up to heaven*). O Zeus, from your seat on Hera's throne* can you see what's going on here?

HERACLES. Is what's happened to me the result of hostility from that quarter, then?

AMPHITRYON. Forget the goddess and attend to your own misfortunes.

HERACLES. My life is ruined. You're going to tell me that some- 1130 thing terrible has happened.

AMPHITRYON. Look! Can't you see the bodies of your sons lying here?

HERACLES. Oh, no! The pain of it! What is this I see?

AMPHITRYON. My son, you made war, a hideous kind of war, on your children.

HERACLES. What's this war you're talking of? Who killed them?

AMPHITRYON. You, your arrows, and whichever of the gods is responsible.

HERACLES. What do you mean? This is ghastly news, father. How did I come to do it?

AMPHITRYON. You were insane. The answers to your questions are all sad.

HERACLES. And am I also my wife's murderer?

AMPHITRYON. Everything that was done here was done by a single hand—yours.

HERACLES. Oh, I am surrounded by a cloud of misery! 1140

AMPHITRYON. That's what makes me grieve for your misfortune.

HERACLES. And did I smash up my own house in my frenzy?†

AMPHITRYON. All I know is that you are overwhelmed by misfortune.

HERACLES. Where did the fit possess me and ruin my life?

AMPHITRYON. It was when you were purifying yourself with fire at the altar.

HERACLES. Oh, the agony! I have murdered my own precious children: why then do I spare my own life? Shall I not go and hurl myself from a sheer cliff or stab my sword deep into my belly? That would be the way for me to avenge the murder of 1150 my sons. Or I could evade the life of dishonour that awaits me by burning their father's† flesh on a fire.

Enter THESEUS.

But here's an obstacle to my resolve to die: here comes Theseus, my friend and relative.* He will see what I have done, and the taint I have incurred by killing my children will be plain to my closest friend. Oh, what shall I do? Where can I go to find freedom from misery? Am I to take to the air on wings or sink beneath the earth?* Come, let me shroud my head in the darkness of my cloak.† For I am ashamed of the terrible 1160 things I have done, and I have no desire to hurt innocent people by infecting Theseus here with polluted blood.

HERACLES veils his head. THESEUS reaches centre stage.

THESEUS (*to AMPHITRYON*). Sir, I have left my companions, young Athenian warriors armed for battle, waiting by the river Asopus. I have come to offer military support to your son, in response to the news we heard in Athens that Lycus had seized the Theban throne and was making war on you. I've come to repay Heracles' kindness in rescuing me from the 1170 underworld, in case you have any need of my strength or my military support. (*He suddenly spots the corpses*) But what's this? Why are these bodies scattered on the ground? Surely I'm not too late. Have I arrived after you have been overtaken by fresh calamities? Who killed these children? Whose wife was this woman I can see here? Children aren't involved in armed conflict, so it must be some new disaster that I've arrived to find.

AMPHITRYON (*piteously*). O lord of the olive-bearing hill* . . .

THESEUS. Why are these first words of yours to me so miserable?

AMPHITRYON. . . . we have suffered horribly at the hands of the 1180 gods.

THESEUS. These children for whom you're grieving—whose were they?

AMPHITRYON. My own poor son was their father. But despite being their father he killed them and endured the taint of their blood.

THESEUS. What do you mean? How did he come to do it?

AMPHITRYON. In a fit of mad confusion, with arrows dipped in the blood of the hundred-headed Hydra.*

THESEUS. Oh, what terrible news!

AMPHITRYON. It's all over with us, all over. We are no more than flimsy creatures of the air.

THESEUS. Please, speak only words of good omen!

AMPHITRYON. I only wish I could do as you suggest.

THESEUS. Here we see how Hera fights. But who is this among
the corpses, old friend?

AMPHITRYON. That's my ... my son. Oh, how much he has 1190
endured! Once he went to the plain of Phlegra to fight along-
side the gods in their battle against the Giants.*

THESEUS. Alas! Is there anyone on earth as ill fated as him?

AMPHITRYON. No, you'll never find another man who has
endured more and roamed more widely.

THESEUS. Why is he hiding himself in misery in his cloak?

AMPHITRYON. He was ashamed to be seen by you, his friend 1200
and kinsman, and concerned about the pollution he incurred
by killing his children.

THESEUS. But suppose I have come to share his pain? Uncover
his head.

AMPHITRYON (*to HERACLES*). Son, uncover your eyes! Remove
your cloak from them and let the sun shine on your face!

*He kneels by HERACLES and takes hold of his knees, hands, and beard
in the ritual gestures of supplication.*

The weight of my body closely rivals my tears. I kneel before
you, take your chin, knee, and hand in my hand, and implore
you, with tears pouring from my old eyes, my son, to behave 1210
less like a proud, fierce lion! Your passionate spirit is taking
you† down an unholy, murderous course; it wants to add woe
to woe, my son!

HERACLES says nothing.

THESEUS. All right. I bid you, sitting there in misery, to show
your face to those who love you. There's no darkness thick
and black enough to hide the disastrous extent of your
troubles.

HERACLES gestures at THESEUS, as if to send him away.

Why do you wave your hand at me to indicate your fear? Are
you worried that I may be tainted by your pollution if you
speak to me? But I don't mind sharing in your misfortune, 1220
because my good fortune is due to you. It has to be dated back
to that day when you rescued me from the realm of the dead
and brought me back to the upper world. I hate it when a
friend's gratitude ages, and when someone is prepared to

enjoy the good times, but not to accompany his friends on
their voyage of misfortune. Get up! Uncover your head, bowed
in misery! Look at me! It is a sign of nobility to endure whatever comes to us from the gods† and not to retreat from it.

    HERACLES uncovers his head and stands up.

HERACLES. Theseus, do you see what's happened to my children as a result of this conflict?*

THESEUS. I've heard about the conflict, and I can see the 1230
troubles you're telling me about.

HERACLES. Why, then, did you have me expose my head to the
light of the sun?

THESEUS. Why? You are a mortal man; you cannot pollute
things that are divine.*

HERACLES. My poor friend, I advise you to flee from the pollution I have incurred.

THESEUS. No avenging spirit can pass between friends.

HERACLES. Thank you. I will not reject you, because I did once
help you.

THESEUS. I was helped by you then, but now I feel pity for you.

HERACLES. Am I really no more than pitiful? I killed my own
sons.

THESEUS. My tears are tears of sympathy for your changed
circumstances.

HERACLES. Have you ever found anyone else with worse
troubles to bear?

THESEUS. In your misfortune you reach all the way from earth 1240
to heaven.

HERACLES. That's why I had steeled myself for death.

<THESEUS. And what will you achieve by dying?

HERACLES. I will defile with my blood the altars of the gods.>†

THESEUS. Do you think your threats concern the gods at all?

HERACLES. The gods look after their own interests; I am repay-
ing them in kind.

THESEUS. Silence! This arrogant talk could cost you worse
suffering.

HERACLES. My hold is filled with woes. There's no room left for
more.

THESEUS. But what will you *do*? Where will your anger take
you?

HERACLES. To death and the underworld, from where I've just
  come.

THESEUS. In saying this you sound like an ordinary man.

HERACLES. You tell me off—but then you're free of disaster
  yourself.

THESEUS. Is this really Heracles speaking, after all he has 1250
  endured?

HERACLES. But I never had to endure so much before. There
  must be a limit to suffering.

THESEUS. Is this really the great benefactor and friend of mortal men?

HERACLES. They do me no good at all. Power lies with Hera.

THESEUS. Greece would find it intolerable if you were to die a
  stupid death.

HERACLES. I have something to say in response to your criticism of me. I shall explain to you that not only is my life not
  worth living now, but it was just as insupportable before. In
  the first place, my father here killed my mother's old father*
  and was therefore polluted with blood when he married my 1260
  mother Alcmene. When the foundation of a family has been
  laid crooked, the descendants of that family are bound to
  suffer misfortune. Moreover, in fathering me Zeus—whoever
  he may be—made me an object of hatred to Hera. Now, don't
  be angry, old man: I think of you as my father, not Zeus.
  Anyway, while I was still an infant at my mother's breast
  Zeus' wife tried to kill me by introducing savage snakes into
  my swaddling clothes.*

  Do I need to mention all the labours I endured once I had 1270
  gained a man's body? Were there any lions or three-bodied
  Typhons* or Giants I left alive? Was there a war against
  hordes of four-legged Centaurs I left unfinished? Once I had
  killed the hydra-hound with its many heads and power of
  regeneration and had completed countless other labours, I
  went down to the realm of the dead to bring Hades' three-
  headed watchdog back up to the light at Eurystheus'
  command.

  Then this was the final labour I had to endure to my
  misfortune—to crown my house with catastrophe by killing 1280
  my own children. My life is so constrained now that it would
  be impious of me to live here in Thebes, which I love so much.

And anyway, if I *do* stay, what temple will I be able to
approach? What gathering of friends will I be able to join?
The curse with which I am afflicted makes it impossible for
people to talk to me.* But am I to go to my native Argos? No, I
can't, because I've been banished from there. Well, then, shall
I make my way to some other community? Am I then to put
up with furtive glances when I am recognized? To be defiled†
by the barbs of bitter tongues, saying: 'Isn't that the son of
Zeus, who once killed his children and his wife? Why doesn't 1290
he get the hell out of our land?'†

I think that one day I shall be so overwhelmed by disaster
that the earth will gain a voice and forbid me to set foot on
the ground. The sea and the rivers will not allow me to cross
them, and I will be like Ixion, bound and tortured on his
wheel.*† So why should I stay alive? What good will it do me
now that I have a useless and accursed life? Let the glorious
wife of Zeus* dance in delight, pounding with her sandals the
gleaming floor of Olympus.† She has got what she wanted:
she has razed to the ground the foremost man of Greece,
foundations and all. How could anyone pray to the kind of
goddess who out of jealousy of Zeus' affair with a woman has
destroyed an innocent man who was the benefactor of 1310
Greece?

CHORUS. Your observation is correct: the only deity involved in
this conflict here is the wife of Zeus.

THESEUS. < . . . >† that would be my advice,* rather than suggesting that you live a life of suffering and misery. But everyone on earth is subject to Fortune—as are all the gods too, if
what the poets tell us is true.* Haven't the gods transgressed
the moral code and had affairs with one another?* Haven't
they defiled their fathers with chains in order to gain kingship?* But they still live on Olympus, without being troubled
by the errors of their ways. So how will you respond to the 1320
charge that you, a mere mortal, are overly concerned about
what Fortune has dealt you, while the gods are not?

Leave Thebes, then, as the law commands—but come with
me to the citadel of Pallas.* Once there, I shall purify you from
pollution, and then present you with a house and a share of
my wealth. I shall give you the gifts I received from my fellow
citizens for saving the lives of the fourteen young people

when I killed the bull of Cnossus;* I have been awarded plots
of land all over Attica, which will henceforth be named after 1330
you and known as such by mortal men while you are alive.*
After your death, when you go down to Hades, all the citizens
of Athens will honour you with sacrifices and works of
stone.* For the Athenians will be graced, in the eyes of
Greece, by the glory they gain from doing good to an honourable man. As for me, this will be the way I repay you for
saving my life. After all, at the moment you are in need of
friends.†

HERACLES. Alas,† these honours make no difference to my mis- 1340
fortunes. But I cannot believe that the gods either acquiesce
in illicit affairs or put one another in chains. I have never
believed these things, nor will I ever be convinced that one
god is master of another. Any true god needs nothing. These
are just the debased tales of poets.* But even in the midst of
my misfortune I have given thought to whether I would incur
the charge of cowardice if I killed myself, on the grounds that
anyone who cannot stand up to disaster would be equally
incapable of standing up to a weapon wielded by a human 1350
opponent. I shall stand fast and endure life. I shall go to your
city, and I am hugely grateful for your gifts. But I did experience a huge number of labours, of course, and I never turned
down a single one of them. Nor did I shed a tear, and I would
never have thought that I would have reached the point I am
at now, with tears pouring from my eyes. But now, apparently,
I must do Fortune's bidding.

So be it. (*To* AMPHITRYON) Father, you can see that I am an
exile, and that I am the slayer of my own children. Dress these 1360
bodies and bury them. Honour them with your tears, since by
law I am not allowed to do so.* Rest them on their mother's
breast and wrap them in her arms—the pitiful family I unwill-
ingly destroyed in my misery. And when you have buried the
bodies in the ground make your home here in Thebes, for all
that you will not find happiness here.† (*To his dead sons and
wife*) Dear children, murdered by your father, the one who
gave you life, you did not live to enjoy the fine future I was
preparing for you, winning by my efforts a life of glory for 1370
you—a fine advantage to gain from a father. And I killed you
too, you poor woman—an incongruous return for your safe

keeping of my marriage bed as you endured your long watch
at home.

Alas for my wife and children, but alas for me too! My
situation is wretched: I am parting company from my wife
and children. O, the sweet pain of kissing them! (*He kisses the
bodies one by one, and then handles his fallen weapons*) O, the
painful partnership of these weapons! I don't know whether I
should keep them or discard them, because as they cling to
my side they will say: 'You used us to slay your children and 1380
your wife. You still have us, the killers of your children.' Shall
I then carry them on my shoulders? What excuse could I have
for that? But shall I lay aside the weapons with which I
achieved the most glorious deeds that have ever been seen in
Greece? Shall I expose myself in this way to my enemies and
die a shameful death? No, I had better not abandon them: I
had better keep them safe, despite the pain they will cause
me.†

O land of Cadmus! O all you citizens of Thebes! Cut your 1390
hair,* grieve with me, and go to my sons' funeral. You will be
grieving for all of us at once—for the dead and for me. For we
have all suffered the same misfortune, laid low in misery by a
single blow from Hera.

Overcome by emotion, HERACLES collapses to the ground.

THESEUS. Get up, you poor thing! You have wept enough!

HERACLES. I can't. My joints have seized up.

THESEUS. Yes, misfortune cuts down even the strong.

HERACLES. Oh, how I wish I could turn to stone, right now, and
forget my woes!

THESEUS. Enough! Give your hand to one who loves you and
would serve you!

HERACLES takes THESEUS' outstretched hand and gets to his feet.

HERACLES. But take care that I don't get blood on your clothes.

THESEUS. Wipe it off. Don't hold back. It doesn't bother me.   1400

HERACLES wipes down THESEUS' clothes.

HERACLES. Now that I've lost my sons, I look on you as my own
son.

THESEUS. Put your arm around my neck. I'll guide you.

HERACLES. I welcome our partnership, but one of us is in a pitiful state. Father, this is the sort of man one should have as a friend.

AMPHITRYON. Yes, the land that gave him birth is blessed with noble sons.

HERACLES. Theseus, turn me around once more. I want to see my children.

THESEUS. Why? Will it ease your pain to have this love-charm?*

HERACLES. But I long to do it. I want to give my father a hug too.

AMPHITRYON (*coming into* HERACLES' *embrace*). Here you are, son! What you want I want too!

THESEUS. Have you forgotten your labours, then?   1410

HERACLES. Nothing I endured before was as painful as my present woes.

THESEUS. The sight of you behaving like a woman will win disapproval.

HERACLES. Do you think I'm pathetic to go on living? You didn't think that of me before.

THESEUS. Yes, terribly. The glorious Heracles has been destroyed by your sickness.

HERACLES. And what were you like in your time of trouble in the underworld?

THESEUS. Where pride was concerned, I had less than anyone.

HERACLES. How, then, can you tell me off† for being devastated by my misfortune?

THESEUS. On your way.

HERACLES. Farewell, father!

AMPHITRYON. And farewell to you, my child!

HERACLES. Please bury my sons as I told you.

AMPHITRYON. But who will bury me, son?

HERACLES. I will.   1420

AMPHITRYON. When will you come back?

HERACLES. After your death, father.† Carry the children back inside—but oh, the pain of such a sad burden!—and I, who have wreaked havoc on my house with deeds of shame, will go in utter misery with Theseus, like a tender in tow.* Anyone who would rather have wealth or strength than good men as friends is a fool.*

Exeunt HERACLES *and* THESEUS. *The bodies are taken back indoors on the ekkyklēma.* AMPHITRYON *follows them into the house.*

CHORUS. In sorrow and in tears we go, having lost our greatest friend.

Exit CHORUS.

CHILDREN OF HERACLES

Characters

IOLAUS, companion and nephew of the dead hero Heracles
HERALD of Eurystheus
DEMOPHON, king of Athens
MAIDEN, one of Heracles' daughters
SERVANT of Hyllus, Heracles' eldest son
ALCMENE, Heracles' mother
EURYSTHEUS, king of Argos
MESSENGER
Some nameless young sons of Heracles

CHORUS of old men of Marathon

Scene: In front of the temple of Zeus in Marathon, on the eastern coast of Attica. Seated on the steps of the temple are the young sons of Heracles and IOLAUS, their guardian.*

IOLAUS. For a long time now it's been clear to me that while one man may deal fairly with his neighbours, the temperament of another is so given over to gain that he is useless to his fellow citizens and difficult to do business with. He is only his own best friend. And this isn't just hearsay for me: I could have lived peacefully in Argos, but because of my sense of honour and my respect for family ties I was the one man who helped Heracles in a great many of his labours,* when he was still among us. And now that he dwells in heaven, I have taken his children here under my wing and I keep them safe, when it is I who need protection myself. For no sooner had their father left the earth than Eurystheus wished to kill us. We fled, however—saving our lives, but losing our city. We roam as exiles from one town to another as people drive us beyond their borders. For on top of all our other troubles, Eurystheus chose to inflict this outrage on us too: whenever he finds out that we have settled anywhere, he sends heralds to convey his demand that we be moved on and banished from that land, arguing that friendship or hostility with the city of Argos is no small matter and also pointing to the success he himself is currently enjoying. They see that I can put up only feeble resistance, and that these lads here are young and have lost a father, and so they banish us, out of respect for those who are stronger. I share the exile of these exiled children and the hardship they suffer is my hardship too. I am reluctant to desert them, in case it is said of me: 'Look, now that the children have no father, Iolaus has withdrawn his protection, for all that he is their kin.'   30

Since we are barred from the rest of Greece, we have come to the territory held in common between Marathon and its neighbours.* We are seated as suppliants at the altars of the gods, begging for help. For we hear that the two sons of Theseus, who are close kin to these lads, govern the land here, having obtained the right by lot as descendants of Pandion.* That is why we have made the journey here to the borders of glorious Athens.

The two who are in charge of this flight are both elderly: there is me with my commitment to these boys, and then   40 there is Alcmene, who has Heracles' daughters safe in her embrace within the temple here, because it is not proper, in our view, for young maidens to draw near a crowd and take their stand at an altar. Hyllus and the oldest of his brothers have gone to look for somewhere for us to establish a stronghold, if we are driven by force out of this land.

Children, children, come here! Take hold of my cloak! I can see approaching us Eurystheus' herald, who hounds us into   50 exile and bars us from every land. You foul creature! Damn you and the man who sent you, for all the evil messages delivered from this same mouth of yours not only to us but to the noble father of these children too!

Enter the HERALD *holding a staff to denote his office.*

HERALD. I suppose you think this is a fine place to have seated yourself, and that you've reached a city of allies—but you're wrong! There's no one who will prefer your feeble resources to the strength of Eurystheus. Go! Why waste your effort? You must get up from here and go to Argos, where death by   60 stoning awaits you as your punishment.

IOLAUS. No, I won't. We shall be protected by the god's altar*
and the freedom of the land we have come to.

HERALD. Do you want to make more work for this arm of mine?

IOLAUS. I'm sure you won't seize me and these boys and drag
us away by force.

HERALD. You'll find out. (*He takes hold of* IOLAUS) It looks as
though you weren't a good prophet about this.

IOLAUS (*struggling*). Over my dead body . . .

HERALD. Clear off! (*He starts to pull* IOLAUS *away from the altar*.)
Whether or not you like it, I shall take these boys away. I
claim them for Eurystheus, because they are his.

IOLAUS. O inhabitants of Athens, dwellers here from time
immemorial,* help us! Although we are suppliants at the   70
altar of Zeus, guardian of the people, violence is being done
to us, and our suppliant wreaths* are being defiled. It brings
disgrace to the city and dishonour to the gods.

Enter CHORUS.

CHORUS. Ah! What cry is this that has arisen by the altar? What
sight will it soon bring before our eyes? Look! There's an old
man sprawled on the ground. You poor thing! < . . . >† Who
has thrown you to the ground in this humiliating way?

IOLAUS. Friends, it's an insult to your gods: this man here is
pulling me forcibly from the base of Zeus' altar.

CHORUS. Where have you come from, old man? Did you travel   80
overland to this confederacy of four towns,* or was the
Euboean coast your point of departure?* Was it the seagoing
oar that brought you here from over the water?

IOLAUS. Mine is no islander's life, friends. We've come here
from Mycenae.*

CHORUS. And what do they call you in Mycenae?

IOLAUS. I'm sure you've heard of Iolaus, Heracles' comrade-in-
arms. I do have quite a reputation.

CHORUS. The name is familiar; I've heard of you before. But tell   90
me, whose young sons are these that you have with you in
your care?

IOLAUS. They are the children of Heracles, my friends, and
they've come as suppliants to you and your town.

CHORUS. Suppliants for what? Tell me, are they anxious for an
audience with the town?

IOLAUS. Their concern is not to be handed over, not to be torn by brute force from the altars of your gods and go to Argos.

HERALD. But that is not what your masters want. You are theirs to command, and they have found you here. 100

CHORUS. Suppliants of the gods deserve respect, stranger, and should not be forced to leave the gods' altars. The august lady Justice will not be treated like this.

HERALD. Banish these slaves of Eurystheus from this land and I shall lay no violent hands upon them.

CHORUS. It would be an impious act for the town to hand over a group of suppliant visitors.

HERALD. Yes, but it's good to stay out of trouble by following 110 the path of sounder judgement.

< . . . >†

CHORUS. Shouldn't you have spoken to the king of this land before going so far? Shouldn't you have shown respect for a free country by not using violence on visitors and pulling them from the gods' altars?

HERALD. Who is the lord of this land and its city?

CHORUS. Demophon, the son of noble Theseus.

HERALD. So the debate over this issue had best take place before him. We've been wasting our time so far.

CHORUS. Here he comes now! He's hurrying here with his brother Acamas to hear your arguments.

Enter DEMOPHON, *Acamas, and attendants.*

DEMOPHON (*to the Chorus-leader*). For all your age you reached 120 this altar of Zeus before men younger than yourself in response to the cry for help. So tell me: what has happened to bring all these people together here?

CHORUS. The suppliants sitting here are Heracles' sons, my lord, and as you can see they have decked the altar with wreaths. And this is Iolaus, their father's faithful comrade-in-arms.

DEMOPHON. But what happened? Why the cry of pain?

CHORUS (*pointing to the* HERALD). It was his fault. In trying to pull Iolaus by brute force away from the altar here, he made the old man collapse to the ground and cry out. It made me weep for pity.

DEMOPHON. His outfit and the way he wears his clothes are 130

Greek, but these are the actions of a savage.* (*To the* HERALD)
You had better tell me—and quickly now—from which
country you have come to our land.

HERALD. I am an Argive, to answer your question. But I also
want to explain why I have come and at whose orders. Eurystheus, the lord of the Mycenaeans, sent me here to bring
these people back. I've come with a mission that is just on
many counts, and also justifiable by argument. For I am an
Argive myself, and these people I'm trying to seize† and take
with me are Argives, runaways from my own country who   140
have been condemned to death by due legal process there. It is
right for us, as citizens, to pass our own binding judgements.*
Moreover, not one of the many others at whose altars we
have relied on exactly the same arguments has dared to bring
trouble down on his own head. These people have come here
to you either because they saw a streak of foolishness in you,
or because they are desperate enough to gamble their lives on
whether or not <you are in fact the fools they take you for>.†
After all, I'm sure they cannot expect you, if you are thinking   150
straight, to be the only one, out of all the Greeks they have
approached, to be stupid enough take pity on their
misfortunes.

Look, weigh things up. What do you stand to profit* by
letting them into your country, or by letting us take them
away? Here is what you will get from us: you will gain for
your city the armed support of Argos and the full might of
Eurystheus. But if consideration of their arguments and tears
makes you soft, armed conflict will have to decide the issue.   160
For you should not suppose that we will let them go without a
trial of steel. What will you say, then? What lands of yours
have been appropriated, what property stolen, for you to go to
war against Argos?* As you bury your dead, on whose behalf
will you say they fell? Which allies would you have been
defending? You'll reap abuse from your fellow citizens if you
foul your feet in bilge-water for the sake of an old man with
one foot in the grave, a virtual nobody, and for these children.
Perhaps you'll say that you can at least gain hope from an
alliance with these boys,† but this too does nothing to remedy   170
the situation you find yourself in. Even when grown up, they
would be no match for the Argive army (in case this prospect

was raising your spirits at all), and meanwhile there's plenty
of time for you to be crushed. No, listen to me: all you have to
do is let me take what is mine and you can gain the Argives as
your allies. Don't do what you Athenians normally do, and
prefer the weak when you could have the strong as your
friends.

CHORUS. It's impossible to come to a verdict or assess an argument until one has heard a clear statement from both sides.   180
IOLAUS (*also addressing* DEMOPHON). My lord, since it is customary in your country for both sides to be heard, I can take my
turn now, and no one will banish me before I have had my
say, as they have done elsewhere. We have no common
ground with this man. I mean, we have been exiled from our
native land:* we no longer have anything to do with Argos,
and this has been ratified by vote. How, then, can it be right
for this man to take us back as if we were citizens of Mycenae,
when they have driven us from the land and we are now
foreigners to them? Then again, do you think it is right for
someone who has been banished from Argos to be banished   190
from Greece as a whole? He would not be banished from Athens, at any rate; the Athenians are not so afraid of Argos that
they will expel the children of Heracles from their land. (*To
the* HERALD) This is not Trachis or some Achaean town.* You
cannot drive us from here as you did from there—wrongfully,
since we were seated as suppliants at their altars—by boast-
ing about Argos as you did today as well. If this should happen, if they decide in your favour, I will no longer recognize
Athens here as a free city. But I know their temperament and
their nature: they will be prepared to die, since decent men   200
prefer honour over life.

   (*To* DEMOPHON *again*) So much for the city. Excessive praise is
invidious, and I myself have often felt annoyed when someone has been over-complimentary. But what I would like to
say to you is that, as the ruler of this land, you are bound to
protect these boys here. Pittheus was the son of Pelops,
Aethra the daughter of Pittheus, and your father Theseus
was her son.* Next I shall trace back the lineage of these boys
for you: Heracles was the son of Zeus and Alcmene, and   210
Alcmene's mother was Pelops' daughter. Your father and
theirs were therefore the children of first cousins.

That's how things stand between you and them in family
terms, Demophon, but I shall also explain the debt you have
to repay to them even apart from the fact that you are related
to them. I have to tell you that as their father's right-hand
man I once sailed with Theseus in pursuit of the girdle which
was the cause of so many deaths.* < . . . >† and he fetched
your father from the gloomy depths of Hades.* These facts are
known throughout Greece. Heracles' sons here require from   220
you a favour in return for these favours. They want not to be
handed over, not to be torn by brute force from the altars of
your gods and banished from your land. For it would bring
disgrace to you in particular, and no less to Athens, if suppliants, refugees, kin—ah, look at them! Look at them and pity
their troubles!—were dragged off by force. (*He bows before*
DEMOPHON and takes hold of his beard in the suppliant gesture)
No, I beg you, by the supplication which these hands perform
in holding you, and by your chin, not to scorn the sons of
Heracles and refuse them your protection. Be a true kinsman
to them; be their friend, their father, their brother, even their   230
master, since nothing could be worse than falling into Argive
hands.

CHORUS. My lord, after hearing this, I feel sorry for the calamity
that has overwhelmed these boys. I have never seen a clearer
case of high birth brought low by misfortune. These boys,
children of a noble father, do not deserve their bad luck.

DEMOPHON. Iolaus, my conscience compels me, for three
reasons, not to spurn your plea. Above all, there is Zeus at
whose altar you sit with this flock of fledglings. Then there is
my kinship with them and the fact that, for their father's sake,   240
they have long deserved my kindness. Thirdly, there is the
possibility of disgrace, which is particularly important to me,
because if I let this altar be robbed by the violent actions of a
stranger, people will think that the land I rule is not free, and
that fear of Argos made me fail to help suppliants. This would
be almost enough to make me hang myself. I could wish that
you had come under happier circumstances, but even now
there is no cause for fear: no one is going to lay violent hands
upon you and the children and drag you away from this altar.

(*To the* HERALD) As for you, go back to Argos and tell   250
Eurystheus what I have said, and add that if he brings a

formal charge against Iolaus and these boys here, he will receive a fair hearing. But you're not going to take them away with you now.

HERALD. Not even if my claim is just* and I successfully argue my case?

DEMOPHON. How could it possibly be just to drag a suppliant away by force?

HERALD. So won't this bring disgrace on me but do you no harm?

DEMOPHON. No, if I let you pull them off, I do suffer harm.

HERALD. Banish them beyond your borders, and then we'll take them from there.

DEMOPHON. You're displaying a coarse temperament if you think you can outwit a god.

HERALD. It looks as though Athens is the place for bad men to come for refuge.

DEMOPHON. The gods' sanctuaries are places of safety for 260 everyone without exception.

HERALD. I'm not sure the Mycenaeans will see it that way.

DEMOPHON. Don't I have authority here?

HERALD. Yes, as long as you're sensible and do the Mycenaeans no harm.

DEMOPHON. Take this harm, then, because I shall commit no sin against the gods.

HERALD. I have no desire for you to go to war with Argos.

DEMOPHON. Nor do I, but I won't let these suppliants go.

HERALD. All the same, I shall seize them and take them, because they are mine.

DEMOPHON. Then your journey back to Argos will be far from easy.

HERALD. I'll put this to the test immediately and see whether you're right.

He makes a threatening move towards the children.

DEMOPHON. You'll regret it—now, straight away—if you lay 270 hands on them.

He makes a threatening move towards the HERALD.

CHORUS. In the name of the gods, please don't be reckless! Don't hit a herald!*

DEMOPHON. I will, unless the herald comes to his senses.

CHORUS (*to the* HERALD). You'd better leave. (*To* DEMOPHON) Don't lay a finger on him, my lord.

HERALD. I'm going, because one man alone lacks the strength for battle. But I'll be back with a mighty force of armed Argives. Countless soldiers await me, with the lord Eurystheus himself at their head. He is waiting on the borders of Alcathous' land,* to see how events here turn out. Once he receives news of your insolence, he will be here in no time to   280 threaten you, your fellow citizens, the land itself, and its crops.* There would be no point in our having amassed in Argos such a huge force of men in their prime if we were to leave you unpunished.

DEMOPHON. Get lost! I am not frightened of your Argos. You were not going to shame me by abducting these boys by force. This city of mine is free, not subservient to Argos.

Exit the HERALD.

CHORUS. Now is the time for forethought, before the Argive army draws near our borders. The Mycenaeans are very fierce   290 fighters, and will be more than usually so in the present circumstances, given that heralds always have the habit of doubling the size of events in the telling. So what tall tale do you think he will tell his king of how terribly he was treated and how he barely escaped being torn apart?

IOLAUS. Children can have no finer gift than a noble and brave father.† High birth is a better defence against misfortune than lowly birth.* So, for instance, when we had reached the utmost depths of adversity, we found friends and kinfolk here, who have proved to be the only ones in all Greece to stand up for these children. Children, draw near and give them your right hands—(*turning to the* CHORUS *and* DEMOPHON) and you do likewise. (*They all shake hands*) Children, they have proved themselves our friends, and so if you ever do return home to   310 your native land, occupy your father's palace, and <regain> his privileges, you must regard <the lords of this land>† for ever as your friends and saviours. Be sure, I beg you, never to raise a hostile force against this land,* but always to regard them as your closest friends. They deserve your respect for having removed from us the enmity of such a mighty country and of the Pelasgian people. Even though they saw that we were destitute wanderers, they did not hand us over, and did not expel us from their land.† (*To* DEMOPHON) Sir, not only in life, but also in death (whenever that may be) by Theseus' side I shall praise you to the skies and raise his spirits with the tale of how you made the children of Heracles truly welcome and offered them protection. I shall tell him how in your nobility you keep your father's glory alive throughout Greece, and how, thanks to your noble parentage, you have turned out to be no less courageous than your father. There are not many of whom this is true; you might perhaps find one man in a thousand who is as good as his father.

CHORUS. Our country has always been willing to take the part of justice and help those who cannot help themselves. That is why we have endured countless trials in defence of our friends—and now I see this fresh struggle looming.

DEMOPHON. You have spoken well, old friend. I am confident that these children will behave as you say: they will not forget the good we have done them. Now, as for me, I shall convene the citizens and dispose them so that I can meet the Mycenaean army in strength. First, I shall dispatch lookouts to make sure that their attack doesn't take us by surprise (for all their men will hasten to help Argos) and then I shall assemble the seers and sacrifice to the gods. You had better leave Zeus' temple and take the children into the palace, where there are people who will look after you, even if I am not there. (*IOLAUS stays where he is*) No, do go into the palace.

IOLAUS. I won't leave the altar. We shall stay here as suppliants and pray for the city's success. We'll go to the palace once you've prevailed in the forthcoming battle. The gods we have on our side are at least the equals of those the Argives have, my lord. For although Hera, the wife of Zeus, is their champion, ours is Athena. Having superior gods is another factor, in my opinion, that contributes towards success. For Pallas* will not tolerate defeat.

Exit DEMOPHON.

CHORUS (*sings*). Not all your proud boasts, Argive stranger,
    will make others pay you more mind.
    Your bragging will not fill my heart with fear.

320

330

340

350

No, may this not be the fate of great Athens,
city blessed with fair dancing-grounds!
But you are not in your right mind,   360
nor is the Argive tyrant, the son of Sthenelus.*

To another city you came, a city the equal of Argos,
and stranger though you were you tried to abduct by force
those who had come to my land as refugees,
suppliants of the gods. You yielded not to our king,
nor urged any just plea. Did you really think
that people in their right minds
would count this behaviour as right?   370

Peace is my pleasure. But I say to you,
evil-hearted king, that if you come to my city,
things will not turn out the way you suppose:
you are not the only one with lance
and bronze-faced shield. You lust after war,
but don't, I beg you, throw this city
of cultured elegance into chaos
with your spear. No, restrain yourself!   380

Enter DEMOPHON, *looking anxious.*

IOLAUS. My son, why have you come with this worried expression in your eyes? Do you have some news about the enemy?
Are they waiting or are they here? What have you found out?
You're surely not going to prove the herald's words false. I'm
quite certain that the general, having met with success so far,
will come to Athens with no little confidence. But of course
Zeus punishes excessive arrogance.

DEMOPHON. The Argive army is here, with their lord Eurystheus. I have seen him myself, since no one who claims to be   390
an expert military commander should use messengers as his
eyes. He has not yet launched his army down onto the plain
here; he is occupying the rocky brow and surveying the
terrain—what I'm telling you is only my guess—to see how
he might best bring such an enormous army within our bor-
ders† and find a safe part of the land to make camp. Moreover, all my own preparations have gone well. The city is
armed, the sacrificial victims stand ready to be slaughtered   400
for the appropriate gods, and the seers are setting about their

sacrifices throughout the city. Once I had assembled all the chanters of oracles, however, I investigated their sayings, both those which have been published and those they have kept to themselves.† In general, there was little agreement among these oracles, but one opinion was conspicuous for being the same in them all: they tell me to sacrifice to the daughter of Demeter a maiden born of a noble father,* for victory over my enemies and safety for the city. Now, you can   410
see that I am eager to do my best to help you, but I shall not kill my own daughter nor force any of my fellow citizens to do so against his wishes—and who is heartless enough to give up his beloved children willingly? People are gathering even now in groups—you could see them if you were there—some arguing that I was right to offer assistance to strangers who had come as suppliants, others accusing me of folly. In fact, civil war is already brewing, in case I do as the oracles order. So you must be sure to help me find a way to keep both   420
yourselves and this land safe, without incurring the displeasure of my fellow citizens. For I am not the kind of ruler they have in the east: I will be treated fairly only as long as I behave fairly.

CHORUS. Is the god really preventing this city, despite its eagerness, from helping the visitors in their hour of need?

IOLAUS. Children, we are like sailors who have succeeded in escaping the fury of a storm, and have come within a hand's span of reaching land, only to be driven by the winds back to   430
sea and away from dry land.* Likewise, we are being repelled from this land when we had just reached what we thought was the safety of its shores. Alas! Why, cruel hope, did you gladden my heart earlier, when you were planning to withdraw your favour before its fulfilment? For there's nothing wrong in what *he* is doing, in refusing to kill his fellow citizens' children, and I can commend even the city's actions. (*To* DEMOPHON) The fact that the gods have decided that this is what should happen to me doesn't undermine my feeling of gratitude to *you*. (*To the children*) But, children, I don't know what I shall do with you! Whatever shall we do? Is there any   440
god whose altar has not been decked with our suppliant wreaths, or any land where we have not already sought protection? It is all over with us, children: we are to be given up!

My own death is a matter of indifference to me, except that in
dying I shall give pleasure to my enemies. But it's you I feel
sorry for, children; it's you and Alcmene, your aged grandmother, for whom I weep. Poor woman, to have lived so long!
And poor me, to have worked so hard for nothing! It was our
fate, then, our fate to fall into the hands of our enemy and to   450
die a shameful and degrading death.

    (*He turns suddenly to* DEMOPHON) But you know what? You
must help me. For I haven't entirely given up hope of saving
these children. Hand *me* over to the Argives instead of them,
my lord. There's no risk to you and you can save the children's lives for me. There's no need for me to be attached to
life. Let it go! And Eurystheus would be overjoyed to have
Heracles' comrade-in-arms in his power, for him to persecute
and abuse. He is a brute of a man. Wise men should pray to
have a wise man as an enemy, not one with a coarse and
arrogant nature, because then they will meet with a good   460
measure of respect and justice.*

CHORUS. Old man, please don't blame the city. The charge that
we betrayed visitors to our land, even if false, would be a
terrible slur against the city's name.

DEMOPHON. Your offer is noble, but it doesn't help. Eurystheus
hasn't brought his army here because he wants you. What
would he gain by the death of an old man? No, it's these
children he wants to kill. Men of high birth growing up are a
source of terror to their enemies, when they have the vigour
of youth and their minds are filled with the appalling treatment their father received. He has to take precautions   470
against all of this. If you have some other plan in mind, one
which better meets the moment, set it in motion, for after
hearing the oracles I have no help to offer and am filled
with fear.

Enter the MAIDEN *from the temple.*

MAIDEN. Strangers, don't think me brazen for coming out like
this. I begin with this request because for a woman, silence,
reserve, and staying quietly indoors are best.* Nevertheless, I
came out because I heard your anguished words, Iolaus. No
one asked me to represent the family, but I suppose I may do   480
so as well as anyone. Since I am deeply worried about my

brothers here and myself, I want to find out whether what's tormenting your mind is that the troubles we've been endur- ing for so long have been compounded by some new blow.

IOLAUS. My child, this is far from the first time that I have had good reason to praise you more than any of Heracles' chil- dren. Although our voyage seemed to be going well, every- thing has changed and once again we find ourselves in dire straits. Demophon here says that the chanters of oracles tell him to sacrifice to the daughter of Demeter no bull or calf, but 490 a high-born maiden, if we are to survive and if this city is to survive. This is what makes our situation impossible, because he says he will not slaughter either his own children or any- one else's. He also tells me—in hints rather than plain words—that if we can't extricate ourselves from this situation somehow, we should find somewhere else to go, while he desires to save this country.

MAIDEN. Does our safety really depend on this condition?

IOLAUS. Yes. (*Ironically*) Apart from that, our situation is fine.

MAIDEN. In that case you need no longer fear the Argive spears 500 arrayed against us. Sir, I am prepared of my own accord, without being asked, to submit to sacrifice and death. What possible excuse could we have for avoiding death when the Athenians are willing to face great danger for our sakes, we ourselves are responsible for adding to their burden, and it is possible for us to save them? That is out of the question. It would be quite absurd for us to sit and wail as suppliants at the altars of the gods, and then show ourselves to be cowards, when we are the children of a father such as ours. Where can 510 you find this sort of conduct among men of honour?

Perhaps you think it would be better if (may the gods forbid it!) this city fell, and I was captured by the enemy, suffered indignities—I, the daughter of a noble father—and then died anyway. Or shall I be a vagabond after banishment from this land? What about the shame I would certainly feel were someone to say, 'Why have you come here with your suppli- ant branches when you are nothing but weaklings, clinging to life? Leave our country. We will not help cowards'? Or again, if these boys died and I remained alive, I could still not 520 expect happiness—the hope of which has caused many people in the past to betray their loved ones. After all, would

any man want to take a maiden without a family as his wife
and to make me the mother of his children?* Since I don't
deserve any of these fates, isn't death preferable for me? The
alternatives might suit another girl, but not one from a family
as notable as mine.

(*To* DEMOPHON) Take me to the place where this body of
mine is to perish, and where it seems best for me to be decked
with wreaths and sacrificed.† Defeat the enemy! This life of   530
mine is freely given, with no reluctance on my part, and I
promise to die for my brothers' sake and for myself. By not
clinging to life I have discovered what is finest, and that is to
die in a glorious fashion.

CHORUS. Oh, what shall I say in response to the maiden's great-
hearted offer to die for her brothers? What words, what
actions could be nobler than these?

IOLAUS. Child, you are truly the offspring of your father! You   540
are the seed of Heracles, sprung from his divine spirit! I am
not ashamed that you spoke out, but I am in agony about the
way things have turned out. I'll tell you a fairer way for matters to proceed: (*To the attendants*) you must call all her sisters
out here, and then let the one chosen by lot die on behalf of
her family. (*To the* MAIDEN) It wouldn't be fair for you to die
without drawing lots.

MAIDEN. I refuse to have my death decided by the random casting of lots: I win no gratitude that way. Don't mention it
again, old friend. No, if you accept my offer, if you are happy
to find in me an eager victim, I give my life to these boys freely,   550
with no compulsion.

IOLAUS. Oh, as if your earlier words were not perfect, there is
even more nobility in what you've just said. Your courage
keeps on mounting, your words surpass one another in excellence. No, I neither command nor forbid your death, my child.
But your brothers will benefit if you die.

MAIDEN. Wisely spoken. You need not worry that you will be
polluted by my blood. Let me die as a free woman should,
fulfilling my boast to be my father's daughter. But come with   560
me, old friend: I want to die in your arms. Stay with me and
shroud my corpse in my clothes—for I am going now to the
horror of sacrificial slaughter.†

IOLAUS. I couldn't stand by and watch you die.

MAIDEN. Well, at least you could ask Demophon here to make
sure that women, not men, are holding me as I breathe my
last.*

DEMOPHON. I'll see to it, you unhappy girl. It would reflect
badly on me too if you were not properly arrayed for your
funeral, for many reasons, not least your courage and sense   570
of justice. Of all the women I have ever met, you are the most
wretched. But now it's time for you to go, if you're ready, once
you have spoken your final words to these boys and the old
man.

MAIDEN (*to IOLAUS*). Farewell, then, old friend. Farewell and, for
my sake, teach my brothers to be like you, with an intelligent
approach to every situation. Their education need go no further; that will suffice. Do your best to save them from death.
You have treated us as your children, raised us with your own
·hands; you can see that I too, in sacrificing myself for their   580
sake, am giving up my chance of marriage.

(*To the boys*) As for you, those of my brothers who are
gathered here, I pray that you may find happiness and everything of which my heart will now be disappointed. Treat the
old man with respect, and also the old woman who is currently inside the temple, Alcmene, the mother of my father.
Honour too our friends here. And if, with the gods' help, your
troubles end and you return home, remember the young
woman who saved your lives, and your duty to bury her.* The
finest burial possible would be only right and proper, because
I did not let you down when you needed me, but died for the   590
sake of my family. Rather than children and the pleasures of
my youth, such a memorial is all my wealth—if there is any
kind of existence in the underworld. But my hope is that there
is none. For if we who are on the point of death are even there
to have cares, I don't know where we can turn. For death is
generally considered to be the most effective remedy for
suffering.

IOLAUS. My dear, your courage is remarkable, greater than that
of any other woman. Rest assured that, in death as in life, you
will be highly revered by us. Farewell, then: I shrink from   600
speaking ill of the goddess, the daughter of Demeter, to whom
your body has been dedicated.

Exit the MAIDEN to her death.

Boys, it is all over with me. Grief is making me faint. Take me, children, cover my head with this cloak of mine, and set me down somewhere. I am appalled by what has happened, and if the oracles turn out to be false, that added disaster will make life unbearable. This is already enough of a catastrophe.

Some of the boys help IOLAUS *collapse on the temple steps and cover his head with his cloak.*

CHORUS (*sings*). No man, in my view, is well or badly off
except by heaven's will. Nor does success
securely attend one house for ever: 610
one fate after another pursues it.
Fate settles one man in a humble station,
brought down from the heights, and gives the pauper
    wealth.†
We are not allowed to evade fate;
wisdom is no defence, and one who does his best
to repel it will always labour in vain.

Iolaus, pick yourself up from the ground.
Submit to heaven's will; don't rack your heart with grief.   620
In dying for her brothers and this land,
the wretched girl has an illustrious death,
and men to come will glorify her name.
Virtue is gained by toil. Her conduct
was true to her father, true to her noble birth.
If you honour the dying of the brave,
I join you in showing such respect.

Enter the SERVANT.

SERVANT. Greetings to you, children. Where is old Iolaus, and   630
  where is your grandmother? Has she left this sanctuary?
IOLAUS (*unveiling himself*). Here I am. Such as I am, I am here.
SERVANT. Why are you slumped on the ground? Why are you
  looking so dejected?
IOLAUS. I have been visited by oppressive personal cares.
SERVANT. Then pick yourself up! Away with dejection!
IOLAUS. I'm too old and far too weak.
SERVANT. But I've come with news that will give you great
  pleasure.

IOLAUS. Who are you? Have we met somewhere before? I can't remember.

SERVANT. I'm one of Hyllus' serfs.* Don't you recognize me?

IOLAUS. You are very welcome. So you've all arrived safe and sound, then? 640

SERVANT. Certainly. And what's more, as things stand at the moment, your happiness is assured.

IOLAUS (*raising himself from the ground and calling towards the temple*). Alcmene, mother of noble Heracles, come out here! There's very welcome news for you to hear! For a long time now you've been pining, worrying about whether the children, now that they've got here, would ever return home.

Enter ALCMENE.

ALCMENE. What's going on, Iolaus? Why is the temple filled with the sound of your shouts? Has another herald come from Argos to treat you with violence? (*To the SERVANT*) I may be weak, stranger, but you should know that while I am alive 650 you shall not abduct these children. Otherwise, I tell you, may I no longer be regarded as the mother of a hero! If you lay a hand on them, you'll have to do ignominious battle with two old folk.

IOLAUS. Don't worry, old woman, have no fear. This is no herald from Argos with a hostile message.

ALCMENE. Then why did you shout? That usually indicates some cause for alarm.

IOLAUS. I wanted you to come out here in front of the temple.

ALCMENE. I didn't realize. Who is this man?

IOLAUS. He brings news of your grandson's arrival.

ALCMENE (*to the SERVANT*). You are indeed welcome for the news 660 that you bring. But if he has set foot in this land, where is he? Why isn't he here? Has something happened to prevent him coming here with you and making me happy?

SERVANT. He is making camp and organizing the army he's brought with him.

ALCMENE (*to IOLAUS*). This message is of no interest to you and me.

IOLAUS. Yes, it is. It's up to us to ask what's happening.

SERVANT. Well, what would you like to know?

IOLAUS (*to the* SERVANT). How big is the army he's come with?
How many troops are there?

SERVANT. There are plenty of them. I can't give you the exact
figure.

IOLAUS. I imagine that the Athenian leaders are aware of all this.   670

SERVANT. Yes, and in fact he has been stationed on their left
wing.

IOLAUS. Really? Are the troops already armed and ready for
action?

SERVANT. Yes, and the sacrificial victims have been brought out
clear from the ranks.*

IOLAUS. How far away is the Argive army?

SERVANT. Close enough for their general to be clearly visible.

IOLAUS. What is he doing? Is he organizing the enemy into
ranks?

SERVANT. That was our guess, but we couldn't hear his orders.
Anyway, I'm off. I wouldn't want my master to engage the
enemy alone—or at any rate without me.

IOLAUS. I'll come with you.* After all, we have the same con-   680
cern: to stand beside our friends and help them as we should.

SERVANT (*hesitantly*). You are normally the last person to say
anything foolish.

IOLAUS. And the last person to fail to join my friends in the
battle's fray.

SERVANT. Sir, your strength is not what it once was.

IOLAUS. But all the same I shall fight as many men as ever.

SERVANT. But the weight you add will hardly tip the scales in   690
favour of your friends.

IOLAUS. My enemies will all give up at the sight of me.

SERVANT. Sight alone wounds no one: the arm has to be
involved.

IOLAUS. What do you mean? May not even my blow pierce a
shield?

SERVANT. You may aim a blow, but you might fall down before
it lands.

IOLAUS. Don't stop me when I'm ready for action.

SERVANT. The spirit may be willing, but the flesh is incapable.

IOLAUS. You can say what you like, but I won't be here to listen.

SERVANT. How are you going to take the field as a hoplite*
when you don't have any armour?

IOLAUS. There are weapons taken in war inside this temple here.* I'll use some of them. If I survive, I shall return them, and if I die the god won't demand them back. Go into the temple, take hoplite gear down from the pegs, and bring it to me. Hurry, now. This lingering at home makes me feel 700 ashamed. Some fight, while others stay behind out of cowardice.

Exit the SERVANT into the temple.

CHORUS. Your pride is not yet brought low by time: it is vigorous, though your body is spent. Why are you making all this effort? There's no point: you will get hurt and our city will gain hardly anything. You have to give way to your age and forget about things which are now impossible for you. You'll never get your youthful vigour back again.

ALCMENE. Are you out of your mind? Do you really mean to leave me here all alone with my grandchildren? 710

IOLAUS. Yes, I do. Fighting is for men, and your job is to take care of them.

ALCMENE. But if you die, where will I find safety?

IOLAUS. Your surviving grandchildren will look after you.

ALCMENE. But what if—may the gods forbid it!—something were to happen to them?

IOLAUS. Then our friends here won't let you down. Don't be afraid.

ALCMENE. That's it, then. That's all I have to pin my hopes on.

IOLAUS. I'm sure that Zeus too is looking out for you in your time of trouble.

ALCMENE. Oh, far be it from me to speak ill of Zeus: he knows whether he is behaving honourably towards me.

The SERVANT returns from the temple, carrying arms and armour.

SERVANT. As you can see, I've brought you a full set of arms 720 and armour. You should dress yourself in it as quickly as possible, because battle is about to be joined and there's nothing Ares hates more than delay. (*He hands the gear to IOLAUS, who struggles with it*) If you're worried about the weight of the armour, you had better walk to the battlefield without it on, and then arm yourself fully once you've reached the ranks. In the meantime, I'll carry it for you.

IOLAUS. That's a good idea. (*He hands it back in relief*) Carry my armour for me, but keep it ready. Give me the spear to hold and support my left arm as you guide me there.

SERVANT. So I have to attend the hoplite as if he were a child, do I?*

IOLAUS. I must walk carefully. We don't want any bad omens.* 730

They set out, laboriously, for the exit.

SERVANT. I wish you could do everything you're eager to do.

IOLAUS. Hurry up. I'll be terribly upset if I miss the fighting.

SERVANT. It's not me slowing us down, you know: it's you. You just think you're coping.

IOLAUS. Can't you see how fast my legs are moving?

SERVANT. I see that you're making good speed in your imagination, but not in reality.

IOLAUS. You won't be saying that when you see me there . . .

SERVANT. Doing what? Well, being lucky, I hope.

IOLAUS. . . . wounding one of the enemy through his shield.

SERVANT. If we ever get there—that's what I'm worried about.

IOLAUS. Oh, my fighting arm! I wish you could be the kind of 740
support in battle you used to be when you were in your prime—as I remember you when with Heracles' help you sacked Sparta!* How I would make Eurystheus turn and flee! He's too much of a coward to face my spear. That's another thing success wrongly attracts: a reputation for bravery. We imagine that someone who's doing well has every skill there is.

Exeunt IOLAUS and SERVANT.

CHORUS (*sings*). O Earth and night-long Moon, and brilliant rays of the god who brings light to mortals, 750
bear my message, shout it loud in the heavens,
to the ruling throne, and in grey-eyed Athena's halls!*
In defence of the land of my birth, in defence of my home,
I am about to cut through danger with my sword
of grey iron because I took in the suppliants.

Though daunting that a city like Argos, prosperous
and renowned for its military might, should nurture 760
anger against my land, it would be an act of cowardice,
my city, to hand over suppliant strangers at Argos' command.

Zeus is on my side;* I have no fear; rightly is Zeus
looking kindly on me—and never will the gods
be made out by me to be inferior to mortals.

But, my lady,* since yours is the land   770
and yours is the city whose mother,
mistress and guardian you are,
send elsewhere the man who is bringing
here the spear-hurling army from Argos.
It would be wrong for my virtue
to be repaid by expulsion from my home.

For you is ever accomplished the honour
of rich sacrifices, nor are you forgotten
on the waning day of the month,* through the songs
of young men or their tuneful dancing.   780
And on the wind-swept hill cries
of celebration ring out to the sound
of the night-long rhythm of maiden feet.

Enter the MESSENGER.

MESSENGER. Mistress, nothing could be more delightful for you
to hear than the news I bring, and nothing more quick for me
to tell:† we have defeated our foes and victory trophies are
being set up bearing the arms and armour of your enemies.*

ALCMENE. My friend, you are most welcome. And thanks to
your news this day brings you your freedom.*† But you are   790
not yet freeing me from one source of grief: I am still afraid
that those whose lives I value may not be alive.

MESSENGER. They are, and every man in the army is praising
them to the skies.

ALCMENE. And what about the old man, Iolaus? Is he still alive?
Tell me.†

MESSENGER. Certainly, and with the gods' help he acquitted
himself splendidly.

ALCMENE. What? Did he really achieve something noble in the
battle?

MESSENGER. He has been rejuvenated! He is no longer an old
man!

ALCMENE. That's incredible! But first could you please tell me
about the battle, and how it turned out well for my loved ones.

MESSENGER. I can tell you everything that happened in a single
report. Once the hoplites had been drawn up opposite one   800
another in a long line, Hyllus stepped down from his four-
horse chariot, stood in the space between the two armies, and
said: 'I call on the commander of the invading force from
Argos! Why can't we leave this land <in peace? I have a plan
that will allow you to retain your personal honour>† and by
sparing her soldiers† you will do Mycenae no harm either.
Instead of battle, why don't you and I fight in single combat?
If you kill me, you can have the children of Heracles and take
them away; if I kill you, you let me keep my ancestral rights   810
and palace.' The troops thought this was a good idea, and
commended not only the attempt to avoid battle, but also
Hyllus' courage. But Eurystheus, with no regard for all the
people who had heard the challenge and with no shame for
his own weakness, ill-suited to a commander, lacked the
courage to meet a brave man in combat and displayed the full
extent of his cowardice. Was it such a man as this who had
come to enslave the offspring of Heracles?

Hyllus returned to the ranks, and since it was clear that
battle was not going to be replaced by single combat, the   820
diviners immediately set about their sacrifices, and straight
away the blood poured in a propitious stream from the necks
of the oxen.* Some were mounting their chariots, others joining side to side under the shelter of their shields.* The Athenian king addressed his troops as befits a man of noble birth.
'Fellow citizens,' he said, 'now it is every man's duty to defend
the land that gave him birth and nourished him.' Meanwhile,
for his part, Eurystheus exhorted the men on his side to
commit themselves to not dishonouring Argos and Mycenae.

At the clear signal of the Tyrrhenian trumpet,* battle was   830
joined. How great, do you imagine, was the noise of clashing
shields? How loud the sound of mingled cries and groans? At
first, the impetus of the Argive army broke our lines, but then
they withdrew. In the next phase the battle settled down, as
men advanced step by step and stood up to their opposite
numbers. Casualties were heavy. There were intermingled
cries:† 'Men of Athens'—or 'Farmers of Argos'—'keep dis-   840
grace from our city!' At last—it was far from easy—with a
supreme effort we forced the Argive troops back into flight.

At this point old Iolaus, seeing that Hyllus was setting off after the enemy, stretched out his hand and begged to be taken on a chariot. Grasping the reins in his hands, he went after Eurystheus' horses. Although I was an eyewitness to what I've said so far, for what follows I shall repeat what I heard from others. As he was passing the hill sacred to Athena Pallenis,* he spotted Eurystheus' chariot, and prayed   850
to Hebe* and Zeus that just for one day he might be young again and make his enemies pay their due. And now you shall hear of a miracle. Two stars stood on the horses' yoke and hid the chariot in a dark cloud. Those with some skill in these matters say that the two stars were your son and Hebe. From out of the murky gloom appeared Iolaus' arms, rejuvenated and with a youthful shape. To his glory, Iolaus captured the four-horse chariot of Eurystheus by the Scironian crags* and,   860
as an incomparable victory prize, he has brought back with his hands bound the general who was once doing so well. The misfortune with which Eurystheus is currently afflicted brings a clear message and a lesson for all mortal men: not to admire anyone for his seeming prosperity until they have seen him die. For our fortunes last for no more than a day.

CHORUS. O Zeus, lord of victory trophies, now I can see the light of a day that has been freed from grim fear!

ALCMENE. O Zeus, it took time for you to notice my suffering, but I am still grateful to you for what has happened. And   870
although previously I wasn't sure that my son lived in the company of the gods, now I know it for certain.*

Children, now at last you will be free of your trials, free from that bastard Eurystheus!* Now at last you will see your father's city, take possession of your rightful land, sacrifice to your ancestral gods! From all of these you were barred while you lived as wretched, wandering outsiders.

(*To the* MESSENGER) But what clever plan did Iolaus have in mind when he spared Eurystheus' life? Tell me, please. For it   880
doesn't seem such a clever idea to me, not to make your enemies pay when you have them in your power.

MESSENGER. He was thinking of you rather than himself. He thought you might like to see him with your own eyes, a prisoner,† subject to your authority. But this was not at all to Eurystheus' liking: Iolaus had to use violence to make him

bow to the inevitable, because Eurystheus didn't want to be
brought before you alive for punishment. But now farewell,
old woman. Please remember the first thing you said when I
was beginning my account, that you would set me free. It's   890
important that people of nobility speak the truth in matters
of this kind.

                                                Exit the MESSENGER.

CHORUS (*sings*). Dancing and the sweet charms of pipes at a
          feast
    give me pleasure;† so too does graceful Aphrodite.*
    But there is also something pleasant, I find,
    in seeing friends who once seemed wretched
    attain good fortune. Destiny the fulfiller, and Life,
    the son of Time, are parents to many offspring.   900

    The course you keep to, my city, is one of justice.
    You should never forget to honour the gods.
    The claim that you ignore them borders on madness.
    There is evidence for this—for there is nothing unclear
    in the message the god gives by constantly
    stripping wrongdoers of their arrogance.

    Old woman, your son has found a place in heaven.   910
    I cannot believe he went down to Hades' halls,
    his body consumed by the pyre's grim flames.*
    In a golden chamber he shares with Hebe a bed of love.
    O Hymenaeus,* you have honoured two of Zeus' children!

    The world is full of coincidences. Athena, they say,   920
    helped their father,* and now Athena's city and people
    have saved these children. She has checked the abuses
    of a man who preferred violence and anger to justice.
    I pray to be spared arrogance and an insatiable spirit!

          Enter the SERVANT *with* EURYSTHEUS *bound.*

SERVANT. Mistress, I shall explain, although you can see what's
    going on: we have brought Eurystheus here to you—
    something you never expected to see and he hoped would   930
    never happen. For he never imagined that he would fall into
    your hands, when he set out from Mycenae with his death-
    dealing arms and his unjust pride to sack Athens. But fate

dealt him the opposite lot, and altered his fortune. Hyllus and noble Iolaus were setting up an image of Zeus the lord of victory trophies as a token of their glorious victory, but they told me to bring this man to you, because they wanted to make you happy. After all, nothing could be more enjoyable than seeing an enemy's luck change from good to bad. 940

ALCMENE (*to EURYSTHEUS*). Here you are, you foul creature! Has Justice caught up with you at last? First, turn your head here towards us and have the courage to look your enemies in the face. For you are overpowered now, no longer the powerful. (*EURYSTHEUS looks at her*) Here's what I want to know: are you really the man—you brute!—who thought he had a right to abuse my son (wherever he may be now) in so many ways by sending him off on missions to kill hydras and lions?* I pass over in silence all the other trials and tribulations you contrived for him; it would take too long for me to mention them all, since in your cruelty you found every possible way to humiliate him. You even had him go down alive to Hades!* And as if all this wasn't enough, you also dared to try to drive me and his children from the whole of Greece, when we were seated as suppliants at the gods' altars, and some of us were old or still young children. But then you found a city of free men whom you could not terrify. You must be put to death like a criminal—but that will be entirely to your advantage, because you should die more than once for all the suffering you have caused. 960

SERVANT. It is not for you to bring about this man's death.

ALCMENE. Then we took him prisoner for nothing. What law is there that allows him to live?

SERVANT. It is the will of those who rule this land.

ALCMENE. Why? Don't they find the killing of enemies good?

SERVANT. No, not when someone has been taken alive in battle.*

ALCMENE. And did Hyllus assent to this decision?

SERVANT. I think he should have gone against the wishes of this land.

ALCMENE. Eurystheus should die—should already be dead.†

SERVANT. The first wrong that was done to him was when he did not die before. 970

ALCMENE. Does it not still count as right for him to be
punished?

SERVANT. There's no one to put him to death.

ALCMENE. I will. Even I am someone, I maintain.

SERVANT. You'll come in for a great deal of criticism if you do
that.

ALCMENE. I love this city—no one can deny that. But now this
man is mine, and I will not have anyone take him away from
me. So let them call me brazen, if they want, and over-proud
for a woman, but this is something that I will do.   980

CHORUS. Woman, I'm sure that though the hostility you feel for
this man is terrible, it is also excusable.

EURYSTHEUS. Woman, you should know that I'm not going to
flatter you or say anything else to save my life from which I
would be bound to incur the charge of cowardice. I did not
initiate the hostility between us of my own free will; I knew
that I was your cousin and therefore a close relative of your
son Heracles. But my likes or dislikes didn't come into it, since
a god was involved: it was Hera who afflicted me with this   990
illness.* Once I had initiated the enmity with Heracles, and
had appreciated that this was the struggle I was engaged
upon, I became a master at devising all kinds of suffering for
him. The hours of night were my constant companions as I
produced plan after plan for dividing and killing my enemies,
so that I would not have to spend the rest of my life with fear
as my companion. For I knew that your son was no cipher but
a man indeed—you see, even though he is my enemy, he will
at least get from me the kind of praise† that is proper to a
hero.*

Once he was out of the way, should I not have tried every- 1000
thing in my power to kill and banish and scheme against his
children? After all, I was hated by them; I was well aware that
they had inherited hostility towards me from their father. My
safety lay in acting in that way. If you had been in my situation, I suppose *you* would not have mercilessly harassed the
hate-filled offspring of the hostile lion, but would have meekly
let them live in Argos! You won't convince anyone of this!

Well, they didn't kill me earlier, though I was ready for it, 1010
and so now, in accordance with Greek custom, to kill me
would pollute the killer. It was sensible of the Athenians to

spare my life, to rate the god much higher than their hostility
towards me. You have had your say and you have heard my
response. If you kill me you will have me known not only as a
polluter, but also as a man of nobility.† But the way I feel is
this: although I do not want to die, leaving this life wouldn't
cause me any distress.

CHORUS. I'd like to give you a small piece of advice, Alcmene:
you had better spare this man's life, since that is what the city
has decided.

ALCMENE. What if he were to be put to death *and* we were to do   1020
as the city wishes?

CHORUS. That would be best.* But how could this happen?

ALCMENE. I'll explain; it's easy. I shall kill him, and then I shall
give his corpse to those of his friends who come to get it. I'll
not be disobeying the city's wishes as far as his body is
concerned, but by his death he will pay me the due penalty.

EURYSTHEUS. Kill me, then. I'm not begging for my life. But
since Athens spared my life and refused to put me to death, I
shall present it with an ancient oracle of Loxias,* which will,
in due course of time, do it an unbelievable amount of good.
(*He turns to the* CHORUS, *as representatives of Athens*) After my
death you Athenians will bury me where I was fated to lie,* in   1030
front of the temple of the divine maiden, Athena Pallenis.* I
shall lie, a resident alien, buried in the land for ever, looking
kindly on you and protecting the city, but unremittingly hostile to these children's descendants when they betray the
kindness you have shown them today and invade in
strength.* For that is the nature of the strangers you championed. If I was aware of all this, why did I come here, rather
than respecting the oracle? Because I thought that Hera was
far superior to any oracle and would not desert me. Be sure   1040
not to let anyone pour libations or the blood of victims onto
my tomb, and then in return I will blight their homecoming.
And so you will gain from me in two respects: in dying I will
do you good and them harm.

ALCMENE (*to the* CHORUS). If it is bound to win protection for
Athens and for your descendants, what are you waiting for?
Why don't you kill the man, now that you've heard what he's
said? He has shown you a path which is completely free of
risk: alive, the man is an enemy; dead, he does you good.

Slaves, take him away, and then kill him and give his body to 1050
the dogs.* (*To* EURYSTHEUS) You see, I don't want you to think
that you might live to expel me once more from the land of
my birth!

< . . . >†

CHORUS. I agree with this. (*To the attendants*) Go, then, slaves!
For there is nothing here we have done that will pollute our
king.*

They all exeunt.

CYCLOPS

Characters

SILENUS, father of the satyrs
ODYSSEUS
CYCLOPS, called Polyphemus

CHORUS of satyrs

Scene: In front of the cave where the CYCLOPS lives. SILENUS is
standing there, with a rake in his hand.*

SILENUS. Thanks to you, Bromius,* I've had plenty of trials
and tribulations, right up to now from when I was in my
prime and (*making an obscene gesture with the drooping phallus that forms part of his costume, or with the rake handle
between his legs*) physically fit. The first occasion was when
you were driven mad by Hera, and you took off, deserting
your nurses, the mountain nymphs.* Next, during the battle
with the Giants,* I took my stand by your side, protecting
your right with my shield,* and slew Enceladus, with a
thrust of my spear straight through the middle of his shield
(*he mimics this with his rake*)—hang on, did I dream all this?
No, certainly not, because I also showed the spoils to
Bacchus.

And now I've got far more to put up with. When Hera   10
stirred the Tyrrhenian pirates into action against you, and
got them to sell you abroad,* I heard about it and set sail with
my sons in search of you. Standing right at the stern I per-
sonally took charge and steered our sound vessel while my
sons sat at the oars and whitened the grey sea into surf as
they searched for you, my lord. But just as we were sailing
close to Cape Malea,* an easterly wind fell on the ship and
wrecked us here on this rocky shore, dominated by Mount   20
Etna, where the Cyclopes, the one-eyed children of the sea-
god, inhabit remote caves—and kill people. We were captured
by one of them, and now we're his household slaves. The
name of our master, the one we serve, is Polyphemus. Instead

of taking part in Bacchic revels, we tend the flocks of a
godless Cyclops.

    My sons, then, being young, are grazing young sheep on
far-distant slopes, while my job is to stay here, fill the troughs
with water, sweep this house, and wait on the godless Cyclops   30
at his unholy meals. I have no choice but to do as I've been
told and sweep the house now with this iron rake,* so that the
cave can be nice and clean for my master, the Cyclops, when
he returns—and for his sheep.

He goes about his business, but looks up as the CHORUS* *enters, with
attendants and sheep.*

But here are my sons, driving their flocks this way. What's up?
I can't believe that the pace of this dance of yours is similar to
the lewd dances you performed to the songs of the lyre when
as Bacchus' companions you went in a riot to Althaea's   40
house.*

CHORUS (*sings*). (*To an errant ram*)
    O son of noble lineage from both your parents,
    tell me, why are you wandering off to the rocks?
    Isn't the gentle breeze this way, and the grassy meadow?
    The swirling river water lies here, in troughs, by the cave,
    where the bleating of your offspring calls you.

    Psst! This way, this way!
    Won't you graze the dewy banks here?   50
    Hey! There's a stone coming your way soon!
    Get a move on! Hurry up, you with the horns!
    Go to the keeper of the fold,
    the fold of the wild herdsman, the Cyclops.

(*To a ewe*)
    Release your swollen udders! Let the lambs you left behind
    in these pens come and get at your teats! Listen to the bleating
    of your little lambs: asleep all day, now they're missing you.
    When will you leave the grassy meadows of Etna's crags   60
    and enter† the abode with its double doorways?†

    There's no Bromius here,
    no dances, no Bacchic revels
    with thyrsus* held aloft, no beating drums,

no drops of green wine* by gushing springs.
Nor along with nymphs on Nysa*
can I sing the song 'Iacchus, Iacchus!'   70
to Aphrodite* whom wing-swift I hunted
with my companions, pale-footed Bacchants.
Bacchus, my friend, my dear friend,
where are you wandering without us,†
tossing your golden-yellow locks,
while I, your servant, attend to one-eyed Cyclops,
an exiled slave, dressed in this poor cloak   80
of goat-skin and lacking your friendship?

SILENUS. Hush, children! Get the attendants to take the flocks
and collect them inside the rocky cave!
CHORUS (*to the attendants*). Off you go, then! (*To* SILENUS) But
why the urgency, father?
SILENUS. Off the beach I can see a Greek ship, and there are
men heading this way towards the cave—masters of the oar,
accompanied by a high-ranking military chap. They're carrying empty containers slung around their shoulders for the
food they need, and flasks for water. Unhappy visitors! Who
are they? They don't know what our master Polyphemus is   90
like, or what an inhospitable land they've come to, or that
their bad luck has led them to the cannibal jaws of the
Cyclops. But settle down now, so that we can find out from
where they have come to Sicilian Etna's crags.

Enter ODYSSEUS *and his men.*

ODYSSEUS. Strangers, could you tell me the whereabouts of a
stream where we could relieve our thirst? And is there anyone
here who might be prepared to sell some food to hungry
sailors? (*Aside*) But what's this? We seem to have come to
Dionysus-ville! I can see a bunch of satyrs by the cave here.   100
(*To* SILENUS) I address my words of greeting first to the oldest.
SILENUS. Hello, stranger.* Who are you, and where are you
from?
ODYSSEUS. I'm Odysseus from Ithaca. I'm the ruler of the
Cephallonians.*
SILENUS. I've heard the name—a sly, glib talker, the son of
Sisyphus.*

ODYSSEUS. That's me. But there's no need to be rude.

SILENUS. From where have you sailed here to Sicily?

ODYSSEUS. From Ilium—from the Trojan War.

SILENUS. What? Didn't you know the way back home?

ODYSSEUS. I was blown off course by storms and ended up here.

SILENUS. Oh, your luck's as bad as mine! 110

ODYSSEUS. You mean you too were driven here against your will?

SILENUS. Yes, while chasing pirates who had kidnapped Bromius.

ODYSSEUS. What is this place and who are its inhabitants?

SILENUS. This hill is Etna, the highest in Sicily.

ODYSSEUS. But where are the walls and fortifications of a township?

SILENUS. There are none. There are no human beings on these headlands, my friend.

ODYSSEUS. Who lives here then? Just wild animals?

SILENUS. Cyclopes, who live in caves, not houses.*

ODYSSEUS. Do they have allegiance to a ruler or is the place a democracy?

SILENUS. They live apart from one another. None of them has 120 allegiance to anyone for anything.

ODYSSEUS. Do they sow Demeter's* crops? What do they live on?

SILENUS. The milk and cheese and meat of sheep.

ODYSSEUS. Do they know of Bromius' drink, the juice of the vine?

SILENUS (*mournfully*). Not at all.* That's why there's no dancing in this place.

ODYSSEUS. Do they welcome visitors? Are they respectful of strangers?

SILENUS. They say that there is no meat sweeter than that of visitors.

ODYSSEUS. What? They enjoy killing and eating people?

SILENUS. There's no one who comes here who isn't slaughtered.

ODYSSEUS (*looking around fearfully*). Where is the actual Cyclops? Is he indoors?

SILENUS. He's away, hunting animals on Etna with his dogs. 130

ODYSSEUS. You know what to do, then, to help us escape from here.

SILENUS. No, I don't, Odysseus. But I'll do everything I can for
you.

ODYSSEUS. We have no bread. Sell us some.

SILENUS. I told you, there's nothing here except meat.

ODYSSEUS. Well, that too is a pleasant remedy for hunger.

SILENUS. There's also curdled cheese and cow's milk.

ODYSSEUS. Bring them out here. Trading needs daylight.

SILENUS. How much will you pay for them?

ODYSSEUS. I haven't got any money on me—but (*producing a
wineskin*) I have wine!

SILENUS. That's welcome news indeed! We haven't had any   140
wine for ages!

ODYSSEUS. Yes, Maron, the god's son, gave it to me.

SILENUS. Maron? The child I cradled in these very arms?*

ODYSSEUS. The son of Bacchus, to put it even more plainly.

SILENUS (*eyeing the flaccid wineskin doubtfully*). Is it on board
your ship or did you bring it with you?

ODYSSEUS. Here it is, inside this wineskin, as you can see, old
man.

SILENUS. There's not enough there even for a mouthful.

<ODYSSEUS. Yes, there is. You'd be surprised.

SILENUS. Are you talking about magic? Do you mean that it
produces . . . ?>†

ODYSSEUS. Yes, twice as much as whatever pours from the
wineskin.

SILENUS. This is the kind of spring I like; it sounds really
excellent.

ODYSSEUS. Shall I first give you a taste of undiluted wine?*

SILENUS. That would be right and proper. After all, a taste   150
invites a purchase.

ODYSSEUS (*producing cups*). Look, I brought cups too, not just a
wineskin.

SILENUS. Come on, splash some in. I want to remember what
it's like to drink.

ODYSSEUS (*pouring*). There you are.

SILENUS. Mmmm! What a delightful bouquet it has!

ODYSSEUS. You saw it, did you?*

SILENUS. No, of course not. I can smell it, though.

ODYSSEUS (*handing him the cup*). Here, have a taste. Then your
praise of it won't be mere talk.

SILENUS. Oooh, Bacchus is inviting me to dance! Yes, yes, YES!

ODYSSEUS. Did it gurgle nicely down your throat?

SILENUS. Yes, all the way to the tips of my toes.

ODYSSEUS (*sure now that he can make this offer safely*). We'll give   160
you money as well, of course.

SILENUS. Never mind the money—just keep pouring the wine!

ODYSSEUS. Well then, why don't you bring out cheeses or lamb?

SILENUS. I'll do that—and I don't really care what my master
might think! I'd go mad after downing a single cup: I'd sell the
flocks of all the Cyclopes and hurl myself into the sea from the
cliffs of Leucas,* if I could just get drunk and let my eyebrows
droop.* Anyone who doesn't enjoy drinking is mad: you can
get *this* (*gesturing to or with his phallus*) to stand up straight,
you can grab a handful of breast, and be ready† to 'stroke the   170
meadow'.* There's dancing too, and all your worries fade into
oblivion. So why shouldn't I embrace a drink that can do all
this, and tell that stupid Cyclops with his one eye in the
middle to get lost.

Exit SILENUS into the cave.

CHORUS. Listen, Odysseus. Can we have a word with you?

ODYSSEUS. Of course. Friends can approach friends, and you're
friends of mine.

CHORUS. Did you Greeks capture Troy and take Helen prisoner?

ODYSSEUS. Yes, and we sacked the entire house of Priam's
children.

CHORUS. And after you'd captured the young woman, didn't
you all take turns to bonk her, since she enjoys having more   180
than one sexual partner? The traitress! All it took was the
sight of the pretty colours of the trousers on his legs and
the golden necklace he wore around his neck, and she was
swept off her feet, and abandoned that excellent little man,
Menelaus.* I wish there were no women anywhere—except
for my use.

Enter SILENUS from the cave.

SILENUS. Look, lord Odysseus! Here for you and your men are
flocks of lambs, the young of bleating sheep, and a generous   190
number of cheeses made from curds. Take them, and then
hurry away from the cave—once you've given me some wine,

(*he eulogizes*) that drink pressed from Bacchus' grape! (*Looking off landward*) Oh, no! Here comes the Cyclops! What shall we do?

ODYSSEUS. We've had it, then, old man! Where can we escape to?

SILENUS. You might not be noticed inside this cave here.

ODYSSEUS. A frightening suggestion, that we should place our-selves inside the hunter's net.

SILENUS. You needn't worry: there are plenty of hiding-places there.

ODYSSEUS. No, I refuse. Troy would cry in pain if I were to run away from just one man, when often, shield on arm, I stood   200
up to a vast horde of Phrygians. (*Pompously*) No, if die I must, I shall die as befits a man of noble blood—or I shall live and preserve my former reputation.

Enter the CYCLOPS. *He carries a huge club.*

CYCLOPS. Hey, get a move on there! What's going on? Why this slacking and Bacchic dancing? There's no Dionysus here, no bronze rattles, no beating drums. How are my young lambs getting on in the cave? Are they running to the teats and already under their mothers' flanks? Are the reed baskets full of cheeses pressed from milk? Come on, give me an answer, or   210
this club of mine will soon make one of you cry! Look up at me, not at the ground!

CHORUS. All right! I have turned my gaze up to Zeus himself, and I can see the stars and Orion.*

CYCLOPS. Is my morning meal good and ready?

CHORUS. It's here. All it needs is a hungry gullet.

CYCLOPS. And are the mixing-bowls filled with milk?

CHORUS. Yes, you can gulp down a whole jar of milk if you want.

CYCLOPS. Is it sheep's milk or cow's milk, or both mixed together?

CHORUS. As you wish. Just don't gulp *me* down!

CYCLOPS. Of course not. I mean, you'd leap about deep in my   220
stomach and ruin me with your dancing. (*Spotting* ODYSSEUS *and his men*) But who are all those people by the cave? Have some pirates or brigands put in here? Here, before my eyes, are the lambs from my caves, tied together with plaited

rushes, a jumble of baskets of cheeses—and an old, bald man
with his forehead swollen from blows.*

SILENUS. Oh, poor me! What a fever I've got from being beaten
up!

CYCLOPS. Who's the culprit? Who pummelled your head, old
man?

SILENUS (*pointing*). It was *them*, Cyclops, because I was trying to   230
stop them stealing your stuff.

CYCLOPS (*ponderously*). Did they not know that I am a god and
the offspring of gods?*

SILENUS. I told them, but they set about stealing your property,
and then they started to eat the cheese,* though I tried to stop
them, and to bring your sheep out here. (*He mimes the following actions*) They said they would tie a three-cubit-long leash*
around your neck, rip out your guts right in front of your eye,
flay the skin right off your back with a whip, and then tie you
up and chuck you into the hold of their ship to sell you to
someone to dig rocks up or to throw into a mill.*   240

CYCLOPS. Really? (*To one of the attendants*) Quickly, go and
sharpen cleavers, put a big bundle of sticks on the hearth,
and light them. (*The attendant leaves*) As soon as they're
slaughtered, they'll fill my belly. First, they'll provide the car-
ver with a hot meal of grilled meat, and then the rest will be
boiled and softened up in the cauldron. I'm fed up with food
from the mountains. I've eaten enough lions and deer, and
had no human flesh for ages.

SILENUS. Yes, master, routine makes a change all the more   250
enjoyable. These are the first visitors to come to your cave for
a long time.

ODYSSEUS. Cyclops, you must also hear what we strangers have
to say now. We came up to your cave from our ship because
we wanted to buy food. (*Pointing to* SILENUS) He offered to sell
us the sheep in exchange for a mug of wine and he gave them
to us, because he'd had a drink. There was no compulsion
involved: he was quite prepared to give them to us, and we
were quite prepared to receive them. But everything he told
you was a pack of lies, made up when he was caught trying to   260
sell your belongings behind your back.

SILENUS. What, me? Damn you!

ODYSSEUS. I will be damned, if I am telling lies.

SILENUS. Cyclops, by your father Poseidon, by great Triton and Nereus, by Calypso and the Nereids,* by the sacred surge of the sea and by all the fishes therein, I swear, best little Cyclops in the whole wide world, sweet master of mine, that I was not trying to sell your things to the strangers. If I am lying, may these foul sons of mine, whom I love more than anyone, meet with foul death!

CHORUS. You can keep your curses for yourself! I myself saw 270 you selling the stuff to the visitors. And if I'm lying, may my father die! But don't wrong the visitors.

CYCLOPS (*to the CHORUS*). I don't believe you. I'd sooner believe Silenus here than Rhadamanthys,* and I rate his honesty higher. (*To ODYSSEUS*) But there are some questions I'd like to ask you. Where have you strangers sailed from? Where are you from originally? In what town were you brought up?

ODYSSEUS. We are Ithacans by birth, but we've sailed from Ilium, after sacking the city. Sea winds drove us off course to your land, Cyclops.

CYCLOPS. So you're the ones who went off to Troy, city on the 280 Scamander,* to avenge the abduction of that evil woman Helen, are you?

ODYSSEUS. We are. We endured that terrible struggle.

CYCLOPS. There's no honour in the fact that you sailed on the expedition against the land of the Phrygians for the sake of a single woman.

ODYSSEUS. It was a god's doing; you shouldn't hold any mortal man responsible for it. But, noble son of the sea-god, speaking as free men we implore you not to be so cruel as to kill those who have come to your cave as friends and in an act of impiety to make them food for your mouth. After all, it was 290 we, my lord, who allowed your father to keep safe the temples where he dwells in the recesses of Greece.* The harbour at holy Taenarum remains intact, as do the caves of Cape Malea, while the silver-laden cliffs of divine Athena's Sunium and the havens of Geraestus are safe.* In short, we kept Greece safe, an intolerable disgrace for the Phrygians.† And you are the beneficiary of all this too, since the cave you occupy here, under Mount Etna with its streams of fire, is on Greek soil.

If you don't like arguments, consider that it is customary practice for sea-worn sailors to be taken in when they come as 300

suppliants, to receive hospitality, and to be supplied with
clothing, rather than having their bodies fixed on to beef-spits
to fill your mouth and belly. Priam's land has bereaved Greece
enough—has drunk the blood of many casualties of war, and
robbed wives of their husbands and parents in their old age of
their children. If you roast and consume those who remain,
making a bitter meal of them, what is anyone to do? No, listen
to me, Cyclops: give up your ravening greed, choose piety and   310
respect rather than the opposite. For ill-gotten gains have
often in the past brought penalties afterwards.

SILENUS (*to the* CYCLOPS). I'd like to give you a word of advice:
don't pass over any of this man's flesh. If you eat his tongue,
Cyclops, you'll become clever and supremely eloquent.

CYCLOPS (*to* ODYSSEUS). The wise, little man, regard wealth as
their god, and everything else as hot air and pretty speech.
I'm not interested in the coastal headlands where my father
has his temples. Why did you bring them up as part of your
defence? Zeus' thunderbolt doesn't make *me* tremble, stran-   320
ger: as far as I am aware, Zeus' powers are no greater than
mine.* Nor am I worried about what Zeus might do in the
future—and I'll tell you why I'm not worried. When he sends
down rain from the sky, I have a watertight shelter in this
cave here; I make a meal of roast cow or some wild animal, lie
down and saturate my belly by drinking down an amphora of
milk, and then I beat my clothing with a noise to rival Zeus'
thunder.* And when the north wind brings snow down from
Thrace,* I wrap myself up in animal skins and light a fire, and   330
then the snow doesn't bother me. Willy-nilly, with no choice
in the matter, the earth produces grass on which my flocks
grow fat. I sacrifice them to no one except myself—not to the
gods, but to this belly of mine, the greatest of deities. Drinking
and eating with no thought for tomorrow—this is Zeus for
anyone with any sense—and not causing oneself the slightest
distress. As for those who complicate human life with customs and rules, I tell them to get lost. I shall never stop look-   340
ing after number one—and yes, that involves eating you. I
don't want anyone to think badly of me, so you'll get hospitality from me, but it will consist in fire, and salt† from my
father,* and a cooking-pot,* which will fit your shredded flesh
nicely once it's boiling. You and your men had better go

inside. I want you to stand around the altar of my domestic
deity and make up my feast!

The attendants start to herd ODYSSEUS *and his men towards the cave.*

ODYSSEUS. Alas! After escaping adversity in Troy and at sea,
I've landed now at the savage and harbourless heart of a
godless man. O Pallas, O divine lady, daughter of Zeus, help   350
me now! Here I face a trial greater than that of Ilium, and I'm
mired deep in danger. And you, Zeus the protector of visitors,
whose home is the gleaming stars of heaven, look down on
these events! If you do not, Zeus, you are wrongly considered
a god, when in fact you are worthless.

Exeunt CYCLOPS, SILENUS, ODYSSEUS, *and his men, into the cave.*

CHORUS (*sings*). Cyclops, let the lip of your broad throat gape
  open.
  Boiled, roasted, hot from the grill, the bodies of the visitors
  are ready for you to munch and crunch and carve into pieces
  as you recline in your thick-fleeced goat-skin.   360

  Don't, no, don't give me a share;
  fill the hull of your boat for yourself alone.
  Away with this house! Away
  with the sacrilegious sacrifice of victims
  which the Cyclops of Etna is celebrating,†
  enjoying his feast of visitors' flesh.

  Cruel Cyclops! Merciless is he who sacrifices strangers   370
  suppliant at the hearth of his home† and eats them boiled,
  and with tainted teeth rends and crunches their flesh,
  hot from the grill < . . . >†

Enter ODYSSEUS *circumspectly and on tiptoe, carrying the wineskin*
              and glancing back into the cave.

ODYSSEUS. O Zeus, what shall I say? I've seen terrible things
  happen inside the cave—the kind of unbelievable deeds you'd
  expect to find in stories, not in real life.
CHORUS. What is it, Odysseus? Has the godless Cyclops really
  feasted on your companions?
ODYSSEUS. Yes. He picked out and weighed in his hands the two
  who were the fleshiest and best nourished.   380

CHORUS. How horrible for you! How were you able to endure it?
ODYSSEUS. The first thing he did, once we were inside the rocky
    cave,† was heap onto the hearth great logs from a tall oak,
    heavy enough to need three carts to carry them. After light-
    ing the fire, he put a bronze cooking-pot to boil on it. Then,
    close to the flames, he laid on the ground a bed of greenery
    from fir trees. After he had milked the cows, he filled a ten-
    amphora bowl with the white milk, and put next to it a cup of   390
    ivy-wood three cubits in diameter and what looked like four
    deep,* and spits made of buckthorn branches, with their ends
    seared by fire and planed smooth along the rest of their
    length. When the hellish cook, loathed by the gods, had
    everything ready, he snatched up two of my companions. He
    calmly cut the throat of the first with the blade of an axe and
    let the blood drain into the bowl of the bronze cauldron, a
    sacrificial vessel worthy of Etna.†* As for the second, he   400
    grabbed him by the tendon at the end of the foot, swung him
    against the sharp edge of a boulder in the cave, and dashed
    his brains out. Then he butchered† them with a vicious knife,
    roasted their flesh on the fire, and threw their limbs into the
    pot for cooking. With tears streaming from my eyes in misery,
    I acted as the Cyclops' servant by his side. The rest of my men
    stayed, cowering like birds, in recesses of the cave, with
    bloodless complexions.
        When he had eaten his fill of the flesh of my companions,
    he relaxed, let rip with a loud belch from his throat—and I   410
    had an inspired thought. I filled his cup with this wine here,
    that Maron* gave me, and served it to him to drink. 'Cyclops,'
    I said, 'son of the sea-god, what do you think of this heavenly
    drink, Dionysus' delight, which the Greeks gather from the
    vine?' Sated with his horrendous meal, he took the cup and
    drank it right down in a single gulp. He raised his hand in
    admiration and said, 'Thank you very much indeed, stranger,
    for the excellent drink you've given me to round off my excel-
    lent meal.' When I saw how much he had enjoyed it, I gave   420
    him another cup, my idea being that the wine would make
    him the worse for wear, and that he would soon get his come-
    uppance. Then he got around to singing. I kept pouring him
    one cup after another and warming his insides with drink.
    The cave resounded with his tuneless singing, accompanied

by the wailing of my shipmates. I sneaked quietly out here, and I intend to save both you and me, if you'd like. So tell me whether or not you want to get away from this brute of a man, and live in Bacchus' halls with the Naiad nymphs.* 430 Your father approved my plan indoors, but the fact is that he is weak and since he's been happily indulging in drink the cup has snared him as thoroughly as bird-lime snares a bird,* and he's in a flap, like the bird's wings.* But you're in your prime. Why don't you save yourself with me and get back your dear old master Dionysus, who's quite different from the Cyclops?

CHORUS. My very dear friend, how I long to see just such a day—a day when I am out of the clutches of the foul Cyclops! For too long now <this beloved siphon of mine (*gesturing with his erect phallus*) has had no partner—nowhere to take 440 refuge.>†

ODYSSEUS. So listen to the punishment* I have in mind for the evil creature, and how you can escape from slavery.

CHORUS. Tell me! I'd rather hear news of the Cyclops' death than the sound of the Asiatic lyre.

ODYSSEUS. Now that he's discovered the pleasures of Bacchus' drink, he wants to go to his brother Cyclopes for a party.

CHORUS. I see. You plan to ambush him when he's all alone in the woods and cut his throat or push him over the cliffs.

ODYSSEUS. No, nothing like that. I have a *subtle* plan.

CHORUS. What is it, then? I've known for ages of your 450 reputation for cleverness.

ODYSSEUS. First, I plan to keep him from this party by telling him that he shouldn't give this drink to the other Cyclopes, but keep it for himself and have a good time. Next, once he's fallen asleep under the influence of Bacchus, there's a branch of olive-wood in the cave, and when I've sharped its tip with this sword of mine, I'll put it in the fire. (*Miming*) Then, when I see that the branch has been seared, I'll pick it up, glowing hot, stick it right into the middle of the Cyclops' eye, and melt the eye with the fire. You know how a shipbuilder spins his 460 auger back and forth with a belt?* That's how I shall turn the brand in the Cyclops' eye—truly the bearer of light!*—and burn out his eyeball.

CHORUS. Oh, how happy, how deliriously happy your inventiveness makes me!

ODYSSEUS. And then, once I've got you, your friends, and the
old man on board my dark ship, my oarsmen, ranged in pairs,
will carry us away from this place.

CHORUS. Could I help blind him? Could I take hold of the brand
too, as people do when a libation is being poured to a god?* I'd   470
love to play a part in this job.

ODYSSEUS. Yes, you must. It's a big brand, and I'll need your
help to manoeuvre it.

CHORUS. I'd lift the weight of a hundred carts if it would help us
to smoke out that cursed Cyclops' eye like a wasps' nest.

ODYSSEUS. Quiet, now. You know the plan. When I give the
signal, do as the architect* says. I don't want to abandon my
friends inside the cave and save just myself.†

CHORUS (*sings*). Come, who will go first,
    and who will be second in line
    to grasp the brand like an oar,
    drive it into the Cyclops' eye,
    and destroy his bright sight?

        Cacophonous singing is heard from within the cave.†

Hush now! Hush! Look!
Drunk and making a foul noise
in a vain attempt to sing,
he is leaving his rocky home,
graceless, out of tune—   490
and due for punishment.
Come, let's educate this dunce
with songs of revelry.
But whether we succeed or fail
he is going to end up blind.

Enter the CYCLOPS, *with* SILENUS. *The* CYCLOPS *carries a cup,* SILENUS
a mixing-bowl.

Happy the man who raises
the Bacchic cry, with welcome streams
of wine filling his sails
and carrying him off to the revel!
His arms around a friend,
and waiting for him in bed

a tender mistress in the bloom 500
of her youth, his hair shiny
and anointed with myrrh,† he sings:
'Who will open the door for me?'*

CYCLOPS (*sings drunkenly*). Oh my, oh my! I'm full of wine,
and full of good cheer too,
happy from my feasting!
I'm as loaded as the hull
of a cargo-ship, all the way
up to the deck that tops my belly.
The joyous freight moves me
to revel in the springtime,
to visit my brother Cyclopes.
Come on, my friend, come on! 510
Hand the wineskin over here!

CHORUS (*sings*). With the lovelight in his eyes
he emerges lovely from his halls.
CYCLOPS (*sings*). <But, oh!> Who loves me?†
CHORUS (*sings*). Lamps await your eye, flesh
your flesh, a slender bride,†
within the cool of your cave.
Soon multicoloured garlands
will consort with your head.

ODYSSEUS. Listen to me, Cyclops, since I hang out with this 520
Bacchus I gave you to drink.
CYCLOPS. Who's Bacchus? Is he a god, with worship and all?
ODYSSEUS. There's no god greater when it comes to life's
pleasures.
CYCLOPS (*belching*). Well, I certainly find it pleasant to belch him
up.
ODYSSEUS. That's typical of him. He does us only good.
CYCLOPS. But how can a god be happy with a wineskin as a
home?
ODYSSEUS. He's perfectly content wherever you put him.
CYCLOPS. Gods really shouldn't clothe their bodies in skins.*
ODYSSEUS. Why not, if it makes you happy? Do you dislike the
wineskin?
CYCLOPS. I hate the wineskin—but I love this drink!

ODYSSEUS. So stay here! Drink and be merry, Cyclops!   530

CYCLOPS. Shouldn't I let my brothers have some of this drink as well?

ODYSSEUS. There's more prestige in keeping it for yourself.

CYCLOPS. But there's more benefit in sharing it with friends.

ODYSSEUS. Boozy parties tend to lead to fist-fights and insult-laden arguments.

CYCLOPS. I may be drunk, but no one will lay a finger on me!

ODYSSEUS. Good sir, it's best to stay at home when you've been drinking.

CYCLOPS. It's a stupid man who refuses to mix drinking and partying.

He makes as if to leave, but ODYSSEUS restrains him.

ODYSSEUS. But it's a wise man who stays home when he's drunk.

CYCLOPS. What shall we do, Silenus? Do you think we should stay?

SILENUS. Yes. I mean, why would you want to share the drink   540
with others, Cyclops?

ODYSSEUS. And look how velvety-soft the ground is with meadow grass.

SILENUS. Yes, and it's so nice to have a drink in the warmth of the sun. Please! Lie down here and rest on the ground.

CYCLOPS (*lying down*). There we are! (*SILENUS puts the mixing-bowl behind the CYCLOPS' back and starts to get himself a drink from it*) Why are you putting the mixing-bowl behind me?

SILENUS. In case someone knocks it over as they pass by.

CYCLOPS. No, you want to drink some on the sly. Put it down where I can see it. And as for you, stranger, tell me your name: what should I call you?

ODYSSEUS. Nobody.* What will you do for me to earn my thanks?

CYCLOPS. I'll leave eating you till after I've finished all your   550
companions.*

SILENUS. What a generous gift you're giving the stranger, Cyclops!

In the process of drawing another cup of wine for the CYCLOPS, he takes a swig.

CYCLOPS. Hey, what are you up to? Are you sneaking a drink of wine?

SILENUS. No, the wine kissed me because I'm so handsome.

CYCLOPS. You'll suffer, because your love for the wine is not reciprocated.

SILENUS. No, I certainly won't. He tells me he loves me for my good looks.

CYCLOPS. Just pour it, and give me the cup only when it's full.

SILENUS. Is it properly mixed? Let me have a look.

He pokes his head right inside the mixing-bowl, where he can lap it up.

CYCLOPS. You'll be the death of me. Give me some immediately.

SILENUS. Definitely not—or at any rate not until I've seen you wearing a garland (*he gives him one*) . . . and I've had a sip as well. (*He takes a quick gulp*)

CYCLOPS. This wine-waiter's dishonest. 560

SILENUS. True indeed†—but the wine is sweet. You'd better wipe your mouth so that you can take a drink.

CYCLOPS (*wiping his mouth*). There. My lips and beard are clean.

SILENUS. So take a drink, once you've crooked your elbow delicately. See how I take a drink—except you can't see me any more. (*He buries himself in the mixing-bowl again*)

CYCLOPS. Hey, what are you doing?

SILENUS (*emerging*). That was a nice long swig.

CYCLOPS (*to ODYSSEUS*). Stranger, take over the job of wine-waiter yourself.

ODYSSEUS. Well, at least the vine and my hand are acquainted . . .

CYCLOPS. All right, then: pour me some.

ODYSSEUS. I am. Just be quiet.

CYCLOPS. That's hard for someone who's drunk a lot.

ODYSSEUS (*giving him the cup*). Here you are. Take it, and drink it 570 all up. A heavy drinker and his cup should come to an end together.*

CYCLOPS. Oh, how much skill there is in the wood of the vine!*

ODYSSEUS. And if you have plenty to drink after a heavy meal, you'll saturate your belly until it has no need of drink and the wine will put you to sleep. But if you leave any in the cup, Bacchus will leave you thirsty.

The CYCLOPS drains the cup.

CYCLOPS. Aaah! I only just managed to swim out of there.
What undiluted pleasure! I seem to see the sky merge with
the earth and all in motion. I see the throne of Zeus and the   580
whole sacred glory of the gods. Shall I embrace them? The
Graces are flirting with me.* Enough! This Ganymede here*
will bring me better relief than the Graces. Somehow I find
boyfriends more enjoyable than women.

SILENUS. Cyclops, no! How can I be Zeus' Ganymede? (*He
endeavours to look his ugliest*)

CYCLOPS. You certainly are—and I'm abducting you from Troy.
(*He grabs hold of him*)

SILENUS. I've had it, children! Horrible suffering is in store for
me!

CYCLOPS. Are you finding fault with your lover? Do you spurn
him for being drunk?

SILENUS. Oh, no! I'll soon see just how bitter wine can be!
                                   The CYCLOPS drags SILENUS into the cave.

ODYSSEUS. Come now, sons of Dionysus, noble children! The   590
man is inside and soon, sprawled out in sleep, he'll be vomit-
ing the meat from his foul throat. Inside his home a smoking†
brand is ready and waiting, and there's nothing left to do but
sear the Cyclops' eye. Now is the time for each of you to show
that you are a real man!

CHORUS. We will have spirits of stone and adamant! But go
inside before my father suffers a fate worse than death! You
can count on us to be ready.

ODYSSEUS. Hephaestus, lord of Etna,* burn the bright eye of
your evil neighbour and be rid of him once and for all! And   600
you, Sleep, child of dark Night, descend undiluted on this
beast, loathed by the gods! After the sheer nobility of his
labours at Troy, don't let Odysseus and his men perish at the
hands of a man who cares nothing for gods or men. If you do,
we shall have no choice but to regard Fortune as a god, and
the gods and their deeds as subject to Fortune.
                                   Exit ODYSSEUS into the cave.

CHORUS (*sings*). Fiercely will the clamp fasten on the neck
of the eater of guests. For soon he will lose   610

his light-bearing eye to the fire! Already
the brand, vast limb of a tree, is buried
ember-red in the ashes. Come, Maron,*
to your work! Gouge out the eye of the mad one,
the Cyclops! That will teach him to drink!
As for me, I want to behold Bromius,   620
my beloved, who adores to wear ivy,
and to leave the Cyclops' solitude behind.
Shall I ever attain so much happiness?

Enter ODYSSEUS.

ODYSSEUS. Quiet, you animals, for the gods' sake! Settle down
and shut your traps! Don't even breathe or blink or clear your
throats! Let sleeping dogs lie, until the Cyclops' eye has met its
match in the fire.

CHORUS (*whispering*). We are quiet. No air can escape our
mouths.

ODYSSEUS. All right. Now you must go inside and take hold of   630
the brand. It's good and hot.

CHORUS. We're just waiting for your orders, to play our part in
events. Which of us should be first to take the red-hot stake
and burn out the Cyclops' eye?

SEMICHORUS A:* Well, I'm standing rather too far from the
entrance to push fire into his eye.

SEMICHORUS B. Yes, and I've just developed a limp.

SEMICHORUS A. Exactly the same thing has happened to me! I
don't know how, but as I was standing here I sprained my
ankle.

ODYSSEUS. You got a sprain from standing?   640

SEMICHORUS A. Yes, and my eyes are filled with dust and ashes
from somewhere.

ODYSSEUS. These allies of mine are no good, completely
worthless.

CHORUS. Just because I feel pity for my back and my spine, and
don't want to have my teeth knocked out, does that make me
'no good'? But I know a really good Orphic song,* which will
get the brand to move all by itself into his skull and incinerate
the one-eyed giant.

ODYSSEUS. I had you sussed a long time ago, but now I can see
what you're like even more clearly. I've got no choice: I'll   650

make use of my own friends. But physically feeble though you
are, at least offer us support. With your moral support, I
might raise courage in my friends.

Exit ODYSSEUS *into the cave.*

CHORUS. I'll do that, with others facing danger in my place.* In
so far as words of support can help, let the Cyclops go up in
flames!

(*Singing*) Ah, thrust bravely, lads, and quickly!
    Burn out the eye of the beast, the eater of guests!
    Yes, torch him, burn him, the shepherd of Etna!   660
    Twist and pull! Beware lest in his agony
    he does something savage.

Enter the CYCLOPS *with bloodied face. He stands just in front of the
entrance to the cave.*

CYCLOPS. Aaargh! The light of my eye has been blackened and
burnt!
CHORUS. I love to hear this paean!* Encore, Cyclops!
CYCLOPS. Oh, I have been ravaged and ruined! But there's no
way you'll get away with it, you scum, and escape from this
rock. I'll stand here in the mouth of the cave and fit my arms
to it.

He does so, moving his hands up and down to cover the gaps.

CHORUS. What are you yelling for, Cyclops?
CYCLOPS. It's all over for me!
CHORUS. Well, you certainly look ugly.   670
CYCLOPS. And desolate too.
CHORUS. Did you fall drunk into the middle of the fire?
CYCLOPS. Nobody brought about my ruin.*
CHORUS. Then no one has done you wrong.
CYCLOPS. Nobody has blinded me!
CHORUS. Then you're not blind.
CYCLOPS. What do you mean? Just look!†
CHORUS. How could nobody make you blind?
CYCLOPS. You're mocking me. Where's Nobody?
CHORUS. Nobody's nowhere, Cyclops.
CYCLOPS. I'll make things plain for you. It's the stranger who

has brought about my downfall, the bastard! He flooded me with the drink he gave me.

CHORUS. Yes, wine is a formidable opponent, hard to overcome.

CYCLOPS. Please tell me whether they've escaped or are still inside.

CHORUS. They're standing quietly under the eaves of the cave. 680

CYCLOPS. On which side?

CHORUS. To your right.

The CYCLOPS moves to his right, allowing ODYSSEUS and his men to slip out to the left.

CYCLOPS. Where?

CHORUS. Right by the rock-face. Have you found them?

The CYCLOPS bangs his head on the low entrance to the cave.

CYCLOPS. No, but I've found further misery. I've banged my head and cut it open.

CHORUS. Yes, and they're escaping.

CYCLOPS (*still fumbling around*). Didn't you say they were here or hereabouts?

CHORUS (*standing on the other side of the entrance*). No, I mean here.

CYCLOPS. Where?

CHORUS. Turn around and come this way, to the left.

CYCLOPS. Oh, no, you're making fun of me. You're taking advantage of my misfortune to taunt me.

CHORUS. All right, I'll stop now. He's standing in front of you.

CYCLOPS. Where are you, then, you villain?

ODYSSEUS. Far enough away from you to protect myself. I 690 intend to keep Odysseus from physical harm.

CYCLOPS. What do you mean? What's this new name you've come up with?

ODYSSEUS. It's the name my father gave me: Odysseus. You've just been punished for your unholy meal. If I hadn't punished you for murdering my comrades, our burning of Troy would have been pointless.†

CYCLOPS. Alas! An ancient oracle is coming true, which said that I would lose my sight at your hands after you had set out from Troy. But it also foretold that in return you would pay the penalty of drifting about on the sea for a long time.* 700

ODYSSEUS. Screw you, I say—and I've already done what I say!
   Now I'm going to go to the shore and launch my ship home-
   ward on the Sicilian Sea.

                              Exit ODYSSEUS and his men.

CYCLOPS. No, you won't. I'll break a rock off this cliff and
   throw it and smash you and your men to pieces! I may be
   blind, but I'm going up to climb through this tunnel here* up
   to the top of the hill.

                              Exit CYCLOPS into the cave.

CHORUS. And we shall sail with Odysseus on his ship, and look
   forward to a future with Bacchus as our master.

                              Exit the CHORUS.

EXPLANATORY NOTES

ALCESTIS

1–6   *Dear palace . . . Zeus' fire*: Zeus, king of the gods and father of the Sun-god Apollo, had killed Apollo's son Asclepius, the great physician, because he had restored the dead to life. Thereupon, Apollo had killed the Cyclopes, the one-eyed giants who manufactured Zeus' thunderbolts (5–6). As Apollo tells us, his punishment for this was to serve Admetus as a hired labourer. This servitude carried with it the status of an outcast, and thus Admetus' hospitality to him was impressive.

8   *host*: the Greek word for 'host' appears for the first time. It means 'guest' as well since the roles are obverse sides of the same relationship. Hospitality will prove to be a key concept in this play. See n. at 559–60.

11–12   *I tricked the Fates and saved him from death*: we are not told why or when it was decided that Admetus must die. According to Aeschylus (*Eumenides* 723), Apollo tricked the Fates by getting them drunk (cf. 33–4).

13   *Hades*: god of the underworld.

22–3   *In order to avoid the taint of pollution in the house*: Apollo and his sister Artemis (cf. *Hippolytus* 1437–8) avoid the pollution of death.

30   *Phoebus*: another name for Apollo.

37   *Pelias' daughter*: Alcestis' father was Pelias, king of Iolcus.

38–63   *Don't worry . . . everything you shouldn't*: this passage is in stichomythia, a dramatic device much favoured by Greek dramatists, in which the characters address each other in single lines. It proves very effective in confrontational scenes such as this. I shall not draw attention to subsequent uses of this device in this play.

40   *this bow and these arrows*: Apollo is regularly portrayed in Greek art with these accoutrements. Perhaps the most famous example is the Apollo Belvedere in the Vatican where he is shown stepping forward to see whether his arrow has hit its mark. His appearance with his bow and arrows at the play's outset will have immediately established his identity.

62   *hated by mortals and loathed by the gods*: Euripides' Death is

evidently not a full-fledged god, rather a figure from folklore; the Greeks would have referred to him as a demon.

65   *Pheres' palace*: Admetus' father Pheres has, like Laertes, the father of Odysseus, on Ithaca (in Homer's *Odyssey*), and Cadmus, the grandfather of Pentheus, at Thebes (in Euripides, *Bacchae* 43–4), handed over the reins of power to the younger man.

66–7   *from the wintry regions of Thrace*: the eighth labour of Heracles, set him by Eurystheus, the king of Tiryns, at the goddess Hera's bidding, was to obtain the man-eating mares of Diomedes, king of Thrace.

70   *gratitude*: the reciprocity involved in gratitude will be (like hospitality) a concept woven into the fabric of the *Alcestis*.

75–6   *For anyone . . . the gods of the underworld*: Death refers to the sacrificial consecration of the victim by the cutting of a few hairs from the brow.

92   *Paean*: the Semichorus here, and again at 220, call upon Apollo the god of healing (among other things).

99–103   *Look, there's no spring water . . . grieving for the dead*: the lustral water would be placed in front of the door so that departing visitors could purify themselves. Locks of hair were customary tributes to the dead. Since the head and the hair signified strength and life, the cutting of the latter symbolized submissive grief. And the cut human hair replicated safely the shorn hair offered from the animal about to be killed.

114–15   *to Lycia . . . the waterless seat of Ammon*: Apollo had an oracle at Patara in Lycia (south-west Turkey), and Zeus had one at the oasis of Ammon (Siwa) in the north-east of the Libyan desert (hence 'waterless'). The point being made here is that no oracle can help Alcestis.

124   *the son of Phoebus*: Asclepius: see n. at 1–6.

159–60   *she washed her pale skin*: as Socrates washed before drinking the hemlock (Plato, *Phaedo* 116b).

160   *their homes of cedar*: cedar oil and even its scent were known for their preservative power (Pliny, *Natural History* 16.76)—hence the suitability of this wood for boxes in which to store fabrics.

162   *Hestia*: the goddess of the hearth.

164–5   *I implore you to look after my children when I am gone*: a Greek audience would have understood the urgent need of the dying wife to safeguard her children against a future stepmother.

172   *myrtle*: this plant had funerary associations for the Greeks.

181   *Some other woman will possess you in my place*: she will change her mind about this, later demanding of Admetus that he does not marry again (305 ff.).

228   *This demands . . . in a noose hung on high*: two favoured Greek ways of suicide were to fall on one's sword (e.g. Ajax) and to hang oneself (e.g. Phaedra, Jocasta).

248   *Iolcus*: Iolcus, about 10 miles east of Pherae, was where Alcestis had grown up: see n. at 82.

254   *Charon*: this mythical figure ferried the dead over the river Acheron (see n. at 443) to the underworld.

305   *a stepmother for these children*: see notes at 164–5 and 181. The stereotype of the evil stepmother is not restricted to ancient Greece.

346–7   *the Libyan pipes*: Libyan because from Libya (the north African coast in general) came the lotus, and the pipes were made from either the wood of the lotus-tree or the stalk of the smaller lotus.

357–9   *If I had the tongue . . . recover you from Hades*: Orpheus' wife Eurydice was bitten by a snake and went down to the underworld. The husband, an unsurpassed musician, followed her there and so charmed Demeter's daughter Persephone and her husband Hades, king and queen of the underworld, that they allowed her to go back with him, making this conditional on his not looking back at her as he guided her to the upper air. Orpheus failed to keep this condition and lost his wife for the second time. Virgil tells the story with unforgettable poignancy in the fourth book of his *Georgics*.

360   *Pluto's hound*: Pluto is another name for Hades. His hound was Cerberus, the terrifying three-headed watchdog of the underworld.

391   *s.d. sinks back and dies*: this is one of a very small number of times that a character dies on stage in a Greek tragedy.

424   *a paean, unaccompanied by any libation, to the god below*: a paean was a song of praise, usually accompanied by libations. Admetus speaks with bitter irony.

428–9   *Any of you . . . cut them short*: this was a mourning custom which was apparently common to all northern Greece and to Persia too.

443   *Lake Acheron*: one of the waterways of the underworld. *Achos*, from which the name is derived, is the Greek for 'sorrow'. See n. at 254.

446–7   *the seven-stringed shell of the hill-dwelling tortoise*: the god Hermes created the first lyre by stretching the strings over a tortoise shell.

We are told that the tortoise was 'hill-dwelling' because there were also water-tortoises.

448–51   *in Sparta . . . all night long*: i.e. at the midsummer festival of Apollo Carneius. The moon is 'aloft all night long' when it is at the full.

458   *Cocytus*: another river in the underworld. Its name derives from the Greek word for 'wail'.

463   *May the earth fall lightly on you, lady*: this poignant and familiar expression is here used for the first time in extant literature.

481   *I am carrying out a task for Eurystheus of Tiryns*: see n. at 66–7.

484   *Don't you know how he treats visitors*: a sinister variation on the hospitality theme.

485   *Bistonians*: a Thracian tribe, they lived near Lake Bistonis.

498   *Ares*: the god of war, he had very strong associations with Thrace.

501   *First there was Lycaon, then Cycnus*: two sons of Ares whom Heracles fought.

505   *Alcmene's son*: Heracles refers to himself. His mother was Alcmene and his fathers were the god Zeus and the mortal Amphitryon, both of whom impregnated Alcmene. She is an important character in *Children of Heracles*, also in this volume.

521   *She both is and is not alive*: as he prevaricates, Admetus is being truthful in so far as her body still exists (it has not been cremated yet) even though she is dead. He later (525, 527) argues to Heracles that, while she is alive, she cannot truly be spoken of as such since she is doomed to death. His prevarications are motivated by the desire of this most hospitable of men not to offend a guest-friend.

548   *to lay on plenty of food*: Admetus knows his Heracles. The great hero is presented as the archetypal glutton in comedy.

559–60   *whenever I pay a visit to thirsty Argos, I myself find him the best of hosts*: Heracles lives on the east side of the Argive plain. It was dry terrain compared with the western part. The adjective is adapted from Homer's description of Argos (*Iliad* 4.171).

The Greeks used a single word for 'guest', 'host', 'stranger', and 'foreigner', subsuming all these identities under the important concept of hospitality (*xenia*). See notes at 1–6, 8, and 484. Admetus has attracted a great deal of criticism in this play, but he espouses this key Greek value with total (some may say excessive (565–6)) commitment and would surely have won admiration for this from a Greek audience. Here it is made very clear that he has a good guest-friend relationship with Heracles.

570   *Pythian Apollo of the sweet-sounding lyre*: Apollo is described as
      Pythian because he slew the Python who occupied the gorge of
      Delphi and, when he took over the sacred spot, he absorbed the
      monster's powers. Among his other spheres of influence, he was
      the god of music.

580   *Othrys*: Othrys is between 30 and 40 miles south of Pherae.

590   *Lake Boebeis*: a slim lake some 20 miles long. Pherae was near its
      southern shores. Mount Ossa towers above it to the north.

592–3 *in the region of the sun's dark stables*: i.e. in the west, where the
      chariot of the sun goes down into the ocean for the night.

593–4 *the Molossians*: they lived some 50 or 60 miles to the west in Epirus.

595   *Mount Pelion*: a rocky promontory to the east of Pherae. The
      Chorus refer to the rocky coast of Magnesia onto which the east
      wind drove Xerxes' fleet in 480 BCE (Herodotus 8.188).

662–4 *you had better produce other sons . . . lay out your corpse*: Admetus
      rejects the fundamental obligations of a son to his father.

684   *not a Greek tradition either*: i.e. the tradition is not confined to
      Pherae; it extends to the whole of Greece.

687   *plethra*: a plethron is a Greek measure of space, amounting to
      10,000 square feet.

703–4 *You should appreciate that everyone loves their life*: Pheres' attitude is
      very different from that of Socrates, who, according to Xenophon
      and Plato, refused to make a break from the prison where he was
      awaiting execution partly on the grounds that it was absurd for a
      70-year-old to try to escape death. Cf. 711.

713   *Then I hope you live to be older than even Zeus*: the reference to Zeus
      in this wish for a long life for his father, delivered by Admetus
      with bitter sarcasm, was clearly proverbial. Pheres takes it to be a
      curse (714): to be granted immortality without eternal youth
      leads to the fate of Tithonus, the beautiful youth endowed with
      immortality by the Dawn. When he became a repulsively withered
      old man, he was eventually metamorphosed into a cicada.

726   *A bad reputation won't bother me when I'm dead*: this sentiment
      would have disgusted a Greek audience.

732   *Acastus*: son of King Pelias (see n. at 37) and therefore brother of
      Alcestis.

743   *Hermes of the underworld*: one of the functions of Hermes was to
      guide the souls of the dead to the underworld.

745   *Hades' bride*: Persephone, goddess of the underworld (cf. n. at
      357–9).

746   *s.d. Exit . . . CHORUS*: for a chorus to exit in the course of a play is remarkable; it only happens twice in Euripides, here and in *Helen* (at 385).

757   *undiluted wine*: the Greeks considered it barbarous to drink wine unmixed with water. They usually mixed at least two or three measures of water with one of wine. See n. at 548.

770–1   *by soothing her husband's anger*: the manservant's comment gives us a glimpse of an unattractive aspect of Admetus' character.

782–5   *All human beings . . . fortune's way*: the translation reflects the rhymes in Euripides' Greek. Since there is normally no rhyme in Greek verse, they are unlikely to have passed unnoticed. The actor playing Heracles can exploit them to stress the comic nature of the character's drunken philosophizing.

791   *Cypris*: the goddess of love, Aphrodite, who was born from the foam of the sea and came to land on Cyprus—hence Cypris.

835   *Larisa*: another Thessalian town, a considerable city in modern Greece.

839–40   *what sort of a son Alcmene of Tiryns . . . bore for Zeus*: see n. at 505.

847   *holding him tight in a rib-crushing grip*: he clearly cannot kill the deathless Death.

851   *Kore*: the name simply means 'the girl'. It is used of Persephone, the queen of the underworld.

915   *pine torches*: torches were traditionally carried in wedding processions.

963   *raced on high through the heavens*: the chorus are here talking about metaphysical speculations. The translator finds himself reminded of the *Rubáiyát* of Omar Khayyám: 'Myself when young did eagerly frequent Doctor and Saint, and heard great Argument about it and about: but evermore came out by the same Door as in I went.'

968–9   *Orphic hymns*: Orpheus (see n. at 357–9) founded a mystery religion which we call Orphism. One of its tenets was reincarnation, and thus it would be a good religion for someone searching for arguments against the necessity of death to investigate. Orpheus, of course, had come back safely from the underworld. In addition, Orphic hymns could be sung over an afflicted person simply as a means of purification.

970   *the Asclepiads*: the guild of priest-physicians who took their name from Asclepius, son of Apollo (see n. at 1–6).

980   *Chalybes*: they lived south of Trebizond (south of the Black Sea) in the hill country. The iron they produced was believed to be peculiarly hard.

1029   *the light events*: such as running and jumping.

1103   *But my victory is your victory too*: i.e. there is a sense in which your friend's victory is your own.

1118   *as if I were cutting off the Gorgon's head*: Medusa, the mortal Gorgon, was a monstrous woman with snakes for hair. Anyone who looked directly at her was turned to stone. In order to decapitate her, Perseus had to work out from her reflection in his shield where to strike with his sword. Like Admetus here, he averted his eyes.

1135   *May the gods withhold their resentment*: Heracles aims to avert any divine anger from the extreme good fortune of Admetus, who has now cheated death twice (cf. 223–5). The gods could show violent resentment at an excess of human happiness.

1143   *But why does my wife just stand there without saying anything*: at this stage of the development of Greek tragedy the freedom to use three actors was firmly established. It must, therefore, have been Euripides' decision to keep Alcestis silent. He thus denies us a conclusion of unalloyed (because mutually expressed) happiness, and this may strike some as disconcerting. But it is of course possible to be convinced by the reason that Heracles now (1144–6) gives for her silence.

1150   *the royal son of Sthenelus*: Eurystheus. See notes at 66–7 and 481.

1154   *the whole surrounding province*: in Euripides' day, Thessaly was theoretically divided into four areas, Thessaliotis, Pelasgiotis (in which was Pherae), Histiaeotis, and Phthiotis, each of them with a separate ruler. These areas may be what is referred to here.

1159–63 *Many are the guises . . . this affair turned out*: the 'stock' ending of four or, with a variation in the first line, five of Euripides' plays.

HERACLES

1–2   *Amphitryon of Argos, who shared his wife with Zeus*: Amphitryon was married to Alcmene. While he was absent, Zeus, the king of the gods, assumed Amphitryon's shape and made love to her. Heracles was the offspring of their union.

3   *Perseus*: the son of Zeus and Danae, he killed the Gorgon Medusa.

4–5   *the crop of Sown Men grew from the soil*: the Delphic oracle instructed Cadmus to found a city and to choose its site by following a heifer until it collapsed from exhaustion. This he did, and on the site he killed a dragon, the offspring of Ares and the god's ancient guardian of the place, with a marble rock. Athena gave him half of its teeth to sow—though Ares is said to have done the sowing at 252–3 of this play—and, when he did this, 'Sown Men' sprang from the ground. They then slaughtered each other. Only five survived, and together with Cadmus they built the citadel of Thebes.

8   *Creon, the son of Menoeceus*: Creon, the king of Thebes, had welcomed Amphitryon when he had arrived there as a suppliant after he had unintentionally killed Alcmene's father Electryon (16–17) in a dispute over cattle stolen by the Taphians. Later he gave his daughter Megara to Amphitryon's son Heracles as his wife (10–12).

15   *the city built by the Cyclopes*: this is Mycenae. Its walls are made up of such vast stones that it was considered that only the giant Cyclopes could have lifted them.

19   *Eurystheus*: this figure and not Heracles had become king of Tiryns and Mycenae only through the scheming of Hera, Zeus' wife, who resented Heracles with remorseless bitterness throughout his life, because he was her husband's son by another woman (20–1).

20   *he would clear the earth of its wild elements*: by performing his civilizing labours.

23   *through the entrance at Taenarum*: one of the entrances to the underworld, of which Hades was king, was a cave in Cape Taenarum in the southern Peloponnese.

24   *the triple-bodied hound*: Cerberus, the watchdog of the underworld. He is usually represented as having three heads, not three bodies as here.

27–30   *Lycus, the husband of Dirce . . . the land's rulers*: the first Lycus had seized power in Thebes, but was eventually deposed by Amphion and Zethus (whose epithet 'white-horsed' has simply been taken over from Castor and Polydeuces). According to the Greek travel-writer Pausanias, the ruins of Lycus' palace were on show in Thebes (9.16.7).

31–2   *Lycus' son (also called Lycus) . . . came from Euboea*: this Lycus seems to have been invented by Euripides. He is said to come from Euboea, an island off the east coast of Greece, because that was the place of origin of the first Lycus. The name means wolf and this is extremely apt for the character of the Lycus of this play.

50   *the Minyans*: from Orchomenus in northern Boeotia, the main rival of Thebes.

51–3　　*We keep to our places here . . . we have no bedding*: for a note on
the significance of sanctuary in the Greek world, see *Children of
Heracles*, n. at 60.

53–4　　*the doors of the house have been sealed against us*: they have been
locked out of their own home.

55–6　　*I see now . . . unable to help us*: the pervasive theme of friendship is
here launched.

60　　　*you destroyed the city of the Taphians*: Amphitryon had gone
against the Taphians to avenge their killing of the brothers of his
wife Alcmene.

90–4　　*Do you need any more pain . . . a hideous torment*: stichomythia, a
device much loved by the Greek dramatists whereby the speakers
address each other in single lines. I shall not draw attention to
this effect later in the play.

104　　　*Everything separates from everything else*: this is the language of
speculation about the physical nature of the universe which was
rife in Euripides' day.

110　　　*like the white-plumed bird*: i.e. the swan, which sang before its
death (hence 'swan-song') and is thus an apt comparison for the
old Chorus, whose white hair lends them another likeness to the
swan.

152–3　　*killing a marsh snake or even the Nemean beast . . . with his bare
hands*: Lycus pours scorn on two of Heracles' labours, reducing
the monstrous Hydra to a mere water snake and suggesting that
Heracles used a snare rather than his bare hands to trap the
Nemean lion. Contrast 419–24 and 359–63.

160–1　　*He carried a bow, a weapon of extreme cowardice*: Lycus' criticism of
the great hero is clearly absurd. However, it is true that, in
Homer's *Iliad*, the bow is the coward's weapon, though it is the
ultimate heroic weapon in the *Odyssey*.

174　　　*the unspeakable charge*: there is a legal colour to this expression. In
ancient Athens an 'unspeakable charge', such as of parricide or
throwing away one's shield in battle, could be grounds for a
prosecution.

177　　　*I hereby call to witness the thunderbolt of Zeus*: Amphitryon invokes
Zeus, the king of the gods and wielder of the dread thunderbolt as
well as the father of Heracles. He refers to Zeus' thunderbolt,
since that is a weapon fired from a distance, just like Heracles'
bow.

178–9　　*planted his flighted missiles into the bodies of the earth-born Giants*:
the Earth-goddess gave birth to the Giants to take vengeance on

the gods for her sons the Titans whom Zeus had imprisoned in Tartarus. When they attacked heaven, the gods were assisted by Heracles, who took his stand on Zeus' chariot and shot his arrows from a distance. The Giants were finished off.

182   *those four-legged molesters, the Centaurs*: these mythical creatures were half man and half horse. When Heracles was being entertained by Pholus, one of the Centaurs, the opening by the hero of a jar of wine led to a fight in which Heracles triumphed.

185   *Dirphys, home of the Abantes, the place where you grew up*: Dirphys is a mountain in Euboea where Homer tells us the Abantes lived (*Iliad* 2.536). Lycus is represented as coming from Euboea (see n. at 31–2).

192   *the cowardice of his neighbours causes his death*: the safety of the heavy-armed soldier depends on a close formation being maintained. Half his body is covered by the shield of the man on his right.

220   *the Minyans*: see n. at 50. After defeating the Minyans, Heracles had forced them to pay a double tribute to Thebes.

233   *those golden locks of his*: young people in Greek tragedy regularly have blond hair.

234   *beyond the bounds of Atlas*: Atlas is a great mountain in northwest Africa. The pillars of Atlas were at the straits of Gibraltar and were the limit of the inhabited world.

240   *Helicon . . . Parnassus*: Helicon, incidentally the home of some of the Muses, is a mountain near Thebes. Mount Parnassus is somewhat further away, in Phocis.

252–3   *Offspring of the earth . . . the dragon of its teeth*: the Chorus of antique Thebans here address themselves. See n. at 4–5.

297   *Did any of the dead ever come back from Hades*: Megara believes that her husband is dead.

311   *No one can ever unordain that which is ordained*: Barlow writes (n. at 275–311) of Megara's 'painfully laboured and wordy' speech that the effect of such rhetorical commonplaces is 'to make it seem as if Megara is making supreme efforts to convince herself of her argument by referring to general principles while knowing that really all she feels is despair which no words can make more bearable'.

339–47 *Zeus, it turns out . . . no justice in you*: this passionate and devastating onslaught on Zeus raises questions which are fundamental to this play.

348–51   *Beside a song . . . golden plectrum*: Phoebus Apollo is the god of
           music, often represented in Greek art with a lyre.

353–4   *whether I should call him son of Zeus or scion of Amphitryon*: Zeus
           was the biological father of Heracles but the play raises the ques-
           tion of whether the god or Amphitryon should be regarded as the
           true parent.

359–63   *First he cleared . . . over his back*: Heracles' first labour was the
           killing of the Nemean lion. Subsequently he wore the head and
           skin of the animal on his head and over his back. This, together
           with his club (471, 942, 993) and his bow, became iconic, making
           him immediately identifiable in artistic representations.

364–74   *Then the wild hill-dwellers . . . Homole*: for Heracles' fight with the
           Centaurs, see n. at 182. Peneus is a river in Thessaly; Pelion and
           Homole are mountains there. The Centaurs tore up trees to use as
           weapons.

375–9   *Then, to the delight . . . the farmers' land*: the goddess of Oenoë is
           Artemis, who had a sanctuary at Mount Artemisium which over-
           looks the place. Euripides represents the golden hind which
           Heracles killed as a menace to farmers.

381–2   *the mares of Diomedes*: see n. at *Alcestis* 66–7.

386   *the silvery waters of the Hebrus*: the Hebrus was a river in Thrace
           where there were silver mines.

388   *the king of Mycenae*: i.e. Eurystheus: see n. at 19.

389–93   *On the coast near Pelion . . . the brutal inhabitant of Amphanae*:
           Mount Pelion, on which the river Anauros rises, and Amphanae
           are in north-east Greece (Magnesia). Cycnus chopped the heads
           off travellers on their way to Delphi and erected a temple from
           their skulls.

394–9   *Then to the maiden singers . . . wrapped tightly round*: Heracles went
           to the garden of the Hesperides, the 'maiden singers', on the
           north-west coast of Africa, to take some apples from it. He had to
           kill the dragon which guarded the fruit.

400–2   *Then he entered . . . the oars of mortal men*: civilizing the sea is not
           generally included among the labours of Heracles. Euripides (cf.
           225) clearly wishes to make the hero's influence even greater
           than it is in the traditional accounts.

403–7   *Then to Atlas' halls . . . with his strength*: Heracles stood in for
           Atlas, a giant who was also the mountain range in north Africa,
           giving him a break from his task of holding up the sky.

410   *across the inhospitable surge of the sea*: i.e. to the area near the
           Black Sea, where lay Maeotis (409), now the sea of Azov.

416–17   *the warrior maid*: Hippolyta, queen of the Amazons, a tribe of
          warlike women. Heracles dedicated her girdle at Hera's shrine in
          Mycenae.

419–21   *Then with fire he destroyed ... Lerna*: the Hydra was a many-
          headed water monster. Every time Heracles cut off a head, two
          would grow in its place. He killed it by cauterizing the wounds
          with fire before the new heads could grow. Its venom was poison-
          ous and Heracles anointed his arrows with it. Lerna is near
          Argos, to the south of the city.

423–4   *the triple-bodied herdsman of Erytheia*: i.e. Geryon who lived at
          Erytheia near or at Cadiz in south-west Spain. Heracles had to
          bring his cattle to Eurystheus.

432   *Charon's oar-blade*: see n. at *Alcestis* 254.

464   *Pelasgia*: another name for Argos.

473   *Oechalia*: Eurytus, king of Oechalia, promised his daughter Iole to
          whoever beat him at archery. Heracles did so, and, when Eurytus
          refused to honour his pledge, he sacked Oechalia, killed Eurytus
          and his sons, and captured Iole.

481   *demons for brides*: the goddesses of death.

482   *the only water I shall bear for you in my misery will be tears*: in
          Athenian marriages both bride and bridegroom would have a
          lustral bath arranged by their mothers.

521–2   *He is just as much your saviour as Zeus the Saviour*: at this joyous
          moment, Megara takes a positive view of Zeus. Cf. n. at 339–47.

538   *Apollo*: the invocation to Apollo shows that Heracles is expressing
          himself colloquially here.

547   *for Creon's death*: see 31–3.

572–3   *Ismenus ... Dirce*: the two local rivers.

581–2   *not do all I can to keep death from my own children*: there is a telling
          ambiguity here in view of what happens later in the play. The
          Greek could mean: 'not do all I can to encompass my children's
          death'.

585–6   *It is typical of you ... to loathe your enemies*: to support your
          friends and harm your enemies was what was expected of a
          Greek. The irony here is that Heracles is later to destroy those
          whom he loves the most.

596   *But in fact I saw a bird on an inauspicious perch*: this explanation of
          why Heracles in fact entered the city unnoticed has not struck
          editors as convincing. It seems 'almost added as an afterthought'
          (Barlow, n. *ad loc.*). It will, of course, prove an omen of what *does*
          befall him after he has entered.

599   *Hestia*: the goddess of the hearth. It was customary to pray to her
        first of the gods on arrival.

608   *Kore*: the name means 'the maiden'. It is used of Persephone, wife
        of Hades and therefore queen of the underworld.

613   *since I had witnessed the rites of the Mysteries I was lucky*: Apol-
        lodorus *(Library* 2.5.12) and Diodorus Siculus tell us (4.25.1) that
        in preparation for his journey to the underworld Heracles was
        initiated into the Eleusinian mysteries, in which Persephone was
        worshipped.

615   *It's being kept in the grove of Demeter Chthonia in the town of
        Hermion*: Demeter Chthonia was the mother of Persephone; the
        town of Hermion was situated at the southern end of the Argolid
        peninsula. According to Pausanias (2.35.3 ff.), there was a ravine
        behind Demeter's temple here from which Heracles was said to
        have brought up Cerberus from the underworld—cf. n. at 23.

619   *I brought Theseus back from Hades, father, and that took time*:
        Theseus, king of Athens, and his friend Pirithous went down to
        the underworld to abduct Persephone, whom the latter wished to
        marry. They both found themselves fixed to their seats by Hades.
        Heracles managed to rescue Theseus but not Pirithous.

639   *the crags of Etna*: is Euripides thinking of the Giant Typhon lying
        crushed beneath the weight of the Sicilian volcano after his con-
        flict with Zeus?

673   *the Graces*: the three Graces, Euphrosyne (joy), Thalia (bloom),
        and Aglaia (brightness), symbolize happiness and beauty in life.

678–9   *I may be an aged singer, but still I shall celebrate Memory*: he may be
        old but he is not senile. He has not forgotten. Moreover, Memory
        was the Muses' mother.

682   *Bromius*: another name for Dionysus, the wine-god, it means 'the
        roarer'.

687–9   *At the gates of the temple . . . the blessed son of Leto*: Delos, an island
        in the middle of the Aegean, was sacred to Apollo. Here Leto had
        borne him and his sister Artemis.

770   *Acheron*: a river of the underworld.

781   *Ismenus*: a river of Thebes.

782   *hewn*: in his edition (Oxford, 1981), Godfrey Bond sums up the
        general puzzlement over this word: 'Thebes is a muddy place, and
        even now the lanes connecting houses in Greece are rough; they
        certainly were not paved or polished in Euripides' time. Paley and
        others regarded the epithet as transferred from the houses which
        bordered the streets. Wilamowitz thought it was transferred to

Thebes from Athens, where there would have been rocky paths worn smooth by traffic.'

784–5   *Dirce . . . Asopus*: local rivers.

790   *O wooded crags of the Pythian god*: Apollo killed the Python, the dragon who protected the wooded gorge at Delphi. He took on its powers and its name (the Pythian god).

791   *the Muses of Helicon*: see n. at 240.

798–801 *O twofold liaison . . . Perseus*: see notes at 1–2 and 3.

808   *Pluto*: another name for Hades, king of the underworld.

814   *s.d.*: this is the only appearance of two gods *ex machina* (on the crane) in the middle of a surviving Greek tragedy. This will have added a strong emphasis to this horrific episode.

820   *O lord Paean*: the name of Apollo in his function as the Healer, a suitable deity to call upon in a time of violent dislocation.

853   *sacrilegious men*: such as Cycnus (see n. at 389–93) and Diomedes (see 382).

858   *I call on the Sun-god to witness that what I do here I do with reluctance*: when the goddess of madness makes this invocation, it shows the brutal malevolence of Hera and Iris in an appallingly chilling light.

870   *Tartarus*: the deepest region in the Greek cosmos, as far beneath the underworld as heaven is distant from earth.

876   *your city-flower*: i.e. 'your national pride and joy'.

883   *Gorgon daughter of Night*: the Gorgon had snakes for hair and her gaze turned men to stone.

890   *Bromius with his thyrsus*: the thyrsus was the wand of fennel, crowned with ivy held in place by a pine cone, which was held by Dionysus (Bromius—see n. at 682) and his worshippers. The god of wine and ecstatic liberation, who was born in Thebes where this play is located, would find what is happening to Heracles and his family particularly distasteful.

907–8   *as you once did in the case of Enceladus*: Pallas Athena, goddess of reason, comes—presumably invisible to the audience—to throw a boulder at Heracles to stop his madness (1004). In the fight with the Giants, she had thrown the island of Sicily on top of Enceladus. In Greek art, she is constantly represented as giving support to Heracles.

911   *I shall summon no diviner other than myself*: i.e. I've already worked that out for myself.

924 *thrown his corpse out of this house here*: he has been thrown to the dogs, as Heracles had promised (567–8).

926–7 *The ritual basket had already been passed around the altar*: in the preliminaries to a sacrifice the basket containing barley (to be scattered over the victim) and the knife were carried round the altar.

945 *well laid with the help of red chalk-line*: the chalk-line (a mason's line to mark where to cut the stone) is red since white chalk cannot be seen on stone.

954 *the city of Nisus*: Nisus was king of Nisaea, a city on the Isthmus of Corinth and thus on the way from Thebes to Argos, where Eurystheus was king.

958 *the Isthmus*: the isthmus of Corinth was the site of the Isthmian games. Hence Heracles' wrestling (959–60).

966 *driven you out of your wits*: the word used here refers literally to the ecstasy of Bacchic worship. This perversion of a life-enhancing madness is embedded in the play's imagery. Cf. 879, 890, 892–3, 897, 1085, 1119, 1142.

986–7 *knees . . . chin . . . neck*: an appeal was strengthened by contact with the knees (in the hope of not being kicked away) and chin (in the hope of averting unrelenting words). The process was called supplication and it was invested with considerable power in the ancient Greek world.

1018 *the daughters of Danaus*: forty-nine of the fifty daughters of Danaus killed their husbands, the sons of Aegyptus, on their wedding night. They were condemned to fill leaking water pots in the underworld for all eternity. (Hypermestra was the one who spared her husband because he had spared her virginity.)

1021–2 *I could speak of Procne's murder of her only child, sacrificed to the Muses*: Procne's husband Tereus fell in love with her sister Philomela, raped her, and cut out her tongue so that she could not betray him, but she communicated what had happened to her sister by embroidering it on a piece of material. In revenge Procne killed Itylus, her son by Tereus. The story of Procne's subsequent transformation into a nightingale is told at *Odyssey* 19.518–23: 'You know how Pandareus' daughter, the tawny nightingale, perched in the dense foliage of the trees, makes her sweet music when the spring is young, and with many turns and trills pours out her full-throated song in sorrow for Itylus her beloved son' (trans. E. V. Rieu). Itylus is described as 'sacrificed to the Muses' because he was the subject of Procne's song. Philomela was metamorphosed into a swallow, Tereus into a hoopoe.

1030   *s.d. ekkyklēma*: a wheeled platform which was rolled out from the
        doors of the stage building. It was used to display a tableau of
        what had happened in the house.

1042   *Quiet, old men of Thebes, quiet*: this moving scene, in which a
        protective figure pleads with the Chorus to keep quiet, is a proto-
        type for the scene in *Orestes* (140 ff.) when Electra tries to stop the
        Chorus from waking the mad Orestes.

1052   *spilled on the ground and yet rising into the air*: 'Blood when shed
        normally falls on the thirsty earth and demands more blood. But
        the horror of Heracles' murder is expressed by a special impossi-
        bility: the blood, having been shed, rises up' (Bond, n. *ad loc.*).

1076   *have yet more kindred blood on his already accursed hands*: Heracles
        has already incurred the wrath of the Erinyes by killing his wife
        and children; this wrath will be further heightened if he kills his
        father.

1077–80 *You should have died earlier . . . the murder of your wife's brothers*:
        see n. at 60.

1103–4 *Sisyphus' rock or Pluto and his queen, the daughter of Demeter*: as a
        punishment for his evil dealing on earth, Sisyphus was con-
        demned to push a stone up a hill for all eternity in the under-
        world. Pluto's queen is Persephone.

1127   *O Zeus, from your seat on Hera's throne*: 'The picture of Zeus as
        sharing his rule with his queen, who is enthroned beside him,
        well expresses the essentially compromising effect of Hera on
        Zeus' status as supreme god' (A. N. Michelini, *Euripides and the
        Tragic Tradition* (Madison, 1987), 270).

1154   *relative*: for Thesus' kinship to Heracles, see *Children of Heracles*
        207–12.

1157–8 *Am I to take to the air on wings or sink beneath the earth*: such un-
        real expressions of the longing to escape are characteristic of
        Euripides' characters as they cry out *de profundis*, but one certainly
        does not expect them from Heracles.

1178   *the olive-bearing hill*: the Acropolis at Athens on which Athena's
        sacred olive tree grew in a porch of the Erechtheum. A supposed
        descendant of this tree still stands in the same place.

1188   *with arrows dipped in the blood of the hundred-headed Hydra*: see n.
        at 419–21.

1190–2 *Once he went to the plain of Phlegra . . . the Giants*: see n. at 178–9.

1229   *this conflict*: the word looks back with bitter irony to his glorious
        labours.

1232   *You are a mortal man; you cannot pollute things that are divine*:

Theseus here goes against the traditional Greek view of pollution. He speaks in the rationalistic spirit of the Athens of the late fifth century.

1258–9   *my father here killed my mother's old father*: see n. at 8.

1266–8   *Zeus' wife tried to kill me by introducing savage snakes into my swaddling clothes*: the infant Heracles succeeded in strangling them.

1272   *Typhons*: see n. at 639. Typhon is not usually described as three-bodied: that distinction belongs to Geryon (see n. at 423–4). According to Hesiod, Typhon had a hundred heads.

1284   *The curse with which I am afflicted makes it impossible for people to talk to me*: Heracles has not yet accepted Theseus' assurance that he will not infect people with pollution.

1298–9   *Ixion, bound and tortured on his wheel*: the first mortal to shed kindred blood, he later (after he had been pardoned by Zeus) tried to rape Hera. His punishment was to be bound forever on a revolving wheel.

1303   *the glorious wife of Zeus*: Heracles refers, with biting sarcasm, to Hera.

1313   *that would be my advice*: some words have clearly fallen out of the text here. Supply something like 'If you were the only one concerned' before this clause.

1315   *if what the poets tell us is true*: these words anticipate Heracles' scepticism at 1346 ff.

1316   *Haven't the gods . . . had affairs with one another*: most famously Ares and Aphrodite (Homer, *Odyssey* 8.266 ff.).

1317–18   *Haven't they defiled their fathers with chains in order to gain kingship*: Zeus had dethroned his father Cronos and imprisoned him in Tartarus. He may have castrated him as well as bound him.

1323   *the citadel of Pallas*: Pallas Athena's citadel was the Acropolis at Athens.

1327   *when I killed the bull of Cnossus*: King Minos of Crete (the island whose major city was Cnossus) demanded a yearly tribute of seven young men and seven young women to be consumed by the monstrous Minotaur (half man, half bull) as a reprisal for the murder of his son. Theseus succeeded in killing this monster.

1329–31   *which will henceforth . . . alive*: they will be called Heracleia.

1332   *works of stone*: as in the sculptures on the Hephaesteum in the agora in Athens.

1346   *These are just the debased tales of poets*: in one sense, Heracles here 'deconstructs' himself since if the gods did not have illicit affairs

(1341–2), he himself could not exist. The key point, however, is surely that he is disowning the divine and committing himself totally to the world of men and its bonds of friendship—see n. at 266–7. The most famous ancient critic of the poets for such 'debased tales' was of course Plato, in *Republic* 2, 3, and 10.

1361   *since by law I am not allowed to do so*: because he must now be an exile from Thebes (1358).

1390   *Cut your hair*: see n. at *Alcestis* 99–103.

1407   *this love-charm*: a remedy for someone sick with love.

1424   *like a tender in tow*: a sad reminiscence of the happy family scene of 629–36. Cf. *Andromache* 200.

1425–6   *Anyone who would rather have wealth or strength than good men as friends is a fool*: a final statement of the friendship theme. See notes at 55–6 and 1346.

CHILDREN OF HERACLES

William Allan, the editor of a new edition of *Children of Heracles* (Aris and Phillips, Warminster, 2002), kindly gave the annotator a manuscript of this before it was published. These notes owe a considerable debt to Dr Allan's excellent work.

1   *s.d.*: since Heracles and his children were worshipped at many other Attic demes, why did Euripides locate his play at Marathon? 'According to Herodotus, the Athenians and Plataeans had camped in the sanctuary of Heracles at Marathon before defeating the Persians there in 490 (6.108.116). Shortly afterwards, to celebrate the victory and commemorate the hero's assistance, the *Heracleia* at Marathon were reorganized and expanded to become a pan-Attic festival . . . Thus, by making the Chorus old men of Marathon, Euripides connects two of the most glorious episodes in Athens' past, the defence of the [children of Heracles] and the battle of Marathon' (Allan, introduction 5).

           The temple is that of Zeus as presider over assemblies and trials and thus a symbol of Athenian democratic debate (L. R. Farnell, *The Cults of the Greek States* (Oxford, 1896), i. 58). So the suppliants are appealing to the people of Attica as practitioners of democracy.

8   *I was the one man who helped Heracles in a great many of his labours*: of Heracles' twelve canonical labours, Iolaus later (215 ff.) boasts that he helped Heracles fetch the girdle of the queen of the Amazons. He also remembers Heracles' sack of Sparta (740–1).

32   *the territory held in common between Marathon and its neighbours*: the so-called Attic Tetrapolis, consisting of the towns Oenoë, Marathon, Probalinthus and Tricorythus. However, as Allan (n. at 32) observes, 'Marathon and Athens cannot be distinguished from each other: the distance between them is blurred in the play.'

36   *Pandion*: an early king of Athens.

60   *We shall be protected by the god's altar*: contact with a holy place should have granted suppliants protection, and by trying to pull Iolaus away from the altar (67–8), the Herald is violating a fundamental Greek value. The original audience would have been appalled. The fact remains, however, that ancient history contains examples of such sanctuary being abused by both Spartans, the descendants of the children of Heracles, and Athenians. Herodotus (6.80), for example, tells how the Spartan king Cleomenes I (reigned *c.*520–490 BCE) used fire to burn several thousand Argive survivors to death in a sacred grove. (Though tried for impiety at Sparta, Cleomenes was acquitted.)

    If Iolaus and the children can be made to lose contact with Zeus' altar, they become vulnerable. In Athens in the mid-sixth century BCE, Cylon and his fellow conspirators took sanctuary in Athena's temple, and when they left it to stand trial they attached a braided thread to the image of the goddess and carried it with them, thus demonstrating their reliance on literal contact with the divine. The thread broke, and the archons (the city officials), claiming that this showed that Athena was refusing Cylon and his followers the rights of suppliants, slaughtered almost all of them. As a result the archons were called polluted men (Plutarch, *Solon* 12.1–2).

    Supplication is discussed in an important and illuminating article called 'Hiketeia' by John Gould (*JHS* 93 (1973), 74–103).

    There is the further point that the play was probably written in the first phase of the Peloponnesian war which Athens and her allies fought with Sparta and hers, and, as Gould notes ('Hiketeia', 74), these two cases of 'a breach of the rights of suppliants [one by Athenians, the other by Spartans] played a dominant role in the diplomatic propaganda of the Spartans and Athenians on the eve of the Peloponnesian War'. Neither side was guiltless of violating divine law and human decency.

69   *O inhabitants of Athens, dwellers here from time immemorial*: the Athenians claimed that their ancestor Erechtheus or Erichthonius had been born from the soil of Attica. Thus we have here 'an

appeal by the helpless fugitives to those who have never been forcibly dispossessed' (A. C. Pearson, n. *ad loc.*).

71   *suppliant wreaths*: suppliants carried branches wreathed with wool.

80–1   *this confederacy of four towns*: see n. at 32.

81–2   *or was the Euboean coast your point of departure*: the island of Euboea was about 15 miles east of Marathon.

86   *Mycenae*: in tragedy Mycenae and Argos tend not to be distinguished from each other.

131   *these are the actions of a savage*: see n. at 60.

139–42   *I am an Argive . . . pass our own binding judgements*: but, as Allan points out (n. *ad loc.*), 'there is no agreement between Argos and Athens governing the return of refugees. Such treaties were made between Greek states, though . . . actual examples of extradition are very rare.'

154   *What do you stand to profit*: the Herald's 'material preoccupations make a thorough cynic of him; he assumes that all the world is interested only in profit and so quite naturally he tries to bribe the judge' (A. P. Burnett).

162–3   *What lands of yours . . . war against Argos*: this is a reminiscence of Achilles' words in the *Iliad* (1.153–6) when he says that the Trojans have done him no personal harm by, for example, rustling his cattle or horses or ravaging his crops.

186   *we have been exiled from our native land*: Allan quotes Friis Johansen-Whittle (on Aeschylus, *Suppliant Women* 387–91): Iolaus argues that '*expulsion* from their city renders fugitives no longer liable to its jurisdiction'.

193–4   *This is not Trachis or some Achaean town*: Trachis is near the Malian Gulf in north-east Greece; the Argive town may be Achaea Phthiotis in Thessaly close to Trachis.

207–9   *Pittheus was the son of Pelops . . . Theseus was her son*: Pittheus was the king of Troezen in the north-east Peloponnese, the vast peninsula which makes up southern Greece and of course derives its name from his father Pelops.

216–17   *I once sailed with Theseus in pursuit of the girdle which was the cause of so many deaths*: Heracles' ninth labour was fetching the girdle of the queen of the Amazons Hippolyta for Eurystheus' daughter Admete. In revenge, the Amazons invaded Attica but were defeated.

218–19   *he fetched your father from the gloomy depths of Hades*: Theseus and his friend the Lapith Pirithous had gone to the underworld, of which Hades was king, to abduct Persephone, Hades' wife. When they failed, they were imprisoned, but Heracles rescued Theseus, though not Pirithous.

253–73   *Not even if my claim is just . . . Don't lay a finger on him, my lord*: this passage is in stichomythia, a dramatic device much favoured by Greek dramatists, in which the characters address each other in single lines. It proves very effective in confrontational scenes such as this. I shall not draw attention to subsequent uses of this device in this play.

270–1   *You'll regret it . . . Don't hit a herald*: a herald was supposedly inviolate and the Chorus are appalled at the idea that their king should attack one. However, in 430 when the play may have been performed the Athenians murdered captured Spartan ambassadors (Allan, n. at 271–3).

278   *Alcathous' land*: i.e. Megara, of which Alcathous was king. This country was on Attica's southern border.

280–1   *he will be here in no time to threaten you, your fellow citizens, the land itself, and its crops*: Eurystheus' proposed devastation of the Attic countryside 'recalls Spartan tactics in the early years of the Peloponnesian War. The aim of such invasions, which were a typical feature of Greek warfare, was the demoralizing and debilitating destruction of the enemy's agricultural infrastructure, including grain, olive trees, and vines. In largely agrarian societies like classical Greece, the devastation of crops would seriously undermine the enemy's ability to continue hostilities' (Allan, n. *ad loc.*).

297–8   *Children can have . . . lowly birth*: 'The contradiction between democratic ideals and the continuing respect for nobility produces frequent tragic discussions of the inheritability of virtue, but on balance the statements on nature versus nurture are surprisingly reactionary' (E. Hall in P. E. Easterling (ed.), *The Cambridge Companion to Greek Tragedy* (Cambridge, 1997), 99).

314–15   *Be sure, I beg you, never to raise a hostile force against this land*: ominous words in 430 BCE, if that was when the play was first performed, for the Spartans, the descendants of the children of Heracles, were to invade Attica that year.

352   *Pallas*: another name for Athena, the goddess of Athens, where she was worshipped under the title of Victory.

361   *Sthenelus*: the son of Perseus and father of Eurystheus.

408–9   *they tell me to sacrifice to the daughter of Demeter a maiden born of a noble father*: the daughter of Demeter, the Mother Goddess of the Earth, is Kore (the girl), whose name was Persephone, though she is never called by it in this play. Human as opposed to animal sacrifice would have struck the Greeks as shocking.

427–9   *we are like sailors . . . dry land*: nautical similes were much loved by the Greek tragic writers. This one surely gains in expressive power from the setting of the play at Marathon, which is on the sea.

458–60   *Wise men should pray . . . with a good measure of respect and justice*: 'Iolaus ends his speech with a general reflection. His preference for a "wise" enemy (i.e., one who treats his defeated opponents decently) is shockingly denied by Alcmene herself in the closing scene' (Allan, n. *ad loc.*).

474–7   *Strangers, don't think me brazen . . . are best*: we may be intended to think of Pericles' notorious words to the women of Athens in his celebrated funeral speech: 'Your great glory is not to be inferior to what God has made you, and the greatest glory of a woman is to be least talked about by men.' Though she breaks the stereotype by speaking her mind, the Maiden certainly shows a proper Attic awareness of the woman's role in these lines.

523–4   *After all, would any man . . . the mother of his children*: a woman's male guardian would arrange her marriage. Thus the loss of all the men in her family would destroy the Maiden's prospects of marriage and motherhood.

565–6   *Well, at least you could ask . . . as I breathe my last*: 'The Maiden's request is motivated primarily by sexual modesty: the body is exposed by sacrifice (cf. *Hecuba* 568–70) and vulnerable to violation after it. However, the major role of women in funeral rituals is also a factor: the female relatives of the dead were responsible for preparing the corpse for burial by washing and dressing it' (Allan, n. *ad loc.*).

588   *your duty to bury her*: the Maiden wants a proper burial in Argos.

639   *I'm one of Hyllus' serfs*: the word can simply mean 'labourer', but in a Thessalian context it means 'serf' and, since Hyllus was the mythical ancestor of the Dorians in that region, the latter seems the more appropriate translation.

673   *the sacrificial victims have been brought out clear from the ranks*: 'the victims are taken out far in front of the lines, as close to the enemy as possible, to urge on the troops' (*Heraclidae*, ed. J. Wilkins (Oxford, 1993), n. at 673).

680   *I'll come with you*: 'The sudden bellicosity of the old man who had so long been prostrate with distress . . . could not but appear as a glaring absurdity' (G. Zuntz, *The Political Plays of Euripides* (Manchester, 1955), 29). Allan (n. at 680–747) suggests that this

'encourages the audience to feel affection for Iolaus, while at the same time inviting them to share the servant's gentle irony and amused disbelief, only to reverse this reasonable attitude in the next episode and so magnify the impact of Iolaus' success'.

Allan also notes that this scene 'brings together two traditional comic figures—the old man and the cheeky slave—and thereby cues the audience for a potentially humorous interaction'.

694   *a hoplite*: the entry under 'hoplites' in the *Oxford Classical Diction-ary* begins: 'Greek heavy infantry. Equipment included bronze helmet of varying shape, corslet, originally of bronze . . . and bronze greaves; sometimes extras such as arm-guards. Most important was a circular shield of wood or stiffened leather, faced with bronze, about 30 inches in diameter . . . Offensive weapons were a thrusting spear, 9–10 feet long, with iron point and butt, and short iron swords, sometimes straight, sometimes curved.'

695–6   *There are weapons taken in war inside this temple here*: it was stand-ard Greek practice to dedicate weapons captured from the enemy—or one's own—in temples, suspending them from pegs on the walls (698). While the temple's god could get angry at the borrowing of his or her weapons, Zeus is unlikely to do so since he presides over supplication and the Argives, whom Iolaus is aiming to fight, have violated that.

729   *So I have to attend the hoplite as if he were a child, do I*: the Greek word used here meaning 'attend as if he were a child' refers to the slave who took the children to school. The ludicrousness of the situation is brought out by the fact that the child here is nomin-ally an adult warrior.

730   *We don't want any bad omens*: if Iolaus stumbled as he set out, that would augur ill.

741–2   *when with Heracles' help you sacked Sparta*: Heracles attacked Sparta to restore Tyndareus to the throne.

754   *grey-eyed Athena's halls*: grey-eyed is an epithet frequently applied to Athena in Homer.

766   *Zeus is on my side*: since he protects suppliants. See n. at 695–6.

770   *my lady*: Athena, protectress of Athens and Attica.

779   *the waning day of the month*: this was 28 Hecatombaeon (the name of an Attic month, late July and early August, when the proces-sion and sacrifices of the Panathenaea, the greatest of Attic festi-vals, took place). The night before there was an all-night torchlit festival when the goddess was celebrated by singing and dancing choirs of boys and girls (780–3). The windswept hill (781) is the Acropolis. Allan observes that 'the audience are reminded of

Athens' greatest celebration of civic harmony and power just as the Athenian army does battle off stage' (n. at 777–83).

786–7   *victory trophies are being set up bearing the arms and armour of your enemies*: the trophy was a wooden frame set up on the battlefield at the point where the enemy first turned (Greek *trop*). The frame was covered with a set of captured enemy armour.

789   *thanks to your news this day brings you your freedom*: 'the sole exception to the inescapability of birth status' in Greek tragedy (Hall, in Easterling (ed.), *The Cambridge Companion to Greek Tragedy*, 112). She suggests that such an offer would be construed negatively. But Allan observes (n. at 488–9) that 'gratitude was an acceptable reason for freeing a slave in fifth-century Athens' and adds, 'The effect of Alcmene's generosity here is to throw her later vindictiveness into even sharper relief.'

821–2   *the blood poured in a propitious stream from the necks of the oxen*: the manuscript reading means 'from the necks of humans', not 'from the necks of oxen'. It seems extremely unlikely that this is right. Helbig's reading makes the necks those of oxen, and is to be preferred. It follows logically on from 399–400 and 673.

823–4   *others joining side to side under the shelter of their shields*: another textual problem. The manuscript suggests that they overlapped with each other. Diggle's reading, translated here, simply means that they were close to one another, and this makes good sense since, as he says, 'the distinctive feature of the hoplite formation is the closeness of man to man'.

830–1   *the Tyrrhenian trumpet*: the Greek trumpet, used to give signals, not as a musical instrument, was considered the invention of Tyrrhenus, an Etruscan king.

849–50   *the hill sacred to Athena Pallenis*: 'Eurystheus is to be thought of as fleeing southwards from the Marathon region, rounding the southern edge of Mt Pentelicon and passing through Pallene, a deme approximately 8 miles east-north-east of Athens ... Eurystheus is finally caught at the Scironian rocks (859–60) close to the Isthmus. Quite a chase! The distance from Pallene to the Scironian rocks is roughly 40 miles' (Allan, n. *ad loc.*).

851   *Hebe*: an apt addressee of a prayer for rejuvenation since she was the goddess of youth. She had also married Heracles after he had died and been deified.

860   *the Scironian crags*: so named because there dwelt the robber Sciron whom Theseus had killed as one of his labours on the way from Troezen to Athens. See also n. at 849–50.

871–2   *And although previously I wasn't sure . . . now I know it for certain*:
         she gains this new confidence from the divine epiphany described
         at 854–7. Heracles' marriage to Hebe had given him everlasting
         youth and brought about his reconciliation with Hebe's mother
         Hera, who had dogged him with persistent malevolence through-
         out his life.

874–5   *that bastard Eurystheus*: the Greek uses a colloquialism (literally,
         'the *destroyed* Eurystheus') which Wilkins (n. at 874) says 'is
         unique to tragedy here and perhaps indicates a certain decline in
         Alcmene from the heroic principles of the daughter of Heracles
         and Iolaus, a decline that will continue'.

894–5   *Aphrodite*: the goddess of love.

910–14   *Old woman . . . the pyre's grim flames*: Sophocles' *Women of Trachis*
         looks forward to the cremation of Heracles on a funeral pyre on
         Mount Oeta without making it clear whether he will be deified.
         There are no doubts here.

917   *Hymenaeus*: god of marriage.

920   *helped their father*: mythology makes Athena the constant helper
         of Heracles, and this is strongly reflected in Greek art (e.g. in the
         metopes of the temple of Zeus at Olympia) and literature (e.g.
         Heracles 1002–4 in this volume; Homer, *Iliad* 8. 362–3).

950   *to kill hydras and lions*: the Lernaean hydra, a many-headed mon-
         ster, and the Nemean lion, two of Heracles' labours.

949   *You even had him go down alive to Hades*: to dognap Cerberus, the
         three-headed guard-dog of the underworld.

963–6   *What law is there . . . taken alive in battle*: Christopher Collard
         observes that 'Euripides brings out the repellent vindictiveness of
         Alcmene by showing her ride down the moral objection that she
         flouts the law (of Athens, where they now are), which forbids the
         execution of captives' (I. McAuslan and P. Walcot (eds.), *Greek
         Tragedy* (Oxford, 1993), 158–9).

990   *it was Hera who afflicted me with this illness*: he claims to be Hera's
         victim since she had made him the agent of her persecution of
         Heracles.

997–9   *I knew that your son . . . proper to a hero*: a handsome acknow-
         ledgement of his enemy's prowess. 'As often in Euripides, a clear-
         cut moral view of the characters is challenged by a surprising
         development in their portrayal . . . Here, there is a double sur-
         prise, as Alcmene emerges as less, and Eurystheus as more, sym-
         pathetic than we had been led to believe' (Allan, n. at 983–1017).

1021   *That would be best*: 'The Chorus-leader's reply is even more disturbing than Alcmene's question, for he immediately accepts her assurance that she will be obeying the city (1020) despite the fact that the city's [law] clearly forbids killing the prisoner . . . The audience see an Athenian Chorus comply with a vengeful murder, and Euripides uses their surprise to highlight the contrast between the optimistic ideals of Athenian justice and the harsher facts of political reality' (Allan, n. at 1021).

1028   *an ancient oracle of Loxias*: Loxias is a name for Apollo, god (among other things) of prophecy. This name—appropriately enough to his at times mystifying predictions—probably means 'ambiguous'.

1030   *where I was fated to lie*: i.e. the oracle has revealed what fate determined.

1031   *Athena Pallenis*: there was a temple of Athene at Pallene. See n. at 849–50.

1035   *invade in strength*: see n. at 314–15.

1050–1   *give his body to the dogs*: Alcmene's savagery knows no bounds, but the execution of this command would not necessarily preclude burial.

1054–5   *there is nothing here we have done that will pollute our king*: but how can they be sure? They have gone along with an act of illegal slaughter which will take place on Attic soil. The play ends on a profoundly disturbing note.

CYCLOPS

1   s.d. *SILENUS*: Silenus, the father of the satyrs, is old, fat, snub-nosed, and bald. He wears a loincloth with a non-erect phallus and a tail.

         Bromius: a name for Dionysus, the god of wine; it means 'the roarer'.

3–4   *you were driven mad by Hera . . . the mountain nymphs*: Hera's persecution of Dionysus was no doubt because he was the off-spring of one of her husband Zeus' numerous extramarital flings (with the Theban Semele). Dionysus left his nurses, the nymphs of Mount Nysa in Thrace, and wandered over a wide area accompanied by Silenus and the satyrs.

5   *the battle with the Giants*: the Earth-goddess gave birth to the Giants to take vengeance on the gods for her sons the Titans whom Zeus had imprisoned in Tartarus. When they attacked heaven, the gods totally defeated them, with Silenus' help, according to his own account here—a likely tale!

6   *protecting your right with my shield*: see n. at *Heracles* 192.

10–12   *When Hera stirred . . . got them to sell you abroad*: Dionysus chartered a ship from some Etruscan pirates who decided to sell him as a slave. The god eventually escaped by changing the sailors into dolphins.

19   *Cape Malea*: the most easterly of the three capes at the south of the Peloponnese, the great peninsula that constitutes southern Greece.

33   *this iron rake*: the joke lies in the fact that Silenus is using a farmyard implement rather than a broom to do the sweeping.

36   *s.d. CHORUS*: the Chorus consist of satyrs, who look like younger versions of their father (see n. at 1 *s.d.*). They are, of course, neither fat nor bald and their phalluses are erect. Here they sing the first surviving pastoral song of Greek literature.

39   *Althaea's house*: when staying with Oeneus, king of Calydon, Dionysus fell in love with his wife Althaea. Oeneus discreetly disappeared from the scene and was rewarded with the gift of the vine.

64   *thyrsus*: a fennel wand crowned with ivy held in place by a pine cone, the thyrsus was carried by the worshippers of Dionysus.

67   *green wine*: green because it possesses its own life and vigour (*Cyclops*, ed. R. Seaford (Oxford, 1984), n. *ad loc.*). In addition, as C. Collard assures the translator, some new wines are green ('vinho verde' both literally and metaphorically).

68   *Nysa*: see n. at 3–4.

69–70   *can I sing the song 'Iacchus, Iacchus!' to Aphrodite*: Iacchus is both another name for Bacchus (= Dionysus) and a shout in his honour. The satyrs would like to be singing to Aphrodite, the goddess of love, because they are notoriously lustful.

102–62   *Hello, stranger . . . cheeses or lamb*: stichomythia, a device much loved by the Greek dramatists whereby the characters address each other in single lines. I shall not draw attention to further examples of this in this play.

103   *I'm the ruler of the Cephallonians*: Cephallonia, the setting of Louis de Bernière's *Captain Corelli's Mandolin*, is an island near Ithaca, Odysseus' homeland.

104   *a sly, glib talker, the son of Sisyphus*: Odysseus, whose trickily inventive prowess is a wondrous source of strength in Homer's *Odyssey*, is generally portrayed highly unsympathetically in Greek tragedy. (His characterization in Sophocles' *Ajax* is the exception that proves the rule.) The tradition that makes him out to be the

son of Sisyphus (see n. at *Heracles* 1103–4) reveals him as the illegitimate offspring of his mother Anticleia (rather than her true son by Laertes). And the Homeric inventiveness has metamorphosed into malevolent scheming. Seaford (n. at 104) remarks that it must be 'disheartening and deflating for Odysseus to find that, epic hero though he is, his reputation for chatter and the unsavoury story of his parentage have preceded him to a faraway island, and that they should be well known even to Silenus'. This satyr play, however, proves to esteem his qualities highly.

118   *Cyclopes, who live in caves, not houses*: as in the *Odyssey* (9.112–15), the Cyclopes have no concept of a collective society. The Cyclops of this play may wish to party with his fellows (445–6, 507–9, 531, 533), but he certainly does not want to live with them. The suggestion in the next line that the place may be a democracy is comically grotesque.

121   *Demeter*: the goddess of corn.

123–4 *Do they know . . . Not at all*: in Homer's telling of the story, vines grow automatically (9.109). Euripides' variation here establishes a situation in which Cyclops can have had no experience of alcohol whatsoever. The rest of 124 asserts that there is no dancing (*chorus*) in this place, setting up polarities relevant to a play performed in the Theatre of Dionysus: if there is no wine, there is no dancing; if there is no Dionysus, there is no theatre; if there is no theatre, there is no dancing and no chorus.

141–2 *Yes, Maron . . . in these very arms*: when sacking the city of Ismarus, Odysseus protected Maron, the priest of Apollo, and his child and wife. Maron gave him some incredibly strong and fragrant wine in return (Homer, *Odyssey* 9.197–211). Dionysus, according to Euripides, was Maron's father and thus Maron was cradled in the arms of his leading attendant Silenus.

149   *a taste of undiluted wine*: it was not accepted practice among the Greeks to drink undiluted wine.

154   *You saw it, did you*: Odysseus picks up Silenus' word 'delightful', which he thinks of as a visual response. His robust common sense would fare ill amid the language used by today's encomiasts of wine.

166   *hurl myself into the sea from the cliffs of Leucas*: it was customary to throw a criminal from the cliffs off the promontory of the island of Leucas (in north-west Greece) at the festival of Apollo.

167   *let my eyebrows droop*: i.e. in a drunken sleep.

171   '*stroke the meadow*': Silenus refers to the female pubic hair.

185–6   *that excellent little man, Menelaus*: the Chorus are sympathetic, if somewhat patronizing, to the Spartan king whose wife ran off with a sexy Asian with exotic trousers and a golden necklace (182–4).

213   *I can see the stars and Orion*: it is unlikely that this means that is night. The jocular satyrs are simply pretending to mistake the Cyclops for Orion, a constellation that looks like a giant.

227   *swollen from blows*: or rather, flushed red from his drinking.

231   *Did they not know that I am a god and the offspring of gods*: in the *Odyssey*, Poseidon is the father of the Cyclops.

233   *they started to eat the cheese*: while the general tenor of the Cyclops story in the *Odyssey* sets a grossly inhospitable monster against the decently Hellenic Odysseus, the fact remains that even in Homer's story the hero snaffles and consumes some of the Cyclops' comestibles before being greeted by his host (*Odyssey* 9.231–3). Thus he traduces a basic tenet of Greek hospitality.

235   *a three-cubit-long leash*: a collar could be put on prisoners before punishment. 'But there is a specific insult here: Solon enacted that dangerous dogs should wear the "three-cubit collar" (Plutarch, *Solon* 24), presumably because a large collar enabled them to be held at a distance' (Seaford, n. at 235).

240   *throw into a mill*: the labour of dragging the mill wheel round was a punishment for slaves.

263–4   *by great Triton ... Nereids*: Triton was himself a son of Poseidon who blew on a shell horn to calm the waves. Nereus was the father of the fifty sea-nymphs, the Nereids, and Calypso was a sea-nymph who had detained Odysseus for seven years on her island of Ogygia and had tried to keep him there with the offer of immortality.

273   *Rhadamanthys*: because he had been so just on earth, Rhadamanthys was appointed a judge of the dead.

281   *Scamander*: one of the rivers of Troy.

290–1   *who allowed your father to keep safe the temples where he dwells in the recesses of Greece*: the idea is the somewhat hyperbolic one that if Odysseus and co. had not vanquished Troy, the Trojans would have sailed over to Greece to sack Poseidon's temples.

292–5   *The harbour ... are safe*: there was a temple of Poseidon at Taenarum, the southernmost point of Greece, a statue and cave of Poseidon at Malea (see n. at 18), and a great temple of Poseidon (graffitized by Lord Byron, among many others) at Sunium in Attica. Its harbour is only 500 yards away from the silver mines at

Laurium, and there was another temple to the god at Geraestus, a headland in the south of Euboea.

321   *as far as I am aware, Zeus' powers are no greater than mine*: out-and-out *hubris*. The Cyclops is not going to come well out of this play.

327–8   *I beat my clothing with a noise to rival Zeus' thunder*: the Cyclops is masturbating.

329   *the north wind brings snow down from Thrace*: snow from Thrace will hardly get as far as Sicily: the dramatist is simply aiming to convey the idea of extreme cold.

343   *salt from my father*: Poseidon, the Cyclops' father, was god of the salt sea.

        cooking pot: a grim twist on the fact that a cauldron was one of the gifts given in hospitality.

390–1   *a cup of ivy-wood . . . four deep*: this vast cup is an elaboration of the ivy-wood cup of *Odyssey* 9.346.

399   *the bronze cauldron, a sacrificial vessel worthy of Etna*: there are textual problems here. If the conjecture 'worthy of Etna' is right, the reference is to the mountain as a volcano, thus a potentially smoking cauldron.

412   *Maron*: the donor of the wine—see n. at 141–2.

430   *with the Naiad nymphs*: i.e. with the water-nymphs, symbolic of freedom.

433   *as bird-lime snares a bird*: one way of catching birds is to smear this glutinous substance on twigs; they will stick to it and be unable to fly away.

434   *like the bird's wings*: this may well be Greek slang for sexual arousal.

441   *punishment*: in the *Odyssey* the Greeks are shut in the cave by a stone that only the Cyclops can move. Thus the blinding of the Cyclops is an essential part of their getaway plan. In this play this is no longer the case. Odysseus is simply—and in Greek terms entirely reasonably—out for revenge.

460–1   *a shipbuilder . . . with a belt*: as at *Odyssey* 9.383–6, the simile sets the modern, mechanically minded Odysseus against the primitive Cyclops.

462   *the bearer of light*: the torch will insert a literally blinding light into the Cyclops' eye. The joke here lies in the fact that it's the eye that is described by these words.

469   *as people do when a libation is being poured to a god*: in a sacrifice, a libation of wine was made over the burning victim. Here the

Cyclops is the victim. The wine is already being poured but the sacrifice (the blinding) is still to come.

477   *the architect*: i.e. Odysseus. Again (cf. n. at 460–1) Odysseus is the inventive modern man pitted against the antediluvian Cyclops.

502   *'Who will open the door for me?'*: a line from a popular love song? In any event, it is the question of the reveller outside his beloved's locked door.

527   *Gods really shouldn't clothe their bodies in skins*: only the lowest orders dressed in animal skins (though in fact Dionysus did).

549   *Nobody*: now we coincide exactly with the famous *Odyssey* story (9.366).

550   *I'll leave eating you till after I've finished all your companions*: this too is taken directly from the *Odyssey* (9.550).

571   *A heavy drinker and his cup should come to an end together*: i.e. one should collapse from intoxication only when one has got to the bottom of the cup.

572   *Oh, how much skill there is in the wood of the vine*: the Cyclops probably means that the vine is very good at causing intoxication.

581   *The Graces are flirting with me*: the Graces were associated with Aphrodite, the goddess of love.

582   *This Ganymede here*: Ganymede was a beautiful Trojan boy who was snatched up to Mount Olympus by Zeus in the form of an eagle to be the cupbearer of the gods and his own catamite (the word is a corruption of the name).

599   *Hephaestus, lord of Etna*: Hephaestus was the blacksmith god, the god of fire. His forge was under Mount Etna in Sicily, the location of this play.

616   *Maron*: the donor of the wine—see n. at 141–2.

635   *SEMICHORUS A*: the Chorus of satyrs split into two as they display their shameful but not uncharacteristic cowardice.

646   *I know a really good Orphic song*: the great musician Orpheus could cause even inanimate objects to move.

654   *with others facing danger in my place*: more literally the Greek says, 'We'll let the Carian take our risks.' The Carians were famous mercenaries.

664   *this paean*: a paean could be song of victory or a plea for healing. Both are appropriate here.

672   *Nobody brought about my ruin*: Euripides is back with the *Odyssey* version of the tale (9.408). Cf. n. at 549.

700   *the penalty of drifting about in the sea for a long time*: Odysseus will
       in fact not reach his homeland of Ithaca for another nine years,
       as the *Odyssey* makes clear.

707   *this tunnel here*: for the first time we discover that the cave has a
       way out at the back.

TEXTUAL NOTES

ALCESTIS

16: This line is spurious and has been omitted; it restricts 'those who were close to him' to his mother and father.

94: Reading, with Willink: οὐ γὰρ δήπου φροῦδός γε δόμων νέκυς ἤδη.

102–3: Reading ὃ δὴ νεκύων πένθει πρέπει with Diggle and Blaydes.

106: Reading τί τόδ' αὐδάσεις; with Hermann.

115: Reading ἐφ' ἕδρας ἀνύδρους | Ἀμμωνιάδας with Nauck.

121: Reading μόνον with Hermann.

132–5: These lines are spurious and have been omitted; they repeat the substance of earlier portions of the ode.

153: Omitting the punctuation at the end of 152 and reading, with Hermann, χρηστὴν γενέσθαι τήνδ' ὑπερβεβλημένως;

207–8: These lines repeat earlier material and have been omitted.

215: Reading αἰαῖ· εἰσί τις; with Wilamowitz, and then ἦ with Zuntz.

218: Retaining δῆλα . . . δῆλα with the MSS.

223: Reading καὶ πάρος γάρ τι τῷδ' with Willink and Heath.

226: Some words, now irrecoverable, but perhaps further interjections, have dropped out of the text.

312: This line is spurious and has been omitted.

321: I suggest reading ἐς τρίτην μοι λαμπάδ'.

397: The text is uncertain.

402–3: Reading μᾶτερ, <μᾶτερ>, ὁ σὸς ποτὶ σοῖσι πίτνων καλοῦμαι στόμασιν νεοσσός with Willink.

411–12: A few words have dropped out of the text.

468: A line of text is missing.

593–4: Although the text is somewhat uncertain, and a word has dropped out, the general sense is clear.

651–2: These lines are spurious and have been omitted; they repeat 295–6 and interrupt the flow here.

818–19: These lines were recognized even in ancient times as spurious.

1094–5: These lines are spurious and have been omitted.

1119–20: These lines are spurious and have been omitted.

HERACLES

119: Reading μὴ πόδα πρόκαμνε with Diggle.

121–3: The text is very corrupt, and certainty is impossible, though the general sense is clear. I follow Willink (who was in turn following Hartung and Wecklein) in reading λέπας ζυγηφόρος πονῶν | ἄναντα βάρος ὄχου φέρων | τροχηλάτοιο πῶλος.

183: I prefer to punctuate with a comma at the end of this line.

219: I prefer to punctuate with a comma at the end of this line too.

226: Reading ὧν ἐμόχθησεν χερί with Triclinius and Diggle.

252–74: Editors are undecided whether these lines are all spoken by the single Chorus-leader, or (as I prefer) by a divided Chorus. My distribution of the lines is little more than a guess.

389: The MS Πηλιάδ᾽ seems preferable, in view of the probable location of Amphanae.

413–14: Reading πλέων χρυσεοστόλου φάρους with Murray and Schenkl.

446: Reading ὑπόσειρ᾽ ἁπαλοῖς ποσίν with Bond.

452: Omitting this line as an interpolation.

757–8: Reading οὐρανίων <ὃς> ἄφρονα μακάρων κατέβαλε λόγον ὡς with Diggle and Willink.

762: The Oxford Classical Text omits this line, which spoils the structural balance of this passage (clearer in the Greek than in English).

767: Reading <νέας> with Wilamowitz.

777: Arranging the words with Hermann to suit the metre.

806: Reading σάν, Ἡράκλεες, with Willink.

845: Reading τιμάς τ᾽ ἔχω τάσδ᾽ οὐκ ἀγασθεῖσας φίλοις.

859: line 860 is transposed by the Oxford Classical Text and most editors to immediately after 870.

862: Reading οἰστός with Wakefield.

870: Transposing 860 (see note on 859), retaining ἀνακαλῶν with L, and reading τάχος ἐπιρροιβδεῖν ὁμαρτεῖν θ᾽ with Kirchoff.

1003: There are a few words of garbled text, perhaps all that remains of a lacuna which originally continued the description of Athena, and explained how the house came to collapse.

1091: Omitting Reiske's added connective.

1142: Reading οἶκον ἀβάκχευσ᾽ ἐμόν with Bond.

1151: Reading τὴν πατρῷον with Allen.

1159: Reading <πέπλων> σκότον with Pflugk.

1211–12: Reading ὃς . . . ἐξάγει with Hartung.

1228: Reading τά γ᾽ ἐκ θεῶν with Headlam.

1241: I have filled the lacuna according to Kovacs's suggestion.

1288: Reading κηλιδούμενοι with Hermann.

1291–3: These lines have been omitted. They are interpolations.

1299–300: Further interpolations.

1304: Reading κρόουσ᾽ Ὀλύμπου λαμπρὸν ἀρβύλῃ πέδον with Diggle and Paley.

1313: A few lines from the beginning of Theseus' speech have been lost. In these lines Theseus presumably weighed up the advantages and disadvantages of Heracles' staying alive, and pointed out that life is always changeable.

1338–9: This sententious couplet has long been condemned, and is duly bracketed by the Oxford Classical Text.

1340: The missing word is most likely γάρ (Barnes).

1366: This line has been omitted as an interpolation.

1386–8: Omitting these lines as intrusions (see Bond's note).

1417: Reading πῶς νουθετεῖς δ' ἔμ' with Wecklein.

1420: Reading ἡνίκ' ἂν θάνῃς, γέρον with Bond, and then omitting 1421 with the Oxford Classical Text.

CHILDREN OF HERACLES

76: One line is missing from the text.

110: Five lines of text are missing.

140: Reading ἐλών with Kayser.

149: A line of Greek is probably missing (according to Diggle), but it would presumably have contained something like this.

169: The text is corrupt, and there may even (if Diggle is right) be a line missing, but this is the approximate sense required.

217: There is a lacuna of a couple of lines.

299–301: These lines are certainly spurious, and have been omitted.

311: The sense of the missing line has been supplied.

319: I retain this line.

396: Reading τοσόνδ' ὅροις with Willink.

405: The line is a corrupt and prosaic interpolation, and has been omitted.

529: Reading στεμματοῦσθαι . . . κατάρχεσθαι δοκεῖ with Broadhead.

558ff.: I translate these lines in the following order: 558, 559, 563, 560, 561, 562.

614: Reading τὸν δὲ πένητ' with Elmsley.

784–5: Reading σοί τε καλλίστους φέρω | κλύειν λέγειν τε τῷδε συντομωτάτους with Wecklein.

788–9: The text is corrupt, but the sense is certain.

793: Reading, without certainty, ὁ μὲν γέρων ἔτ' ἔστιν Ἰόλεως; λέγε with Diggle.

805: There is a lacuna of indeterminate length. Whatever else it contained, it might well have included the sentiments enclosed in brackets.

807: Reading ἀνδρῶν with Hartung.

838: Reading ἦν δ' ὁμοῦ κελεύματα with Murray.

884: Reading ἁλόντα with Heimsoeth.

892–3: Reading ἡδὺ καὶ λίγεια λωτοῦ χάρις ἀμφὶ δαῖτα with Bothe and Willink.

969: Reading ὁρᾶν τὸ φῶς ἔτι with Diggle.

999: Reading γ' ἔσθλ' <οἷ>α with Diggle.

1015: The text seems sound.

1052: There is a lacuna of indeterminate length. There are two important loose ends: the play needs to resolve the question whether Eurystheus' body is to be given to the dogs (1050) or properly buried; and Alcmene needs to persuade the Chorus to go along broadly with her wishes rather than those of Demophon, to whom they have previously been loyal. There are four fragments extant which are attributed to this play, but are not found in the text as it stands. (There is also one line in Aristophanes' *Knights* which is said to be a parody of a line from our play.) My own opinion is that the lacuna at this point of the play is not long, and that these fragments have been misattributed. But just in case one or two of these fragments belong here, or in an earlier lacuna (e.g. to do with the otherwise remarkably overlooked self-sacrifice of Heracles' daughter), or come from a different version of the play, I translate them here:

Fr. 852: Anyone who honours his parents during his lifetime is dear to the gods in both life and death. But I would not have anyone who refuses to honour them join me in sacrificing to the gods or launch a boat for a shared sea voyage.

Fr. 853: There are three virtues which you must cultivate, child: to respect the gods, your parents who brought you up, and the common customs of Greece. If you do so, you will be crowned for ever with the fairest of reputations.

Fr. 854: Although it is frightening to be a sacrificial victim, it brings glory. Not dying is not frightening, and there is pleasure in it.

Fr. 949: And to give parents the respect they are due.

CYCLOPS

60: Reading ἀμφίθυρον with Seaford.

62: Reading εἴσει with Seidler.

74: Reading οἰοπολῶν with Nauck.

146: The most plausible idea seems to be to posit a lacuna, which I fill roughly according to Kassel's suggestion.

170: Reading παρεσκευασμένον with Blaydes.

295–6: Reading τά θ' Ἑλλάδος, | δύσφορον ὄνειδος Φρυξίν, ἐξεσώσαμεν with Seaford.

343: Reading πῦρ καὶ πατρῷον ἅλα λέβητα τ' with Kovacs.

365: Reading ἃν ἀνάγει with Jackson.

370–1: Reading (after various editors' emendations) νηλής, τλᾶμον, ὅστε δωμάτων | ἐφεστίους ἱκτῆρας ἐκθύει ξένους.

374: A line is missing.

382: Reading στέγην with Musgrave.

395 ff.: The text is corrupt, lines are out of order, and one or two lines may have been lost; but the best sense is gained by reading Seaford's text: τὸν μὲν λέβητος ἐς κύτος χαλκήλατον, | σφαγεῖον Αἰτναῖόν γε, πελέκεως γνάθοις | ἔσφαζ᾽ ἑταίρων τῶν ἐμῶν, ῥυθμῷ τινι, | τὸν δ᾽ αὖ . . .

402: Reading διαρταμῶν with Paley.

439–40: The text is irredeemably corrupt, but enough survives of the original to guess at the approximate sense.

480–2: These three interpolated lines have been omitted from the translation; they merely repeat the substance of 479, and no editor deems them authentic.

487: There is an ancient stage direction to this effect in the transmitted text of the play. While almost certainly not written by Euripides himself, it is correct.

499–501: Reading ἐπὶ δεμνίοισί τ᾽ ἄνθος (Dindorf) . . . μυρόχριστον λιπαρὸς βόστρυχον (Musgrave).

513: No one can be certain about this line, but I think (with Diggle) it reads best as a plaintive cry from Polyphemus.

514–15: Reading λύχνα δ᾽ ἀμμένει σὸν ὄμμα | χρόα χρώς, τέρεινα νύμφα with Stinton.

560: Reading <ναί> with the Aldine edition.

593: Reading πνέων καπνόν with Diggle.

674: Reading πῶς; ἴδε σύ with Seaford.

694: Retaining κακῶς with L.

Bhagavad Gita

The Bible Authorized King James Version
   With Apocrypha

Dhammapada

Dharmasūtras

The Koran

The Pañcatantra

**The Sauptikaparvan (from the
   Mahabharata)**

**The Tale of Sinuhe and Other Ancient
   Egyptian Poems**

Upaniṣads

ANSELM OF CANTERBURY   **The Major Works**

THOMAS AQUINAS   **Selected Philosophical Writings**

AUGUSTINE   **The Confessions
On Christian Teaching**

BEDE   **The Ecclesiastical History**

HEMACANDRA   **The Lives of the Jain Elders**

KĀLIDĀSA   **The Recognition of Śakuntalā**

MANJHAN   **Madhumalati**

ŚĀNTIDEVA   **The Bodhicaryàvatàra**

The Oxford World's Classics Website

www.worldsclassics.co.uk

- Information about new titles
- Explore the full range of Oxford World's Classics
- Links to other literary sites and the main OUP webpage
- Imaginative competitions, with bookish prizes
- Peruse the Oxford World's Classics Magazine
- Articles by editors
- Extracts from Introductions
- A forum for discussion and feedback on the series
- Special information for teachers and lecturers

www.worldsclassics.co.uk

American Literature

British and Irish Literature

Children's Literature

Classics and Ancient Literature

Colonial Literature

Eastern Literature

European Literature

History

Medieval Literature

Oxford English Drama

Poetry

Philosophy

Politics

Religion

The Oxford Shakespeare

A complete list of Oxford Paperbacks, including Oxford World's Classics, Oxford Shakespeare, Oxford Drama, and Oxford Paperback Reference, is available in the UK from the Academic Division Publicity Department, Oxford University Press, Great Clarendon Street, Oxford OX2 6DP.

In the USA, complete lists are available from the Paperbacks Marketing Manager, Oxford University Press, 198 Madison Avenue, New York, NY 10016.

Oxford Paperbacks are available from all good bookshops. In case of difficulty, customers in the UK can order direct from Oxford University Press Bookshop, Freepost, 116 High Street, Oxford OX1 4BR, enclosing full payment. Please add 10 per cent of published price for postage and packing.